D0686531

THE CONFESSIONS OF
A REFORMER

THE CONFESSIONS OF
A REFORMER

by

FREDERIC C. HOWE

Introduction by
James F. Richardson

THE KENT STATE UNIVERSITY PRESS
Kent, Ohio, and London, England

© 1988 by The Kent State University Press, Kent, Ohio 44242
All rights reserved
Library of Congress Catalog Card Number 87–31111
ISBN 0–87338–361–3
Manufactured in the United States of America

First published by Charles Scribner's Sons, 1925

The paper in this book meets the guidelines for permanence and durability of the Committee on Production Guidelines for Book Longevity of the Council on Library Resources.

Library of Congress Cataloging-in-Publication Data

Howe, Frederic Clemson, 1867–1940.
    Confessions of a reformer / by Frederic C. Howe ; introduction by James F. Richardson.
        p.   cm.
    Reprint. Originally published: New York : Scribner, 1925. With new introd.
    Includes index.
    ISBN 0–87338–361–3 (alk. paper)
    1. Howe, Frederic Clemson, 1867–1940.   2. Social reformers—United States—Biography.   I. Title.
H59.H6A3 1988
362'.924—dc19
[B]   87–31111
                                                                                            CIP

British Library Cataloging-in-Publication data are available

INTRODUCTION

CONFESSIONS OF A REFORMER is an important political autobiography. Originally published in 1925, the book details the odyssey of Frederic C. Howe from the small-town America of the post–Civil War decades, where stifling orthodoxy—whether religious, political, or economic—was the norm, to the heady excitements of Baltimore, Cleveland, and New York during the Progressive Era, to the disillusionment stemming from repressive governmental actions during World War I and the postwar Red Scare. Howe's career is significant precisely because it encompassed so many of the major themes of American history from the early 1890s to the mid-1920s. His graduate work at Johns Hopkins (Ph.D. 1892) fired him with enthusiasm for the possibilities of a society led by an enlightened class open to positive change; his travels to Europe convinced him that American cities could also be beautiful, humane, and cultured; he responded warmly to the political leadership of Cleveland's Mayor Tom L. Johnson (1901–09) and President Woodrow Wilson (1913–21), who had been a favorite professor of his at Hopkins; and he suffered from watching his former hero, President Wilson, in his second term preside over a government that used its power to impose conformity and hound dissidents.

Throughout his career, Howe was both doer and writer. While he was never a profound thinker, his articles and books demonstrate his belief in the power of information and ideas to help transform government and society. Like other progressives, he reveled in the prospect of positive social change under the direction of trained intelligence. In the optimistic atmosphere of the early 1900s, he and his colleagues believed that their generation had an opportunity to escape the dogmatisms of the past and to achieve a secular salvation in the form of economic and social justice. While Howe does not cite William James or John Dewey, he shared these philosophers' belief that humans live in an open universe of possibilities and choices, not in a closed, deterministic system of absolute laws. He thought it incumbent upon men like himself, who had the advantages of formal education, to show "the people" how their aspirations for a better life could be realized and to hold public office to make those promises reality. At various times, Howe was a city councilman, a member of the Ohio Senate, and a federal official.

In retrospect, the Progressive Era of the late 1890s to the entrance of the United States into World War I in 1917 is one of those periods of questioning and innovation thought of as an age of reform. Others are the New Deal years of the 1930s and the tumultuous 1960s with its civil rights movement and President Lyndon Johnson's Great Society legislation. The issues and trends of these reform thrusts are by no means identical: the American economy was certainly more robust during the Progressive Era and the 1960s than it was during the Great Depression of the 1930s. The New Deal had to cope with massive joblessness; at no time during the 1930s did the unemployment rate go below 14 percent, and during bad years it reached 20 to 25 percent. Economic stagnation in the 1930s delayed marriages and kept the birth rate low. Restrictive public policy held immigration to a minimum; indeed Mexican Americans suffered from forcible repatriation during the decade. The combination of low birth rates and limited immigration produced a population profile characterized more by stability than growth or change.

By contrast, the Progressive Era and the 1960s were periods marked both by sharp increases in the number of Americans and substantial change in their composition. In the years before the outbreak of war in Europe in 1914, the United States absorbed millions of newcomers, mostly from central, southern, and eastern Europe. Sustained movement from rural America to the cities resulted in the 1920 census showing for the first time more than half of all Americans living in urban communities. Most immigrants and those who migrated to cities were young, as Howe was when he made the move from Meadville, Pennsylvania, to the wider worlds of Baltimore, New York, and Cleveland.

Youth is surely a theme of the 1960s. So many of the baby boomers of the post–World War II period came to an age when their presence and their buying power exerted influence upon the country, especially its popular culture. Another important theme of the 1960s is civil rights, the search for equality by blacks in white America. In August 1963, Martin Luther King, Jr. made his "I Have a Dream" speech at the mammoth Washington rally, and it seemed as if the nation were well on the way toward breaking down racial barriers. Less than five years later King was dead, the victim of an assassin's bullet, and the civil rights movement was in disarray.

Howe's generation was not much interested in the condition of Afro-Americans; Woodrow Wilson even imposed segregation among federal employees where it had not existed before. The progressive agenda focused more on the implications of concentrated economic power, how to curb monopoly, maintain competition, and preserve opportunity for small businessmen in an increasingly oligarchic economy.

Despite the differences in emphasis among these reform movements, there are some important parallels. The Progressive Era, the New Deal, and the 1960s all began with a rush of optimism, a shared belief that the moment had arrived when outmoded ideas and policies would be superceded by fresh thinking; bastions of privilege and injustice would give way to demands for innovation and greater equality. In each instance, for a few years at least, these demands for change achieved legislative and institutional expression. During the Progressive Era, the transformation began on the municipal and state level—where Howe was an active participant—and then reached the federal government. Both the New Deal and the 1960s focused on the national level from the beginning.

Whatever the level of government, the limits of reform soon became apparent. The New Deal was essentially over by 1938. Historian Allen J. Matusow has entitled his history of liberalism in the 1960s *The Unraveling of America,* a designation which accurately conveys his interpretation. Howe's experience in Cleveland before 1911 taught him how difficult it was to overcome the resistance of important interests threatened by reform demands. Even President Wilson minimized the impact of such innovative legislation as the Federal Reserve System (1913) and the Federal Trade

Commission (1914) by the conservative character of the administrators he appointed to these agencies. In each reform era, therefore, action for change brought reaction to limit the impact of that
change.

One more important common theme remains to be discussed:
war. Each of these reform thrusts lost whatever vitality persisted
when the United States became a belligerent in a major international conflict. When the United States entered World War I in
1917, the Wilson administration made prosecution of the war its
chief concern, even at the expense of the civil liberties of those who
questioned our involvement. During World War II, President
Roosevelt announced that Dr. New Deal had been replaced by Dr.
Win-the-War. Lyndon Johnson feared that "the bitch of a war" in
Vietnam would destroy the woman he really loved, his Great Society; Johnson's expression of concern is a fairly apt description of
what did in fact happen.

During World War I, journalist Randolph Bourne wrote an es-
say entitled "The State," whose theme is that war and repressive statism go hand in hand. Howe, like other progressives,
had put his faith in purposeful social action and contributed to its
realization. When he came to write his *Confessions* in the 1920s, he
had suffered the disillusioning impact of the war, the flawed peace
settlement, and the postwar Red Scare, where the federal government carried on a systematic campaign against dissidents and radicals. Political power was in the hands of business-oriented conservatives who promoted rather than resisted consolidation of
corporate domination of the American economy. So the dominant
tone of the book fits an interpretation of the 1920s as an interval of
conservatism following a period of reform. Naturally, Howe could
not in 1925 anticipate the New Deal, although he did have hopes
that new leadership would arise to rekindle the spirit of reform.
When the New Deal did begin in 1933, Howe, then sixty-six years
old, played an active role in it.

Confessions of a Reformer is the story of Howe's public life; it is
rarely confessional in the sense of Jean-Jacques Rousseau or St.
Augustine. We get some glimpses of the inner man—his rejection
of his childhood religious inheritance and his desire to make a

mark on the world through his writing and his public service come through. So too does his craving for variety, for new places and new experiences.

Fred Howe was a restless man not content to choose an endeavor or profession early in life and then spend a career plowing the same narrow furrow ever more deeply. At another time he might have been a religious seeker moving from church to sect and back in hopes of finding an answer to the big question of how shall I and the rest of mankind be saved. In his actual life span of 1867 to 1940, he moved from the middle-class Protestant pieties of Meadville and its Allegheny College to the intellectual excitement of Johns Hopkins to the rough and tumble world of New York journalism in the early 1890s to the often reluctant practice of law in Cleveland and a more congenial involvement in the city's emerging reform politics under Mayor Tom L. Johnson. From 1911 to 1914 he was the director of the People's Institute in New York City, and in 1914 he served the federal government as commissioner of immigration at New York's famed Ellis Island, where he remained until 1919. During the 1920s he spent much of his time either in Europe or on Nantucket Island, largely out of the public eye. Fortunately, he lived long enough to be an active participant in the New Deal. The years from 1933 on were more congenial to someone of Howe's temperament than the 1920s had been.

For most of his life, Howe was an active writer, expounding his views on democracy, equality of opportunity, the evils of monopoly, and the lessons Americans could learn from English and German cities on how to create beautiful and corruption-free communities. The best expression of these aspirations is in his *The City: The Hope of Democracy*, published in 1905. Like other reform-minded persons, before the war he thought ideas and information more powerful than interests and that intelligence properly applied could end abuses and promote social well-being. He was particularly influenced by the ideas of Henry George, who in *Progress and Poverty* (1879) had argued that growing wealth and growing poverty went hand in hand because a disproportionate share of the social product went to the land owner. The land owner was in effect a monopolist just as were those who controlled natural resources like coal and iron, or who succeeded in obtaining franchises to provide street railways and other public services—the so-called natural monopolies.

In these views, Howe followed the lead of Tom Johnson, a street railway entrepreneur who became the antimonopolist mayor of Cleveland in 1901 and served until 1909. Johnson attracted a core of able young men in his fight against "Privilege," his term for those who reaped the benefits of a growing industrial city with little cost or risk to themselves. His disciples included Newton D. Baker, Cleveland's law director under Johnson, mayor of the city from 1912 to 1915, and subsequently secretary of war under President Woodrow Wilson. Baker, like Howe, had been a student of Wilson's at Johns Hopkins. Peter Witt, a blacklisted union man, lacked Howe and Baker's formal education and social polish. What he did have was a slashing and vitriolic style that took the skin off his numerous opponents. He once described golf as a game that needlessly prolongs the lives of some of our most useless citizens. Howe, a cradle Republican, supported Democrat Johnson as a member of Cleveland's city council, and then switched parties to become a Democratic state senator in Ohio.

Howe's profession at this time was the law, knowledge of which was acquired reluctantly and under great pressure when newspaper work was hard to come by in the depressed years of the 1890s. According to *Confessions of a Reformer,* he never loved the law; he wanted variety and change while the law governed present conduct by a set of often outmoded past rules. The old rules that survived were those which benefitted employers rather than employees. Howe was particularly incensed at the law's treatment of those killed or injured on the job. Lawyers who represented workers or their survivors in such cases were condemned by their peers as "ambulance chasers" while those who represented corporations were leaders of the bar. Paradoxically, Howe was himself associated with two leading establishment figures, James and Harry Garfield, sons of the former president of the United States. The Garfields supported Howe in his political activities, no matter how much business the firm lost because of Howe's connection with Johnson, some of whose policies were hated by Cleveland's elite.

Johnson and Samuel "Golden Rule" Jones of Toledo, another wealthy businessman, have always been cited by historians as leading examples of municipal progressives. Progressivism was not a single unified doctrine; rather, it was a diversified set of responses to the realization that the United States had become an industrial nation dominated by big businesses and big cities. Included in progressivism were movements for honest, efficient, and more expansive municipal government, weakened corporate domination of state legislatures, strengthened public control or public ownership of utilities, democratization of the political process and weakened party organizations, women's suffrage, expansion of government's power to regulate business, and adoption of social welfare legislation.

Not everyone who could legitimately be called a progressive supported all of these proposals; in some instances they might be contradictory. For example, supporters of honesty and efficiency in government often sought to limit popular participation; they wished not only to weaken party organizations but also to raise the class level of those chosen for public office and eliminate local and lower class influence from municipal government. The city manager form of city government with its nonpartisan-at-large elections of a small council which would in turn appoint a chief executive, is a classic example.

The Cleveland Chamber of Commerce, an organization of leading business and professional men, played an important role in the city's public life. Its committees prepared well-researched and well-written reports on various public issues. The chamber had more information and a better grasp of the implications of proposals than did the city council. The chamber supported Mayor Johnson where it thought his policies would enhance Cleveland's reputation as a desirable place to live and do business; one such policy was development of the Group Plan, Cleveland's version of a monumental civic center. Fred Howe, as State Senator in Ohio, played a leading role in the adoption of the legislation authorizing Cleveland to proceed with this project, one in keeping with national trends at the time.

In the 1890s and 1900s, various cities around the country sought to improve their downtowns by building monumental railroad stations, such as Pennsylvania Station and Grand Central Terminal in New York, and major public structures. Known as the "city beautiful movement," this form of urban planning drew inspiration from the famous White City built for the Columbian Exposition in Chicago in 1893, whose guiding spirit was architect Daniel Burnham. Here for almost the first time, Americans saw a city rationally planned and with its buildings conceived in relationship to each other and to the street pattern. Burnham then went on to oversee the revival of the L'Enfant plan for Washington, D.C. in 1901 before being invited to Cleveland to chair the planning committee for the Group Plan the following year. Both Tom Johnson and the Chamber of Commerce wanted Cleveland's major public buildings grouped around an expansive mall to present to the world a visible embodiment of the city's wealth and power, to show that an American industrial city was more than smoke and soot, that it could match the great public squares and buildings of Europe.

Where the chamber and Mayor Johnson and his followers emphatically parted company was over the issue of the ownership and control of public utilities, especially street railways. Before 1910, the automobile was a luxury item, and most city dwellers either walked to work or rode the electrically powered street railways, known as trolleys. Because the trolleys used public property, operators needed the approval of city governments in the form of franchises. Franchises conveyed valuable property rights to the holders in raising the value of real estate along lines, and street railway promoters were often the owners and developers of adjacent real estate. Until rising costs reduced profits, the provision of transportation itself was also a money maker. Mark Hanna, until his death in 1904 Tom Johnson's great opponent in Cleveland, referred to his street railways as his savings bank. Johnson, whose own fortune was based on street railways, advocated public ownership. Only in this way could the corruption of government by those seeking franchises be avoided. Otherwise those fighting corruption in government were doomed to failure because they refused to get at the source of corruption. Also, the monopoly conveyed by franchises enriched a few people at the expense of the city's workers, who endured tedious, overcrowded rides so that promoters and stockholders might benefit.

Because Ohio's constitution forbade public ownership of street railways, Johnson, Baker, and Howe had to resort to a variety of unsatisfactory expedients to try to achieve the substance of public ownership without the legal form. These efforts encountered the implacable opposition of the city's monopolistic street railway entrepreneurs, law firms tied to them, the Chamber of Commerce, and banks, which profited from the status quo. The prolonged struggle cost Mayor Johnson his health and his fortune and ultimately led, not to public ownership, but to enhanced public control over the private company.

Howe and others of Johnson's circle found that political opposition led to social ostracism. Not unnaturally, Howe wanted to be accepted and respected by men of his own class—those who came from old stock backgrounds and enjoyed extensive formal educations and above-average incomes. The bruising street railway battle made that difficult; while his law partners did not desert him, others of his circle did. Here was direct evidence that interests were indeed stronger than ideas or information and that while many business and professional men were prepared to devote time, energy, and some money to the improvement of their city, they would draw back and turn hostile if their basic interests were threatened.

Johnson, Baker, and Howe were not socialists. Johnson had made a lot of money, liked the good life, and continued to tinker with money-making schemes during his mayoral years. From the end of his service as secretary of war until his death in 1937, Baker was one of Cleveland's and the nation's best known and most highly compensated lawyers. Howe opposed socialism because he associated it with regimentation and the stifling of creativity. Although he never used quite this language, Howe wanted a reformed capitalism, one with genuine equality of opportunity, no undue profiting from rising land values, and no monopolistic control of natural resources of public utilities. As Howe was not a deep or systematic thinker, the reader will not encounter in this book a probing examination of the complexities of reconciling individual freedom with social well-being. What the reader will experience is the continuing perplexity of a man of good will whose life, like that of many others, involved a continuing unlearning of what he thought he knew.

A case in point is his attitude toward the Constitution and constitutionalism. At Hopkins, Woodrow Wilson and other faculty members inculcated a veneration of the Constitution and a perception of its drafters as wise and experienced men whose knowledge of history and political principles enabled them to solve the great riddles of creating a governing framework for a free people. Later Howe came to view the framers as men afraid of democracy and the popular will who built a government designed to thwart rather than encourage constructive change. The manner in which Ohio's constitution protected the economic interests of monopolists by forbidding municipal ownership of street railways was a compelling local example. If action designed to protect workers or otherwise threaten corporate interests successfully made it through the legislative maze, where corporate lobbyists abounded, judges appointed from the ranks of safely conservative lawyers could find some constitutional provision that it violated. Like other Progressives, Howe chafed at the courts' functioning as a third house of the legislature. He supported the recall of all public officials, including judges, so that those who frustrated the popular will could be removed by popular vote.

Howe's most satisfying public service in Cleveland was his last one, that on the tax commission to reappraise property. Following Ohio law, the city had not reassessed in ten years and so did not reap the revenue benefits of rising land values after 1900. Johnson and his followers had contended since coming into office that small homeowners paid more than their fair share because of the undervaluation of industrial and commercial real estate. As followers of Henry George, they also wanted to tax land more than buildings so that speculators who held land hoping to profit from rising values would pay more than those who used their land for productive purposes. The Ohio Constitution of 1851 required that all property be assessed at 100 percent of its market value, a requirement never observed. Counties vied with each other in underassessing so that their residents would pay less to the state. Railroad land was taxed according to the number of miles of track in a particular county, not the value of the land on which the track stood. Within cities assessments varied widely from one parcel to another because of political influence among landowners and incompetence among assessors. Newton Baker estimated that property in Cleveland was assessed at anywhere from 10 to 110 percent of true value.

Howe was proud of the fact that he and his colleagues in the reassessment of 1910 were able to redress many of these inequities. They had to tax improvements as well as land values because of constitutional requirements, but they were at least able to reduce the comparative burden on the small homeowner. What Howe does not tell us is that at the same time when Cleveland's tax duplicate, the total value of assessed property, more than doubled, the state legislature imposed stringent limitations on the power of all units of government in the state to raise revenue. Over the next decade the city accumulated millions of dollars of operating deficits because the state prevented it from taxing its citizens adequately. The state eased these prohibitions in the early 1920s, and for a brief period the city enjoyed some financial stability. The Great Depression that set in after the stock market crash of 1929 again turned Cleveland from the "City on a Hill" of the Johnson years to a city in a hole.

These developments occurred after Howe left Cleveland for New York in 1911. During his first sojourn in New York in the 1890s he was a young man struggling to make a career as a journalist in a highly competitive marketplace and a depressed economy. Now he was a financially secure man in his forties, able to escape the despised practice of law for something more engaging. Howe notes that by this point in his life, he was financially free to pursue his own bent. What he does not tell us is whether this freedom came from the successful practice of law or from some other source.

In any event the New York of 1911 and the next few years offered a great deal to Howe and his wife, Marie Jenney Howe, whom he had married in 1904. In Cleveland, Howe had discouraged his wife's career aspirations; in that conservative city a working wife meant that her husband had failed in his basic responsibilities as provider. The unspoken corollary was that men then did not have to fear economic competition from women. In New York, where Greenwich Village was just entering into its greatest period of cultural innovation, feminism flourished in the advanced circles in which the Howes moved. He notes the stimulation they received from the bright young people who visited their West 12th Street apartment. Howe was one of the older liberals found at Mabel Dodge's famous salon, one of the many times and places where America was in the process of losing its innocence.

Howe's position as director of the People's Institute provided opportunities to interact both with members of New York's elite and the more intellectually ambitious of the immigrants from the Lower East Side. Charles Sprague Smith, former professor of German at Columbia University, founded the institute in 1897 at Cooper Union. Cooper Union, located just north and west of the most densely populated Jewish section of the city, provided a 1600-seat auditorium where many of the country's more interesting minds could lecture on and debate socialism, housing issues, and labor problems before audiences rich in political passion and intellectual involvement although poor in money. For all the valuable opportunities it afforded, however, the institute never escaped a measure of condescension toward its immigrant constituency.

Howe provides some indirect evidence of this point when he says that before he became commissioner of immigration at Ellis Island in 1914 he never thought much about immigration. Yet in Cleveland, where he was so active in local affairs, three quarters of its population in 1910 were either foreign born or had at least one foreign-born parent. In New York at the same time the corresponding figure was four-fifths. Howe and others of his background were more likely to do things *for* the immigrant poor than to do things *with* them, a not surprising attitude in view of the ethnic and class divisions characteristic of American society (and most others that one can cite).

At Ellis Island, where Howe remained until 1919, he labored to make the processing of new arrivals as humane as possible and to

promote employment opportunities. He established what later became the United States Employment Service. Like other middle
managers he had his difficulties both with those below and those
above him within his own organization. He shared other educated
Americans' enthusiasm for the British civil service, which recruited many of the best and brightest of that society; he had a
much lower opinion of the career bureaucrats under his supervision who were more interested in their privileges and prerogatives
than in serving their clients. Howe also experienced periodic political pressure on issues such as the "white slavery" scare, where
young immigrants were viewed by concerned old stock moralists
primarily as potential prostitutes or pimps. In trying to preserve
humanity and perspective, Howe had to contend with a superior in
Washington, himself of immigrant background, who wanted to
show others how tough, not how understanding and compassion-
ate, he was.

Howe had come into the federal service because of his long-
standing admiration for President Woodrow Wilson. This respect
turned to condemnation with the Wilson administration's repressive actions against civil liberties both during and after World
War I. Immigration officials bore the brunt of this campaign because of the fear of foreign-born dissidents and radicals. So long as
deportation was considered an administrative and not a judicial
proceeding, the foreign born were relatively easy targets of repressive governmental action. Howe and Louis Post struggled hero-
ically to slow down, indeed to derail, this campaign of deportation.
Others like him who had championed strong leadership and the
positive state had some rethinking to do when they saw the uses to
which political power could be put.

Howe made one more attempt to serve Wilson when, surpris-
ingly, he attended the Paris Peace Conference as an expert in Near
Eastern affairs. He writes of his interest in this region, although it
is unlikely that his knowledge could have been extensive. The various scholars and other experts who made up "The Inquiry," the
name given Wilson's panel of specialist advisers, found their work
largely ignored in the actual drafting of the treaties.

After the war, Howe largely withdrew from public life. In the early 1920s he was in his fifties, content to spend much of the winter in Europe and the summer on Nantucket Island. He did conduct a "School of Opinion" on Nantucket whose "faculty" included writers Floyd Dell, Bruce Bliven, and Sinclair Lewis.

Howe's political activity during these years came through the Conference on Progressive Political Activity, organized in 1922 under the leadership of the various unions of railroad workers. The railroad unions, known as brotherhoods, were interested in the adoption of the Plumb Plan, a form of nationalization of the railroads. Other progressives participated because they saw the conference as a vehicle for supporting reform candidates and proposals. In 1924 it became the nucleus of the progressive effort to elect Senator Robert M. La Follette of Wisconsin as president. La Follette had been a leading progressive Republican before the war and staunchly opposed the entrance of the United States into the war. His followers hoped that since both major parties had nominated conservatives, Calvin Coolidge for the Republicans and John W. Davis for the Democrats, the progressives would do well. Coolidge ascended to the presidency after Warren Harding died in office in 1923 but largely escaped being tarnished with the scandals associated with the Harding administration. Davis was a compromise candidate for the Democrats whose convention witnessed a titanic struggle between the followers of Governor Alfred E. Smith of New York and William G. McAdoo.

Although neither Davis nor La Follette would prevent Coolidge's election, the Progressive candidate, who had been nominated in Cleveland, won a plurality of the city's votes. This result disturbed the city's elite mightily. Business leaders worried about the city's reputation for radicalism; they were afraid that entrepreneurs would avoid Cleveland because of its strong construction unions and the political philosophy represented by the vote for La Follette. The metropolitan area vote went for Coolidge because of the suburbs' strong support for the Republican candidate.

Confessions of a Reformer does not discuss the differences in voting patterns between city and suburb and their implications for his earlier book title, *The City: The Hope of Democracy*. *Confessions* does indicate Howe's love of cities and his hope that American cities could acquire the more positive characteristics of

English and German municipalities. But by the mid-1920s many families who could afford to had left the city for low-density, high-income suburbs where they could be assured of "good" (i.e., socially homogeneous) schools and sufficient control over land use to prevent businesses from encroaching upon their residential areas. Urban residential land had long been divided along lines of income, race, and ethnicity. The city of Cleveland itself constituted a series of ethnic villages. What was different by the 1920s was that old stock, above-average income people were no longer part of the same polity as more recent arrivals, new immigrants and blacks, or the less successful of their own kind. They sought not only more space and newer housing but also a refuge from the cosmopolitanism ("cosmo" is Cleveland shorthand for ethnic) and political complexity of the city.

Before 1910 Cleveland leaders often assumed it was simply a matter of time before the suburbs became absorbed into the city. As late as 1916 the Chamber of Commerce established a committee on annexation to promote the political integration of city and suburbs. By 1924, the committee on annexation had become the committee on cooperative metropolitan government, one more instance where the title gives away the plot. Chamber leaders now assumed the continuing independence of the suburbs; after all this was where most of them lived by choice. What the chamber did seek was an arrangement that would combine some governmental functions while leaving schools and land use control in local hands.

Though many of these developments lay in the future, especially the explosive growth of suburbia after World War II, it is worth noting that by 1925, the year *Confessions of a Reformer* was originally published, the pattern of socially superior suburbs fiercely committed to maintaining their political independence was well established. Various attempts to bring about metropolitan government in Cleveland, from the 1920s to the 1950s, failed. In recent decades a number of single-function metropolitan area agencies have been created. Unfortunately since no general government encompasses the metropolitan area as a whole, these agencies often lack accountability to anyone other than themselves.

Howe lived for another fifteen years after the publication of this memoir. With the inauguration of Franklin D. Roosevelt as president of the United States in 1933 and the creation of the New Deal, Howe's brand of liberalism was back in style. In the mid-1920s prosperity and a concern for cultural conformity dominated political life, with a majority of voters ready to "keep cool with Coolidge." The depression of the 1930s with its massive unemployment engendered a desire for government action, a desire that FDR and his colleagues were more than ready to satisfy. Agriculture was a particularly troubled sector of the economy. After unprecedented prosperity during World War I, growers of the great staple crops such as wheat and cotton faced hard times even during the 1920s. The world-wide depression of the 1930s made their lot, and that of virtually all farmers, much worse. One of the New Deal's major innovations was the Agricultural Adjustment Administration, which Howe joined in 1933 as consumer counsel. The old progressive, now sixty-six years old, joined a group of younger liberals such as Chicago lawyer and later Federal Judge Jerome Frank in seeking to protect the interests of consumers. This group's goal was to prevent programs for farmers from gouging food buyers. Within the agency, the urban liberals were regarded as an exotic lot by the veteran agricultural professionals. One famous anecdote involves a citybred lawyer demanding, "But what does this do for the macaroni growers?"

Apart from social origins and cultural styles were serious conflicts of policy. The agricultural specialists, more committed to the interests of large commercial farmers than of tenants or consumers, won the internal battle and drove the liberals either out of the agency or into impotence within it.

Howe stayed on for a while as a special adviser to Secretary of Agriculture Henry Wallace. In 1937 he left to become a consultant to the Philippine administration on rural issues. At the time of his death on August 3, 1940, he was associated with the Federal Monopoly Committee.

With this final assignment, Howe's political career had in a sense come full circle, from the antimonopoly orientation of the Johnson years in Cleveland to this federal effort. Neither succeeded in achieving its stated goals. Public ownership of Cleveland's transit system came only when private enterprise saw no profit in it, while the New Deal's approach to the issue of concentrated economic power was half-hearted, inconsistent, and self-contradictory.

Yet it would be wrong to regard Howe's career as a set of failures. Throughout his life, he set himself to something more than just making money. As a young man he had a vision of what a good city could be and worked hard to make that dream a reality in Cleveland. In New York he was an active participant in some of the most exciting cultural developments of the twentieth century. The flowering of bohemian Greenwich Village and the thirst for knowledge, political debate, and cultural expression among East European Jewish immigrants in the years before the United States entered World War I constituted important sources of energy, creativity, and inspiration both then and for later decades. Unfortunately, the war unleashed demands for repression and conformity, demands which Howe's former hero, Woodrow Wilson, too readily supported. In this bleak political climate, Howe found his job as commissioner of immigration a "nightmare." His participation in peacemaking and the postwar international settlement was not much better.

Confessions of a Reformer reflects his disappointment with the failure of old stock, Protestant, middle-class America, his people, to lead the way in the creation of a more open, generous, and humane society. He was not without hope. He saw great possibilities in the leadership of the railroad unions, a specific confidence that proved to be quite unfounded. However, the general point that reform would once again rise was valid.

When this book first appeared in the mid-1920s, the progressive impulse associated with the prewar period was more faint than throbbing. In the White House, President Coolidge deliberately set out to reduce the role and significance of government. Agencies established to regulate business acted more as promoters of consolidation than opponents of monopoly or combinations in restraint of trade, while unions and social legislation faced an especially hostile judiciary. In the private sector innovation flourished, and industries such as automobiles, motor trucks, movies, radio,

and electric power experienced rapid growth. Howe was less exhil-
arated by prosperity than troubled by America's cultural and political shortcomings. At this stage of his life, he was ready to let
other, younger people bear the burden of struggle. Like St. Paul in
another context, he had fought the good fight. The New Deal years
showed that the old battler still had a couple of good rounds left in
him.

Historians rightly warn against too facile parallels between past
and present. Still, it is intriguing to think that Calvin Coolidge is
one of Ronald Reagan's heroes and that the era of Reagan will
soon come to a close. No one can predict the shape of American
politics in the 1990s, but somehow it would not be surprising if that
period had more in common with the Progressive Era or the New
Deal than the 1920s or the 1980s. If so, Fred Howe would be
pleased.

James F. Richardson

CONTENTS

CHAPTER I

BEGINNING

I AM not nearly as old as the records of births in Meadville, Pennsylvania, make me seem. My life really began in the early nineties instead of the late sixties. It began at Johns Hopkins University. Under the influence of Richard T. Ely, Woodrow Wilson, Albert Shaw, James Bryce, I came alive. I felt a sense of responsibility to the world. I wanted to change things. It was not very clear what I wanted to change or how I should go about it. It had to do with politics. Also with economics. My mind found new authorities. They were intellectual rather than moral, social rather than personal.

From Professor Richard T. Ely I learned that the industrial system was not what I had assumed it to be in Meadville, where my father was a manufacturer on a small scale; not a kindly family affair, like my father's furniture store, in which he employed his brother, his nephews, and other good-looking and engaging young men who came and went in our house as guests. Employers, I now learned, were capitalists. They exploited their workers. They were not considerate men who got rather less than their employees out of the enterprise. Those friendly young men who sang and joked and took me on picnics, occasionally went to a saloon and had a glass of beer. That distressed me. Ought I to tell my father about it? Surely he would remonstrate with them if he knew. One man was always in domestic difficulties. He overdrew his account by several thousand dollars. Such problems of personal conduct I heard discussed at home. They were the only serious ones that business, to my boyhood knowledge, presented.

In the new world that took shape for me at the university, industry was a grim affair of mines and mills, of trusts and monopolies, in which men were numbers rather than human beings. There was conflict in it, division of people into those who owned things and those who worked for the people who owned. There were strikes, bloody sometimes like civil war, in which men hated one another. Little children were slaves in cotton-mills and sweat-shops; men in mines worked twelve and fourteen hours a day. There was menace in the industrial system; there was need of change.

Politics, too, had been simple matters in Meadville. The Andrews Brothers, lieutenants of Matthew Stanley Quay, looked after all the offices. They personally selected the candidates and advised men whether or not they should run for office. They gave me railway passes on which I travelled to and from the university. Few persons questioned the right of two amiable gentlemen—one of them editor of the Meadville *Republican*, the other a man with no apparent vocation—to advise men whether they should be a candidate or get an appointment. It did not seem improper that every one in the county should go to them to have things done at Harrisburg or in Washington by Mr. Quay. In the opinion of my relatives—and that opinion had been mine—Mr. Quay was maligned by disgruntled men who had not gotten the county printing or some job they wanted. He was a good organizer. He kept his word, rewarded his friends, and punished his enemies. He was a member of the church. That was political morality enough for Meadville. He was known as the "political leader," and people leaned on him much as they leaned on the church. Authority was a necessary and desirable thing. It existed unquestioned. There was something unthinkable to me about being a Democrat—Democrats, Copperheads, and atheists were persons whom one did not know socially. As a boy I did not play with their children. The Republican Party and the Methodist church divided our allegiance. Their authority was unquestioned. They were the guardians of morality, respectability, and standing.

At Johns Hopkins new authorities took the place of the old. Mr. James Bryce lectured on the failures of democracy and the need of the scholar in politics. I had brought from home a mild distaste for the word democracy; it savored of objectors to Senator Quay. But I did not know that it had failed. I was not aware that everything was not as it should be. My friends and relatives were not only content with things as they were; they were stanch believers in the system which freed them from responsibility and left them free to go about their business, leaving the primaries, conventions, and elections to excellent men who were pillars in the church and respected because of their conventional virtues. Mr. Bryce's *American Commonwealth* was at that time a work of Biblical authority. When he visited our seminar on politics, professors and students accepted his opinions as beyond and above question. He talked about the spoils system, about the corruption of cities, and the decay of a sense of responsibility among the kind of people whom I knew. That was what impressed me most: the kind of people I knew had neglected their duties.

I had not been interested in politics; I had accepted conditions as I found them, as I accepted business. They were approved by the people I knew; the political system included the local judge, a member of the Methodist church. It had his approval, and it had the approval of my relatives. I might become a part of it some day.

I was interested in getting a job—perhaps in my father's store. I dreamed about homesteading out West, in Kansas or Nebraska. That suggested adventure. I admired the big brick residences of citizens who had found oil in Bradford, Oil City, or Ohio; I envied their social life outside our own. I fancied myself pioneering, going out as these men had done, and returning to know them and their families. Life meant business, getting on in the world; the business one was in determined one's social position. My ambition was to make money and to enjoy the pleasures that possessors of wealth enjoyed. I should have liked to be the county judge —but that was out of the question. I did not envy my college professors, though they seemed tremendously wise. They were disagreeable, prone to be critical of me in the classroom. I never thought of being a scholar. The law seemed to me a distinguished, a difficult, profession. I was desperately afraid of being pushed into the ministry, which maiden aunts and Sunday-school teachers urged on me. One of the terrors of my boyhood was that I might get drawn into it. Every one agreed in admonishing me against the saloon; it was the symbol of everything bad, the cause of the downfall of some of our relatives. If one went into saloons, one became a printer or a tramp; one associated with disreputable women.

In these years I wanted what the people around me wanted; wanted to get on in the world; to make money—though I had little hope of ever making much. My mind was empty of enthusiasms. I thought as those about me thought. My world was bounded by the block in which I lived, by my relatives, by the

Methodist church, although I always sought escape from it; by the college on the hill. I submitted to college as a tedious experience that had to be gotten through with, and looked forward to graduation as the day when a decision would have to be made for which my previous life and associations gave me no help.

At Johns Hopkins individual authorities took the place of my small-town herd. Professor Ely showed me a cruel industrial system, Woodrow Wilson and James Bryce the evils of party politics. Mr. Bryce said that America, with no leisure class devoted to statecraft, as in Great Britain, was to be saved by the scholar. Unthrilled by eloquence—for Mr. Bryce was a dull lecturer—I accepted his creed of responsibility and service. Democracy must be salvaged from the hands of spoilsmen and politicians; it must be salvaged even from Senator Quay and the Andrews Brothers.

This change did not come immediately. It did not come vividly; as old moralities left me, new ones imperceptibly took their place. I accepted them from men whom I respected, just as I had accepted my previous opinions from men who were esteemed in Meadville. I was accustomed to moralistic authority. These new authorities, too, had a moralistic flavor.

Doctor Albert Shaw, editor of *The Review of Reviews*, stirred my imagination as did none of the other lecturers. He lectured on municipal administration and painted pictures of cities that I could visualise—cities that I wanted to take part in in America; cities managed as business enterprises; cities that were big business enterprises, that owned things and did things for people. There was order and beauty in the cities he described. They owned their own tramways and gas and electric lighting plants, and they made great successes of them. Good men ran them, business men, who gave up their business interests to do so. This kind of objective politics I could understand; I could think of material things more easily than economic abstractions. There was something in my mind that seized upon order, on plans, on doing things the way business men did them in their own shops and factories. I was familiar with this sort of thing; it was about the only academic subject that fitted in with my background, to which something inside of me responded. I read with zest Doctor Shaw's two illuminating books on municipal government in Great Britain and on the Continent of Europe. These pictures of cities gave me my first political enthusiasm. I desired to be an editor and writer, as was he, so that I could further the ideas I had gotten from him. I wanted to go to Europe and see for myself the cities he had described, to study their machinery, their municipal enterprises, their splendid streets, parks, and public buildings.

I do not know why out of all the things I heard at Johns Hopkins this was the thing that gripped me most. Perhaps it was partly my herd instinct that found expression in this dream. I cared about beauty and order in cities—cities that chose for their rulers university men, trained as I was being trained. Possibly because I was disorderly myself, I wanted order. And I hated waste. That I had been taught to esteem a cardinal sin, and American cities, I was told, were wasteful because they were ruled by politicians, whose only interest was in jobs.

Woodrow Wilson, though our greatest lecturer, gave me no such pictures. He dealt in abstractions about the Constitution. He was interested in political forms, in the fathers of the Republic, especially in the Virginia statesmen, who were writers of great documents. He inspired an admiration for the British constitution, which he counted even more perfect than our own. Mr. Wilson was a brilliant speaker, and it was his brilliance as a speaker rather than what I got from him that made me take every course he offered. In his lecture-room it was not always clear to me what I believed; but I felt that we had departed from the ideals of the fathers and were indifferent to our responsibilities to the state. Listening to him, I got hints of impressions received at home, when preachers lamented our lukewarmness to Christian ideals, our neglect of responsibility to the church. A note of moral passion in his speech was familiar to me. Great men had departed from Capitol Hill; the Senate no longer reverberated to the high morality of earlier days. Democracy was not concerned over issues of great constitutional import. Politics had become a struggle of vulgar interests, of ignoble motive, of untrained men. We were abandoned to money-making in politics, as we were in our personal relations. We had permitted the government to be seized by spoilsmen and politicians. It was from them that democracy must be reclaimed.

I learned about Socialism. But it did not interest me. It was not believed in by the men I knew. I read Henry George, but the Single Tax seemed altogether too easy a reform to be taken as a social philosophy. Nor was it believed in by my professors. I had a hazy sense of the brotherhood of man, but was not greatly moved by it. I liked my own new kind of people—of that I was clear; educated, university people, who read books and talked about them. I had a strong belief in the superiority of the Anglo-Saxon. English-speaking people were the chosen people; they must be looked to to carry on civilization.

The new world into which I was emerging was still moralistic. I got its new moralities, the moralities of educated men, of scholars, of intellectual reformers. There were evils within the State to be corrected and abuses without. America required new leaders; without them democracy must fail. The people were misled, because business men and educated men had not taken the trouble to instruct them. The people were hungry for guidance; of that we were clear—guidance which we, the scholars, alone could provide. To this brotherhood of service I belonged. I was one of the chosen; one of the remnant that Matthew Arnold wrote about. The purple robe of doctor of philosophy dedicated me to this service, as it gave me a distinction which seemed rare in my world. The Johns Hopkins motto was *Veritas Vos Liberabit.* Through the truth we would redeem the world.

Atlas had nothing on the Johns Hopkins men of the nineties. We felt that the world had been wished onto our shoulders. And I rather enjoyed the burden that I was to carry. I accepted it with conscious satisfaction, though without any clear idea of just how to go about it. I had lost one set of moralities, which had never been very clear to me. The new ones were only less uncertain.

It was a distinction to be on intimate terms with men who had studied abroad, with recognized scholars, to whom the mind was very important. From them I had unlearned many things; I took pride in that, more pride than in my limited acquisitions of something new. I was initiated into a new order; the order of scholars whose teachings had changed me, would change the world.

CHAPTER II

MEADVILLE, PENNSYLVANIA

THERE was nothing in my inheritance to make me want the world any different. None of my ancestors ever crusaded. They took no part in the Revolutionary War; they were not Abolitionists; they escaped service in the Civil War. My mother's people were Quakers in a direct line of descent from the little band of settlers which Gustavus Adolphus sent out from Sweden in the early days of the seventeenth century to build a Swedish colony on the shores of Delaware Bay. There was no meeting-house in Meadville, and, like many Quakers, my mother's family had joined the Methodist church. Her grandparents were farmers who had drifted west till they came to rest in the very centre of what was later the town of Meadville, Pa. There my grandfather laid off a big city block and settled his five children around him.

My paternal ancestors came from the north of Ireland in the eighteenth century. They were what is known as Scotch-Irish, which means that they were Scotch Presbyterians who went over to Ireland and took the land away from the Irish and gave them their Scotch brand of religion in exchange. Like my mother's people, they came to this country poor, to get a new start in life. Only those who had little to lose came to America in those days, in sailing-ships which often took months in the crossing. They settled in northeastern Pennsylvania, and when other settlers trod on their heels they packed up their few possessions and trekked to the western part of the State. My father came to Meadville as

9

a young man and there he married my mother. There I was born and lived to my twenty-fifth year.

Neither of my parents had any interest in reform. They did not want the world changed. It was a comfortable little world, Republican in politics, careful in conduct, Methodist in religion. Religion to me was a matter of attending church, of listening to long and tedious sermons, of irritable, empty Sunday afternoons, church sociables, and Wednesday-evening prayer-meetings. To the older people it meant rivalry with Presbyterians and serious differences about the minister, the choir, and the power of a rich trustee who contributed generously to the church. Life revolved about our church, which was the finest in town. My father was president of its board of trustees. The neighbors whose opinions counted belonged mostly to it, although they might be Presbyterians. Unitarians were beyond some pale. Church activities and sectarian points of view bulked large in our lives, even though my mother had a gentle Quaker tolerance and kindliness and my father a quiet broadmindedness which was unusual in the community. Fellow churchmen did not understand his going across the public square on Sunday evenings to hear a Unitarian minister who had formerly been a Methodist and had renounced Methodism. The apostasy of Doctor Townsend had been in the nature of a public disgrace, hardly less than a crime. Lifelong friends shunned him. Yet my father, without discussion or defense of his action, forsook his own pew of a Sunday evening and went to hear strange doctrine.

My sisters and I were allowed to go to church or not, as we pleased. That was a rare departure from the Methodist pattern. I went to Sunday-school because I was in love with my Sunday-school teacher. I coveted the seat next to her during the Sunday-morning lesson and at parties which she arranged for us with the girls of Ida M. Tarbell's class, who sat near us in the big chapel.

I went to prayer-meetings on Wednesday evenings more often than to church on Sunday mornings. "Getting" religion, to my mind, was a catastrophic experience that changed a person in the twinkling of an eye. It should come young. It meant eternal damnation if it never came at all. Old people with quavering voices told about it at the Wednesday-evening meetings—told over and over again how it had happened to them. Repetition hardly staled the curious emotional appeal of their testimony. I wondered why my father never gave "testimony." As president of the board of trustees, it seemed to me that he ought to. I wondered if he had gotten religion. He never talked about it at home. In his consistent silence, when other brethren and sisters discussed their souls' salvation, he failed to live up to my conception of him, as he failed to live up to what the neighbors expected when he went to the Unitarian church. To experience religion seemed to me like a great climacteric; a tremendous personal drama that miraculously changed sinful nature. I drifted about the outskirts of the prayer-meetings getting hints of the drama, glimpses of the invisible scene where it was staged.

I escaped, more than my sisters, from the Methodist espionage of conduct. I went to the only dances in town, in the hall of the Taylor Hose Company. I played cards surreptitiously with a colored driver in the barn. And with my father's connivance I went to the theatre. That was a secret between the two males of the family. A smile and a meaning look at supper prefaced those happy evenings. I would meet my father casually in the yard when the meal was over. After a little banter he would say: "Like to go to the Opera House to-night to see Booth?" Or it might be Barrett, Joe Jefferson, Florence, Modjeska, or Lotta. I saw them all from inconspicuous seats in the top gallery. So much concession was made to "What will the neighbors think?"

These were purple spots of freedom, but what the neighbors might think seriously conditioned our lives. Watchful eyes observed us in all we did. There was a sense of being clamped down, stiff in a mould made for one. My mother was a neighborly person, ministering to the needs of every one on our street; but she was sensitive to their opinions and prejudices, deeply unwilling to have them flouted. And I rebelled against espionage, hated it, chafed under it. I sought ways of escape.

One escape was the Erie Canal. It ran through a shabby part of the town, and its banks were lined with shacks where wild, delightful Irish boys lived, with whom I was forbidden to play. Their mothers smoked pipes, their fathers worked on the railroad. They did not have to bother about their clothes, about keeping them whole or clean. They lived in the midst of adventures. I thought them happier than kings, and ran away whenever I could to play along the banks of that tempting waterway, which spelled romance to me. It went on and on, far down the valley to other towns. One could go as far as Pittsburgh by canal and by the Allegheny River, and Pittsburgh seemed a tremendous and probably a very wicked place. It was the big world that some time I might see, as some men I knew had seen it. They talked about it when they came to our house, although they had not been there for years. It was the event of their lives, and it grew in significance as the visit receded. Once I fell into the canal, thereby justifying my mother's fears and prohibitions. In punishment I received my first and only whipping. I took it ungenerously, with brooding and a sullen wish that some day I might make my father sorry for having inflicted it on me.

Another escape was the public library. I devoured books of adventure, reading them gluttonously, locked in my room, hurrying through the chapters in order to take the book back the next day and start another. I lived in the adventures I read about —of the sea, of the West, of the outside world.

But the refuge I loved best was the printing-office of the Meadville *Democrat*. I played truant from school to sit in wonderment in the old loft where its presses whirred. I made friends with the pressmen and printers, dabbled in printers' ink, played at typesetting. When the other boys went swimming, I slipped away to the printing-office. If I did not come home at night, my father looked for me there, and found me sometimes asleep back of the presses.

I remember my boyhood through a haze, as of a tranquil, bright September day. There was no sharpness, no struggle, little reproof. My mother kept a large house immaculate, entertained guests, raised her children and saw them with unremitting care through school and college. Her anxieties were all for us. The family worries had to do largely with money. Although my father's furniture store and factory were prosperous when I was a lad, there never seemed to be money enough to go around, and the weekly budgetary discussions on Saturday night were distressing times. My mother kept house on a very small allowance, but there was minute examination at the supper-table of the next week's necessary outlay. She put off as long as possible the moment of asking for her housekeeping money, and approached the subject nervously. There was no friction and no quarrelling, but a sharp line was drawn between necessary and unnecessary expenditures. I learned that extravagance was a cardinal sin and that money was not to be spent lightly. Small monetary units and a low scale of expenditure were early established for me. "Take care of the pennies and the dollars will take care of themselves" was a maxim far more deeply ingrained in my mind than any of the Ten Commandments. *Poor Richard's Almanac* was a much-quoted guide, and the end dramatically held before a spendthrift child was the poorhouse. My mind got a pattern of life from these Saturday-night talks. Right living was living carefully, avoiding debts of any kind, and husbanding for some distant future when sickness and old age would overtake one. My sisters and I got the pleasures we wanted if they could be provided, but we felt the sacrifices involved in them. We got a money measure of life and a fear of prodigality from which I, for one, have never escaped.

My father had a refuge of his own from the obligation of thrift. He loved horses; therefore, keeping half a dozen horses in the big barn in the rear of the house did not seem to him an extravagance. And we had a farm about a mile from town. Thanks to this rift in economy, I lived much in the open, riding, driving, breaking mustangs, knowing many of the joys of country life.

As I grew older and understood him better, I came to see in my father a person of distinction. Distinguished not in wealth or in honors, but in his way of living and his treatment of his children. He had a quiet independence of judgment and a humorous and tolerant quality that did not fit into the intellectual pattern of Meadville. He was a poor business man. I found that out as I grew older. From the time I entered college, the furniture store and factory were in a bad way, and one summer when he set me to collecting unpaid bills I understood why the weekly housekeeping discussions had been so distressing. I found a ledger, far bigger than the family Bible, in which he kept his accounts; few of them were balanced. In the safe there were bundles of promissory notes in sums running all the way from a few dollars to several hundred. My father apparently trusted everybody, and everybody seemed to love him in return, but without finding it necessary to pay their bills.

When my sisters and I finished high school we went to Allegheny College, not because we had any love of learning but because it was the proper thing to do. The income from my father's business was somehow stretched to suffice for all of us. Allegheny was one of the two colleges in Meadville that gave to the town the modest name of the "Athens of the West." Allegheny was thoroughly sectarian. Progress toward a degree was made easy for men who said they were going into the church or into foreign missions. Many of our professors were retired ministers or missionaries, who knew none too much about their subjects. Professions of faith were rather more important than scholarship, and revival meetings were the great events of the winter. I found study a bore. None of the subjects stirred in me the least enthusiasm and I cut classes as often as I dared. I was never able to make head or tail of the sciences, mathematics, Latin, and Greek. As far as I can recall, I went through college without having an enthusiasm awakened, yet I wanted to know things, to be admitted to the secrets of life. My classmates seemed to get as little out of the course as I did. Because the college failed to satisfy us, we created activities of our own. Mine were in college journalism. I planned in class and fraternity politics to get the posts I wanted. The first thrill of my academic life came from getting out the commencement edition of the college weekly. I worked on it day and night. I could hardly wait for the summer vacation to end to take up the work again. The furtive and forbidden amusements of theatregoing, card-playing, and dancing were but slightly diverting as compared with the joy of working over an editorial column.

The winter revival meetings at the college found me inwardly rebellious, outwardly passive. They were thoroughly organized. Freshmen and sophomores were allotted to the seniors, who took us on long walks, during which they inquired about our souls. Night after night they herded us into the Stone church. There revivalists prayed, worked on our fears, made us feel that we were eternally damned if we went without their particular brand of religion. Under the influence of Moody and Sankey hymns I went to the mourners' bench the second winter. I crept forward to be prayed for by strangers for sins of which I was ignorant and for a salvation that seemed at best dreary. I did what relatives, friends, and older college students expected me to do. I had no conviction of sin, no sense of guilt, or of being abandoned. And nothing happened. The great change that was promised did not come over me. Convinced of my own callousness, and rather sick at heart because of it, I found myself hating every one engaged in the proceedings and wishing heartily to escape. I had gone through the ordeal of being prayed for, of confessing a desire for regeneration, and had found no relief; no heavenly manna had fallen my way. I was resentful of religion, and deliberately refused from that time on to attend revival meetings, scandalizing and grieving my teachers and friends.

Physical escape from the embraces of evangelical

religion did not mean moral escape. From that religion my reason was never emancipated. By it I was conformed to my generation and made to share its moral standards and ideals. It was with difficulty that realism got lodgment in my mind; early assumptions as to virtue and vice, goodness and evil remained in my mind long after I had tried to discard them. This is, I think, the most characteristic influence of my generation. It explains the nature of our reforms, the regulatory legislation in morals and economics, our belief in men rather than in institutions and our messages to other peoples. Missionaries and battleships, anti-saloon leagues and Ku Klux Klans, Wilson and Santo Domingo are all a part of that evangelistic psychology that makes America what she is.

This particular brand of evangelistic morality became bone of my bone, flesh of my flesh. It was a morality of duty, of careful respectability. It was the code of a small town, of the Sunday-school, of my church. I had no rights as to my own life; danger lurked in doing what I wanted, even though what I wanted was innocent. One's desires were to be suspected; they were in some way related to lustful things, and lust in thought was as bad as in deed. One might hate Democrats, Unitarians, persons outside of one's own church; one could be sharp in business, possibly corrupt in politics, but one could not forget that life was a serious business, that duty should be always before one's eyes, that one should be diligent in things distasteful, and that self-fulfilment meant getting on in the world, being assiduous to church-going, rather exhibitive in attendance on revivals, the holding to one's particular church denomination, and the avoidance of even the appearance of careless morals, drinking or association with men of questionable opinions.

The important thing was to live as other men lived, do as other men did, avoid any departure from what other men thought. Not to conform was dangerous to one's reputation. Men who had strange ideas, who protested, who thought for themselves, were quietly ostracised. When people passed their houses there were side glances between the men; some remarks that sounded very damning to me at that time. There were other men, bankers and department-store keepers, of whom stories were whispered about women they had been seen with, of their trips to New York, of sharp advantages they had taken of other men. But these things did not seem to matter so much as did dissention from established ideas. It was a distinction to be stopped by them on the street, to be nodded to from their carriages, to be called by one's given name. Somehow they seemed to be permitted to do things that other men did not do. They had a freedom from their neighbors, from a code of living that was always demanding something unpleasant of me.

I conformed, but departed when I dared. In town and at college I resisted claims made upon me; decisions made by others; the dulness of classrooms, of chapel exercises, of conformity. I did not fit in as other boys did, and was conscious of questionings on the part of neighbors, my college professors, most of whom were friends of my family.

It was rumored that when I came up for a degree and various professors made unfavorable comments in faculty meeting on my scholarship and attendance, President David H. Wheeler asked how long I had been at Allegheny.

"Five years," he commented, on hearing the secretary's reply. "Well, any one who can stay at this institution for five years deserves a degree." And to that estimate of the worth of sectarian education pronounced by a man of genuine culture who was oddly out of place in it, I owe perhaps my bachelor's degree.

The five years at college had been very nearly barren for me. The inflexible pattern of American collegiate life left almost no impress on my mind. It had neither variety nor inspiration; it stimulated neither revery nor inquiry. What was offered was not what I wanted. It was not what any one wanted. College created no strength within me with which to face the world. My real life was outside of the classroom, in politics, fraternity life, in journalism and ephemeral college activities.

During the summer months I worked in my father's factory. I was successively finisher, cabinet-maker, and upholsterer, but I was more interested in playing practical jokes or paying off grudges on my fellow workmen than in learning the trade. The men in turn made it unpleasant for me. They thought that I was spying on them or might take away their jobs. My summer spent in the office reduced the bundle of promissory notes in the safe by very little.

The summer of my junior year I went to Chautauqua Lake and got a job as night-clerk in a hotel. That was gay and more to my liking. But I had very little free time. I went on duty at six o'clock and remained in the office until nine or ten the next morning. One night the owner put a heavy-caliber revolver in my hand and told me I would have to police the place. One of the cooks was drunk and was threatening to kill every one in the kitchen with a meat-cleaver. I paced up and down the basement kitchen all night, frightened at every sound.

One of my duties was to balance the books, over which I usually agonized during the night. One morning about three o'clock I was clapped on the back, and woke up to see my employer standing over me. Several thousand dollars were spread out on the desk in front of me, and the big hotel safe that contained the jewels of guests was wide open. The morning before when I went off duty a girl had suggested that we take a walk. We did not get back until nightfall, so I had had no sleep. Hard characters made the neighborhood of the hotel none too arcadian; I expected sharp justice to be meted out. But it was tempered—possibly because I danced well. And I came back as clerk summer after summer.

At Chautauqua I heard some lectures on political economy by Richard T. Ely, of Johns Hopkins. They made me want to know more about the big world outside of my little home town. I met John H. Finley, later president of the College of the City of New York and now on the New York *Times*, who was then a student at Johns Hopkins and was doing editorial work on *The Chautauquan*, a periodical published by the Assembly. John Finley, I realized suddenly, was doing what I most wanted to do. He was writing for a newspaper. And I found that I had a definite ambition. I would become an editorial writer on a city newspaper. In order to be that I felt that I should know something about economics, history, politics. Apparently Johns Hopkins was the place where one should study these things. Therefore I would go to Johns Hopkins. I had saved a few hundred dollars; that would be enough for a start and I would work my way through. For the first time in my life I had a definite, serious desire to do something, not because somebody expected me to do it or because it was there to do, but because I genuinely wanted it. I was also under the glamour of a Ph.D. degree. It seemed to me a hallmark of intellectual power. It might open doors to wealth and distinction. And I was not indifferent to wealth. Men in Meadville were comfortable on nine hundred dollars a year; few made more than twelve hundred out of their business. Given the magical degree, I might in time earn fifteen hundred dollars a year. And that would be a princely income.

CHAPTER III

JOHNS HOPKINS

In the fall of 1889 I set out for Baltimore with my earnings as a hotel clerk increased by a hundred and fifty dollars given me by my father. I realized later how much it had cost him to gather together even that sum, for a hundred dollars bulked larger in those days than five hundred does to-day. Before my departure he took me to the best tailor in town and had me outfitted with a cutaway suit. It was very expensive, made of broadcloth with broad satin stripes running up and down the material. It would usher me into the big world. This kindness of my father's caused me more unhappiness than any unkindness I ever experienced at his hands. The striped suit made me a marked man. In classrooms and on the street it proclaimed the small town from which I came. It was far too good to be discarded; my sense of thrift and regard for my father would not permit of that. So it had to be worn. It was my first hair-shirt.

When I had paid the fees and cast up the cost of board and necessary incidentals, I realized for the first time how meagre were my financial resources. At Allegheny students with three hundred dollars a year were courted by fraternities and looked up to as scions of wealth. At Johns Hopkins twice that was needed just to get along. I had three hundred dollars in hand and three years of study to look forward to. The struggle that was in store for me seems now, as I look back on it, one of the best things that ever happened to me. It forced me to be resourceful and to stand on my own feet.

But I nearly went shipwrecked within a few weeks after my arrival. Baltimore seemed very big and I did not feel at home in the university. It was confusing to me, a student from a sectarian college, to be cast on my own resources; to be permitted to come and go as I willed. Informal methods of study without recitation were new, and I was badly prepared for study. I had done no real work at college and had no scholarly enthusiasms. Nor had I any friends. To forget my loneliness I went to the theatre, sitting in the topmost gallery. One night I saw Julia Marlowe in a Shakespearian rôle and fell desperately in love with her. I had never cared much about girls; at college I felt uncomfortable with them. But I was ready to sacrifice everything to be near Julia Marlowe. I determined to be a super, and got as far as the stage entrance, but my courage failed me. I did not miss a performance the week she was in Baltimore. I followed her to Philadelphia and spent a week there. I would have gone farther, but the hopelessness of it and my rapidly failing bank-account sent me back to Baltimore, where I was lonelier and poorer than ever.

One evening at dinner I met William Gard, now of the Metropolitan Opera House. At that time he was a newspaper man. He took me under his wing and secured a position for me on the Baltimore *American*, doing university sports. After a while I began rewriting articles on popular economics, which I sold to Baltimore and Pittsburgh papers. An article on prison reform that I sent to *The Christian Union*—now *The Outlook*—brought me in a check for fifteen dollars. I was lifted out of myself by this encouragement. Something of mine would be printed in a form more permanent than a daily paper. I treasured the check for a long time, unwilling to cash it, confident, when I looked at it, that success had really come.

My financial troubles were eased that winter in a way that I was rather ashamed of. Returning to Baltimore after the Christmas holidays, I changed cars at Harrisburg about four in the morning and found a seat in the smoker with a young travelling man, who told me that he sold pickles in Maryland for H. J. Heinz. He was a fine-looking fellow, with the carriage and voice of William Jennings Bryan. Several weeks later he called at the boarding-house where I lived. He was much embarrassed, but finally floundered into telling me the purpose of his visit.

"I've been asked," he said, to make a speech at a big dinner Mr. Heinz is giving in Pittsburgh next month to his agents. I'm frightened to death. I don't know what to say."

He paused dolefully. Then he made a clean breast of it.

"Mr. Howe, I want you to write a speech for me; you're a college man, it won't be hard for you. I'll never forget it if you will."

Amused at his tribute to a college education and in a hurry to get rid of him, I said: "Yes, I'll fix you up something to say; don't worry about it."

I forgot about my promise until he called a couple of weeks later. When he found that the speech had not been written, he was in a panic. I told him to come and get it the following evening, and sat down in fancy with the two hundred assembled pickle agents of H. J. Heinz before me.

I dwelt on the distinguished sons of the Commonwealth of Pennsylvania and their contributions to America. On William Penn, Benjamin Franklin, and James G. Blaine; I talked of the Continental Congress, the Declaration of Independence, the resources of the Keystone State. Then I launched into pickles and the boon of fifty-seven different varieties. I closed with a peroration. The glory of the Keystone State would never die. It had encircled the world. Its most distinguished son was H. J. Heinz.

When the pickle drummer appeared at my rooms a week later, I was apprehensive. Had I gotten him into trouble with my mock-serious flourishes? I should have remembered that what was fun to me was bread and butter to Mr. Heinz's aides. But my fears were groundless. The drummer was expansive in his enthusiasm about himself. He was an orator. Apparently he had not only delivered a great speech, he had written it. He called, not to express the gratitude he had promised, but to tell me about his achievement. He had captured the convention, and Mr. Heinz had rushed from the head of the table to congratulate him. Every one had taken the speech seriously; it was a brilliant appreciation of one of America's great men. To the two hundred drummers the fifty-seven varieties were a title to greatness. Pickles were blazoned over the world. The name of Heinz was a household word, pictures of his factories were displayed on thousands of billboards. The speech had been reprinted in several languages and was being distributed all over the country.

My friend's conversion into an orator was not the end of the incident. He was later appointed general manager for the State of Maryland, and sent me a check for fifty dollars in tacit recognition of my share in his advancement. Somehow the story leaked out. That winter I wrote speeches for greengrocers, for travelling men, for food conventions of divers sorts. And my finances flourished more than my self-esteem.

Ultimately I made my expenses by newspaper work. At first I wrote the university gossip, and covered athletics and university activities of all kinds. I knew the other university reporters, and when they quit their jobs I hastened to secure them. I utilized material of my instructors in special stories, which I sold to Pittsburgh and Baltimore papers. I looked after the publication of one of the scientific societies which had its headquarters in Baltimore. I did some syndicate writing and took over the publication of my fraternity journal. During my second and third years I earned enough to feel free from worry. In fact, I earned more than I did years after graduation.

My reveries during these years were always of a metropolitan newspaper, of a noisy city office with men rushing in and out, of the make-up room; of the press-room, where dirty-fingered and dirty-faced men worked far into the night in a chaos of confusion. I worried not a little over my lack of scholarly enthusiasms. I had none. I worked hard and read diligently what was assigned, but it was a good deal of a grind. Neither history, economics, nor jurisprudence gave me half the thrill that came from an assignment to write up a football game for one of the Baltimore papers. I felt somewhat wronged when I was not awarded a fellowship at the end of the second year, but comforted myself with the explanation that my failure was due to having to work my way through the university. But the real reason was that I was not interested in scholarship as such; I was preparing for the trade of journalism. In the back of my mind was the consciousness that if necessity drove me to it, I could take up teaching. For Johns Hopkins provided an assurance of easy entrance into the academic world.

Daniel C. Gilman, the president of Johns Hopkins, was a great educator. He had been selected by the board of trustees and given a free hand in working out the plans for the university before its doors were opened for students. He determined that the endowment should be spent on men rather than on buildings, and that the university should be devoted primarily to graduate work. Up to that time America sent her advanced students abroad, especially to Germany, for study. The men whom he gathered about him as instructors brought with them an atmosphere of the German university, of its freedom, its unconventionality, its enthusiasm for research work. American universities had followed the models of Oxford and Cambridge. They were church institutions; they emphasized the classics; they were designed primarily for the education of the sons of gentlemen. Doctor Gilman selected as instructors men of enthusiasm, of independence, of courage.

The university had been endowed by Johns Hopkins, with money made out of whiskey. The endowment seemed magnificent at the start, but year by year it had declined owing to the depreciation in the value of the stock of the Baltimore and Ohio Railroad, in which a great part of the funds was invested. No one talked about the great wealth of the university; there was no financial agent touring the country to build up a huge endowment. And if "Uncle Daniel," as President Gilman was affectionately called, had any financial worries, he kept them to himself. The university was not a showplace. It was very badly housed in a group of old lofts and residences on Howard Street, close by the business section of the city. There was none of the magnificence of the present-day university. Little had been done to the old buildings except to cut out partitions so as to provide lecture-rooms with long tables running down the centre and comfortable chairs in which the students sat with their notebooks. There was no campus. There were no college publications; athletics were negligible. Students learned how to use books and how to enjoy their minds. Teachers and students alike felt a dignity and enthusiasm in their work.

My subjects were political economy, history, and jurisprudence. Professor Ely, whose lectures had attracted me to the university, was head of the department of political economy. He was an economic radical, critical of old traditions and of accepted authorities. Adam Smith, Ricardo, and John Stuart Mill wrote, he said, about the world as it had been in the days of our grandfathers, when there were no railroads, when large-scale industry was not known, huge aggregations of capital had not appeared, and the industrial revolution had just begun. Traditional political economy was a science a hundred years out of date. It was without reality. Text-books talked about the universality of competition; Professor Ely told us that competition was coming to an end. They outlined laws of rent, of profits, of demand and supply that were inoperative. They pictured a society of struggle, while Professor Ely showed us a world of monopoly, an economic feudalism that was fast taking the place of the theoretical world of freedom and equal opportunity.

Under his teaching I found myself wrenched loose from the economic theories current in Meadville. Men who came under his influence learned to look at the world with inquiring minds and to challenge the finality of established things.

The year I took my degree Doctor Ely left Johns Hopkins to go to the University of Wisconsin. There a few years later he was tried by the Board of Regents for alleged socialistic teaching. It was, I believe, one of the first heresy trials in the universities. Doctor Ely was vindicated and a tablet was put up on the campus as a monument to academic freedom, but the trial sent a chill through political economists everywhere and aided effectively in transferring discussion of social questions from the universities to the street-corners and the radical press.

Johns Hopkins in my time and during the first quarter of a century after its founding was as free as a privately endowed university could be. Accustomed to constraint, I wondered at this freedom. I wondered at the intimacy between professors and students, at the possibility of meeting distinguished teachers as human beings. As I gradually became accustomed to this new freedom, I myself pioneered into new fields of thought. I learned how to work, how to use books. I met men who were not afraid to use their minds, not afraid of what they might find if they looked for the truth. Religion was completely overlooked in this scheme of things. Its taboos were disregarded. The Old and New Testaments were material to be dug into, like other historical material. Unscholarly as I was by nature, I came to love Johns Hopkins with a peculiar affection, as did other men of my time. We likened it to the mediæval universities of Paris, Padua, or Bologna, to which men tramped across Europe for the privilege of sitting under some great teacher who expounded the wisdom of the East. We too were masters and pupils, living simply, badly housed, indifferently fed; just a group of enthusiasts interested in a rediscovery of the mind. We took pride in the achievements of all the departments; whether of Basil M. Gildersleeve in Greek or Ira M. Remsen in chemistry. In the department of history and politics, in which I belonged, we lived and worked in an intimate way with Herbert B. Adams and esteemed him a great teacher. We felt his freedom from intellectual prejudices, his encouragement of us to discover our own enthusiasms in our own way. We felt a comradeliness in him, as if he had been an older and wiser fellow student. We knew that he respected our choices; we learned to share in his scorn of stupid conventions, and caught from him a sense of education as a pleasurable thing, full of drama and excitement.

We were proud of our department, housed on the top floor of an old building on Howard Street. It was lined with book-shelves running to the ceiling. Here forty of us took a few lectures a day and did our reading. Here we gathered at night and worked over our doctors' dissertations. Men of distinction who happened to be in Baltimore were brought into our semimonthly seminars, to give us a glimpse of what was happening in the world outside. Simon Newcomb, the astronomer, a big, lusty, joyous man, lectured to us on economics, as did Fabian Franklin, the mathematician, and later one of the editorial writers of the New York *Evening Post*. Doctor Franklin was one of the kindliest of men, a teacher who spared no effort of sympathy to help his students.

As I became adjusted to university life I found a companionship such as I had never known. We read widely in history and political science under direction from our instructors. We worked together at night in our department and met in the fraternity houses on Saturday evenings. There were *bemuesste koepfer* here and there in the various departments who never seemed quite ready to face their examinations for a doctor's degree.

Among the students whom I knew best was Newton D. Baker. He was an undergraduate while I was in the graduate department, but we took many of the same courses and roomed together for two years. He was definitely preparing for the law and already gave promise of the distinction he has since achieved as a lawyer and public man. He was a brilliant speaker, a constant reader, and remembered what he read. Things seemed to lodge in his mind properly classified and to come out again when he needed them. Mr. Wilson knew him at that time as a serious student, but his interest in him dated further along to the Baltimore convention, where Baker made a remarkable speech that contributed to Mr. Wilson's nomination.

I had grown up in Meadville with Charles Homer Haskins, now dean of the Graduate School at Harvard, and followed him to the university. We had been together at Allegheny College, where he was a prodigy. He was teaching seniors Greek and Latin when he was himself a sophomore. He was the youngest man who had ever taken a doctor's degree at Johns Hopkins. Other men in the department of political science whom I knew best were David Kinley, now president of the University of Illinois; Westel W. Willoughby, with whom I roomed for a time and who is now director of the department of political science at Johns Hopkins; Edward A. Ross, the distinguished sociologist at the University of Wisconsin; and Charles D. Hazen, professor of history at Columbia. We were very serious-minded. Sunday was the one day when we felt that we had a right to take liberties with time. Then we slept late and took long tramps in the country. There was little to distract us from the great adventure of education on which we were engaged; an occasional dance in the gymnasium, an evening in the comfortable beer saloons around the university, glimpses of the charming hospitality of the city, were incidents in the great business of making ourselves scholars. Our own relationships and interests sufficed us, and the outside world seemed very far away. There was a spirit of courage and restless inquiry communicated from instructors to students. Among the gifts of the university to us were open-mindedness, a willingness to make sacrifices for the truth, a passion for change. Johns Hopkins taught men to think, not what to think.

We were encouraged to be ourselves, to find our own lives, to make our own decisions. Education was not a thing of books alone, it was to be taken wherever one could find it. We were free to do part of our work in Europe, where most of our instructors had studied. Such an adventure was always in the minds of my roommate, Westel W. Willoughby, and myself, and in the spring of 1891 we took second-cabin passage on the old liner *New York*. We landed in England and went to Oxford. But Oxford was not very hospitable. We went on to Berlin and took lectures in history and political science. We heard von Treitschke, the Prussian historian whose teachings of the divinity of kings and the necessity for military force shocked many German students at that time.

We lived in students' quarters and ate at students' restaurants, where enough food with a stein of beer could be bought for from twenty to thirty cents. When we went to the theatre it was in the topmost gallery at a negligible cost, and our excursions were made on foot with packs on our backs. Our total expenses averaged less than a dollar a day. But when, by the end of the summer semester, we turned toward home, we were broke. Walking seemed the cheapest method of locomotion, and we tramped for days through Saxon Switzerland. We worked our way to Carlsbad, where I remembered that a cousin of my father's spent his summers. By our united efforts I was made as presentable as possible and mustered up courage to go to the villa to which I had been directed. But my father's cousin had left

the week before for Italy. I think that I was relieved. I should not have known what to ask him
for. We got to Munich, and there an acquaintance
lent us money for a tramp into Italy and back over
the mountains to Switzerland. In Lucerne a draft
for an insignificant sum put us on our way to Liver-
pool. Our passage home had prudently been bought
before leaving America.

From many of the evils of American education
Johns Hopkins was conspicuously free. Censorship
of thought, mental docility, waste of enthusiasms, of
adventure, of individuality—all were foreign to it. It
was free from fear. It was as unlike the timid small
college from which I came as it is unlike the universities of to-day, which seek their presidents from
among business men, lawyers, good money-getters,
and in which freedom of teaching is being subordinated to the desire for a big endowment. The teachers, not the trustees, determined what was to be
taught and how they should teach it. There was no
placating of possible donors, no mirroring of the
views of an economic class. In the nineties at Johns
Hopkins I had the good fortune to be born into the
world of thought, to be associated with men to
whom honesty was a matter of course, and to whom
courage was the first essential of a gentleman and a
scholar.

Johns Hopkins freed me from many small-town
limitations. It gave me new authorities, but they
were still authorities outside of myself. I continued
to think as others thought, only now I was thinking as
did wise men, men who paid little attention to the
church, but who had a worshipful veneration for
some scientist or teacher under whose influence they
had fallen. I accepted these new authorities as quite
natural. Acceptance fell in with my earlier assumption that authority was proper, necessary, probably

the first of the moralities. Not till years after did I come consciously to believe that I had a right to be my own authority. And not until I had made serious mistakes did I awaken to the belief that I had some rights of my own in the world, the right to pursue my own enthusiasms, to choose what was agreeable rather than what was not. Duty was always first; happiness was to be scrutinized.

CHAPTER IV

WOODROW WILSON—VIRGINIAN

OUR greatest lecturer, as he was the most distinguished graduate of the department, was Woodrow Wilson. Austere, never inviting intimacies, he kept quite by himself at the university. I lived at the same boarding-house with him on McCullough Street for several winters, where he occupied a modest bedroom, and fraternized absently with the half a dozen men who lived there. He was a raconteur of good stories and a brilliant conversationalist. But he spent most of his time in his room by himself preparing his lectures and writing.

I permitted no conflicts to interfere with his courses. I read religiously the books he suggested as prescribed reading. What he had achieved I might also achieve if I were diligent enough. I absorbed his conceptions of disinterested statesmanship, of government by *noblesse oblige*. That early discipleship gave me, years later, clews to the understanding of the powerful, baffled, lonely personality who took us into the Great War.

The Wilson whose words I accepted then as I did a quarter of a century later was a child of Calvinistic forebears, of Virginia backgrounds, of university enthusiasms. He never escaped from the church, the reveries of student days, from love for his native State. They explain his written words, they made him what he was.

He studied at the University of Virginia as a Virginian should. No university left a stronger stamp

35

on its students than did the foundation of Thomas Jefferson. At Johns Hopkins he continued the study of history and politics. There he lived in the lives of the Fathers of the Republic. He read their State Papers, studied the debates of the Constitutional Convention, and idealized them as philosopher-statesmen who had left imperishable monuments to liberty in the written word. These Virginia gentlemen had not only won liberty by the sword, they had made it permanent by great documents—the Declaration of Independence, the Bill of Rights, the Federal Constitution. They had laid the foundations of democracy, industrial as well as political. Only those students who lived in the atmosphere of Johns Hopkins during these early years know the veneration in which the men who gave these written monuments to the world were held.

At Johns Hopkins, Woodrow Wilson fell under the spell of Walter Bagehot, one of the greatest of British essayists. He urged his students to read and reread Bagehot as he himself had done. His *Congressional Government* was said to have been inspired by Bagehot's *British Constitution*, as were many of his essays on public men. Bagehot gave the student Wilson that which his mind wanted; a picture of what a great constitutional statesman should be. Through Bagehot's eyes he saw British statesmen as he saw himself. They were drawn from the best families, trained from youth for the service of the state. They grew up in the atmosphere of Oxford and Cambridge, and were exalted by traditions of disinterested public service. They had no private ends to serve; because of their independent wealth they were influenced only by the welfare of the empire. They were the natural rulers of the constitutional state. England was a gentlemen's country. And Mr. Wilson believed in gentlemen, in selected men, in the platonic sense of the term. To Woodrow Wilson the scholar it was easy to idealize a country that put its scholars in politics and kept them there as it kept Arthur Balfour, James Bryce, and other men of his own type.

A love of English institutions was strong in Mr. Wilson even during his student days. He organized then a debating society known as the University Commons, modelled after the Oxford Union. Its proceedings were carried on as are the proceedings in the House of Commons. There was a ministry and an opposition. Weekly debates were staged on current political issues, and ministries rose or fell on votes of confidence. As a dissertation for his doctor's degree Mr. Wilson had written *Congressional Government*, which was considered the best book written by an American on our form of government. It treated the British constitution with its responsible ministries sitting in Parliament as better fitted than our own for popular government.

Woodrow Wilson loved England as the mother of civil liberty and of parliamentary government. She had given us the Magna Charta, the Bill of Rights, and Petition of Rights. She had exiled the Stuarts for their betrayal of English liberties and had called in Cromwell and William of Orange to re-establish them. In his mind England was the literal mother of America. From her we had taken our political institutions. Also our system of jurisprudence. His chief criticisms of the American Constitution related to those features which failed to follow the British parliamentary model. It was this love for British forms that led him to read his messages to Congress in person and to treat himself as a Premier rather than as a President. As a matter of fact he was better fitted by temperament to serve as a parliamentary leader than as a President, and he would have felt much more at home at Westminster than in Washington.

Mr. Wilson gave us no glimpse of the economic background of the English ruling class. There was always the assumption that these public men were not moved by private gain. It was never hinted in his lecture-room that the British landed gentry, bankers, and business men enacted laws to protect their own class and group; looked out, in short, for their own interests. Nor that the House of Lords was in the nature of a private corporation representative of special interests even more than the United States Senate. He was not interested in economics.

Woodrow Wilson prized the blood of his forebears. It was the blood of the Washingtons, Jeffersons, Madisons, Lees which flowed back in its purity to old England. During the Peace Conference Mr. Wilson went to Buckingham Palace, to the old Guildhall, to Carlisle with a pride of birth, which the British never failed to keep alive before his eyes. He was the kin, the equal, of the men he sat among from the British Parliament. He loved England as did they. His blood was the same as theirs. He knew her history better than did most of his English associates, and he was proud of the service which he had been able to render to the mother country.

Another university influence permanently affected Woodrow Wilson. At Johns Hopkins history was studied from original sources, from American State Papers, from *The Federalist*, from the writings of the Fathers; the text-book was secondary. We were directed to read and reread the writings of the Presidents, especially of Washington, Jefferson, and Madison. We read the debates of the Constitutional Convention, the letters of these early men. This reverence for State Papers lived on in President

Wilson as it did in all of his contemporaries. It exalted the written word; it made him careful of his official addresses and communications to Congress. Just as he gathered his pictures of men out of their public utterances, so subsequent historians would judge him from the same source. His other addresses may pass away; his *History of the United States* may be forgotten; the things he did may be condemned; but generations hence students in the universities and statesmen at the Capital will find the Woodrow Wilson of his own reveries, the Woodrow Wilson that he wanted preserved in the State Papers written by him to his contemporaries.

Woodrow Wilson the President is to be found in these early influences. He never outgrew them. He lived in a world of dreams rather than with men. His reveries were of English and American statesmen, himself among the number; they were the reveries of the student, of the admiring biographer, of the historian of the Victorian age, when men were measured by ideological standards rather than by the more realistic standards of to-day. He was always religious, Calvinistic. He loved Virginia, the Mother of Presidents, and esteemed great documents as the most enduring of deeds. His heroes had phrased liberty, had inspired movements, had given the world charters of freedom. They had won great victories by the pen.

CHAPTER V

JOURNALISM

WHEN I descended from the platform on Commemoration Day in May, 1892, with a certificate conferring on me a doctor's degree, I felt assured that it, if not my abilities, would be recognized as a matter of course. I had great confidence in that certificate of scholarship, but I wondered a little that it had been conferred on me; I did not feel scholarly, I had not been able to master the abstractions of political economy, I was not soaked in history as were some of my associates. And I had never had any great enthusiasm for any of my subjects. But that the degree was an invaluable possession I had no doubt. It would open doors, command friends, assure a job; of that there was no question. Only a few men had taken advanced degrees at that time. Johns Hopkins was the first and almost the only American university that emphasized postgraduate work. A Hopkins Ph.D. was a distinction of which I was infinitely proud. I should have no difficulty in finding a position. Journalism was my goal, but I was not unwilling to consider a good academic post as a stopgap. The only position offered, however, was as instructor in political science at an Indiana college; a Johns Hopkins man was being dismissed from it because he smoked a pipe and refused to conduct chapel exercises. The salary was nine hundred dollars a year, a sum which I had easily earned at newspaper work at the university.

But I was not greatly interested in salaries. They were quite secondary. I had found something that had evaded me on the mourners' bench at Allegheny College. I was one of the chosen. I had had a great opportunity. I must pass what I had learned on to others; especially must I justify my superior knowledge of economics, of politics, of history. I must make war on the evils that had been disclosed to me. The political boss must be exiled, the spoilsmen must be replaced by trained men. The business man must be awakened to responsibility and led to take a disinterested part in municipal politics; he must bring his experience to the administration of the city as did the business men in England. The trusts, which were then rising to power, must be curbed or destroyed, while the public-utility corporations of the cities must be either owned or regulated in the interest of the public.

There was a strong moralistic quality to my philosophy. I was one of the elect. The motto of Johns Hopkins, *Veritas Vos Liberabit*, meant that salvation was to come through the mind; it must come through men who were trained to know the truth and to carry it out to others.

This was my priesthood of service. Other men had gone out to it. Walter Page, Albert Shaw, John Finley were carrying on the Hopkins tradition in journalism—why should not I?

In the fall I went to New York. There I found a cheap and crowded boarding-house on West Tenth Street near Sixth Avenue with three other men from Allegheny College who had drifted to New York to do newspaper work or to study. The other boarders were for the most part shop-girls from the Sixth Avenue department stores, newspaper men who were down and out, and a motley array of men and women who professed to have known more prosperous days. Every morning they went out in search of a job, every evening they returned empty-handed. The atmosphere of the place was one of failure, of lost illusions, of wrecked hopes. It was a descent for me, but it would not be for long. Of that I felt sure. Our room, containing two double beds, was soon discovered by other men, and not infrequently one or more would spend the night there curled up in chairs or stretched out on the floor before the fire. For this was during the hard times of the winter of 1892, when the newspapers had reduced their staffs owing to the industrial depression. But I had no fears. I had worked my way through the university, had earned substantial sums without great effort, and now that I had definitely set my hand to journalism I would quickly rise, as other Johns Hopkins men had done.

I determined first to try the New York *Times*. I should have preferred to go to *The Nation* and *The Evening Post*, then edited by Lawrence Godkin, Horace White, and a group of other intellectual liberals, but that was far above me. *The Times* appealed to me as a free-trade paper.

After many days I managed to see the city editor.

I told him who I was and my unusual preparation for editorial work. I had studied history and political economy. I was familiar with historical jurisprudence. I had travelled abroad; had been editor of several college publications. Very few men were as well equipped as I was. We should have a new deal in politics. Trusts and monopolies should be destroyed. Possibly the railroads should be owned by the government. Labor must be treated with more consideration. Most important of all, a new type of men should be drawn into politics. I had prepared my creed of service for the interview. *The Times* seemed the best of all mediums for the propagation of my ideas, and I was eager to begin.

The city editor—I think his name was McGuire

—listened tolerantly. He told me one did not begin as an editorial writer; one had to work his way up; one must be familiar with the traditions of the paper, with the city of New York. He was rather sharp in his comments on my contempt of reportorial work. That was the only way to begin, he said. Moreover, many men were out of work. The industrial depression had hit the newspapers as it had everything else. Finally he said:

"You may sit around here if you want to. I will send you on any assignment that cannot be covered by our regular staff."

I sat around for days. I was there on time. I read the files of *The Times*. I was faithful in small things. Nobody paid any attention to me, and finally I began to think I had been forgotten. I could not afford to be forgotten. My board bill was five dollars a week, and pretty soon I should be unwelcome at West Tenth Street.

I ventured to call the attention of the city editor to the fact that I was there and wanted to earn my salary.

He smiled at the word salary. I was working on space. "Here," he said, "is a call for an up-town fire. Beat it and get back as quick as you can."

That fire story was a remarkable bit of literature. It was at least a column long. That meant four dollars. I lingered in the hope that the city editor would notice it; possibly I might be permitted to see the proofs; but that was denied me. I went to bed happy and was up in the morning earlier than the milkman. The story was not on the front page; it was not on the second page. I finally found a few lines hidden in an obscure corner. Not a word of my fine writing did it contain.

I ate little breakfast. I hated McGuire; felt that he should be fired. Some weeks later I resigned—

rather I just stayed at home. My weekly earnings scarcely paid car-fare.

I tried other papers without success. I was not known anywhere. My doctor's degree seemed a liability; soon I ceased to mention it. I was willing to begin anywhere if I could be assured a wage sufficient to live on. But New York was filled with discharged newspaper men, and those whom I came to know seemed to be very capable.

In the big room in which four of us lived on the street floor of the boarding-house, no hours were observed. Typewriters were at work long into the night from the four corners of the room. The food was bad. A glass of beer and a free lunch was a substitute to be preferred. A loan of fifty cents was the maximum that any of our callers suggested. Most of us walked to and from Park Row to save car-fare.

A number of the men who loafed that winter in our room have risen in their professions. At that time some of them had pawned almost everything they possessed. There was a tradition that a pawn-broker would loan more on a vest than it was worth, in the expectation that the coat and trousers would follow. Some of the men speculated in vests in order to pawn them. When we meet to-day we never speak of that winter. It is as though it had never been. Yet, as I look back upon it, there was nothing very terrible about our poverty. We talked about it and lived with a feeling of failure hanging over us, but there was little depression. I think I felt the situation most, for I had been eight years preparing for journalism. I felt that I was equipped for any opportunity. Even at the university I had been earning a comfortable income from newspaper work. But other men were worse off than I was, and, anyway, poverty is not a terrible thing to youth. Physical discomforts meant little. We had a roof to cover

us, enough food—such as it was—to keep us from
starving, and, as a last resort, we could go home.
That, however, seemed too humiliating to consider.
In my case, going home meant adding another mouth
for my father to feed.

An old reporter living at the boarding-house
talked to me about his work. He was out of a job
and drank heavily.

"It's all very well now, my boy," he said. "You
like feeling important; you like getting the news
before any one else does; you enjoy being sent to
dinners and receptions. Newspaper work is full of
thrills, but look at me. I'm an experienced reporter.
At forty I am in the discard. I may never get another job. A hundred things may make or break
you. The city editor may be changed. He makes a
sweep of the office. You make some trifling mistake,
or violate some tradition of the paper. There were
a hundred such traditions on *The Sun* when I worked
under Dana. You don't dare marry. You may
possibly rise to five thousand dollars a year, but
that is close to the top, and the chances are you will
be glad of fifty a week ten years from now.

"And when you reach my age, it may be the East
River for you."

That was a common expression of the men who
were out of work. Occasionally we heard of one of
the shop-girls who had taken that road of escape.
There seemed to be much of that kind of despair in
1892.

A bright spot in that gray winter was my acquaintance with Walter H. Page. He was one of the
early graduates of Johns Hopkins, where he had
done brilliant work under Basil Gildersleeve in
Greek. After graduation he turned to journalism,
and felt that his work was in the South, from which
he came. He would free the Southern mind from its

mediæval theology and from the negro question. He would make a daily paper which he acquired in Raleigh the forum of the new South. He told me about his experience. A dispute arose between Presbyterians and Baptists over a question of doctrine. Mr. Page ridiculed the intolerance of both sects, scouted their claims to infallibility, and exposed the stupidity of the controversy. That week he said he lost half his circulation. Some petty political question arose a short time after. Mr. Page questioned the infallibility of the Democratic Party. That week he lost the other half of his circulation. In a short time he said he was almost the only reader left. Then he went to New York and wrote for *The World* and *The Evening Post*.

Mr. Page took pains to aid me. He entertained me at his home in the country, where he would philosophize in an intimate, kindly way. He was a wonderful talker, full of warm enthusiasms. One day he asked me to go with him to call on Mark Twain, who had just landed from Europe. We went to the old Everett House on Union Square. Mr. Page wanted some new Huckleberry Finn stories, and pleaded for them in vain. Finally Mr. Clemens said in his deliberate way: "All my life I have been a slave. I have had to get up in the morning, I have had to write an article or get ready for a lecture, I have been pursued by managers, publishers, and, worst of all, by dinners which I thought I wanted to go to when I accepted the invitation but which I hated when the evening came around. I have been a slave all my life—to engagements and to other people. That's over now. I made one resolution on the steamer coming home, and that is that I will make no engagements, that I have to keep, of any kind."

Arguments were vain. Suddenly Mr. Clemens interrupted them. In his inimitable drawl, "Mr. Page," he said, "my wife told me this morning that I must find a place to live. I can't pay much rent; I don't know how to find a house. If you will find one for me that we can move into to-morrow, perhaps I will write you some Huckleberry Finn stories."

Mr. Page consented with alacrity. He found the house, but I do not remember ever seeing the Huckleberry Finn stories that Mr. Clemens prudently had not promised.

By Christmas-time I was ready to do anything on a daily paper. But the training on which I had spent so many years had no value; it seemed to be a disability in the eyes of managing editors. I came to fear building my future on the capriciousness of journalism, on its uncertainties, on the apparently inevitable failure at forty or fifty which seemed to have been the fate of the men I met that winter. It was too precarious, too hard getting started. And I finally gave up. I gave up reluctantly, knowing that I loved the newspaper game, remembering my passion for the old Meadville printing-office, my enthusiasm for the college paper at Allegheny. The hope of an editorial position had sent me to Johns Hopkins. And had lured me to New York. A vocational psychologist, had there been any in those days, would undoubtedly have told me to stick to the work that I most wanted to do. I loved everything about a printing-plant from the smell of printer's ink to the apparent chaos that prevailed. I loved the intensity with which men worked, the abandonment of the reporters, the comradeship, the competition, the devotion of everybody from the printer's devil to the man at the top to his particular paper.

The maxims of *Poor Richard's Almanac*, on which my childhood had been nourished, were ghostly men-

tors in my mind. They challenged my personal
desires. I must establish myself. I must justify
quickly the long years of preparation. I had been
brought up on a kind of hair-shirt morality, the assumptions of which were that one ought to be doing
what one liked least; that suffering is good for character and that distasteful work is an excellent and
profitable thing. According to this devastating morality the fact that I loved newspaper work was a
reason for suspecting it and giving it up; according
to Poor Richard's maxims of thrift the reason was
twofold.

But I was wrong. I did not know until years
afterward that I only did well the things I liked to
do. For years I tried to do well things that I disliked. I always failed. Even when I seemed to succeed I had a sense of failure. Success was dead-sea
fruit. Nature seemed to lay down one rule for life:
"Refuse to be yourself and you court failure. Worse,
you insure disaster." Nor did working at things
that were uncongenial strengthen my character.

The reverse was true. I shirked the things I did not
like to do. My mental training came from things
that were easy for me, not from tasks that were
hard. Things uncongenial made little impression on
my mind. I could not remember facts that did not
interest me. My mind refused to assimilate them.
Any attempt to force me to be something I was not
seemed to do violence to some natural law.

When I turned that winter from journalism to the
law I did violence to myself. It offers security, was
the argument that I used. It opened doors to politics. Through it I might achieve independence and
return to writing. Through it, too, I could get into
reform work, for the lawyer speaks with authority
and can devote himself to outside matters without
injury to his profession. Marshalled together, the

arguments were convincing, and I enrolled in the
New York Law School, intending to do two years'
work in one and go up for my examination the following June.

CHAPTER VI

THE POOR MAN'S CLUB

TIME seemed very precious to me at twenty-five, and I felt that I must be fulfilling my Johns Hopkins traditions. There was a pressing need in me to help the world along. If I could not write editorials, at least I could work for some cause. I had no right to permit a day to pass without something to its credit. A Johns Hopkins friend offered to introduce me to Doctor Parkhurst, who was engaged in one of his many crusades to clean up the morals of New York City. His organization had agents, mostly unpaid, whose business it was to watch the saloons, to report on violations of the Sunday-closing law, on the sale of liquor after hours, on the Raines law hotels, which existed all through the lower part of the city, and other violations of the numerous regulatory laws of the city and the State. Doctor Parkhurst appointed me captain of the assembly district which included Greenwich Village.

A vocational adviser again might have told me that I was not really interested in this sort of work, in regulating people's habits, or putting them into jail. Less wise in my own person, I took it for granted that I was zealous about enforcing the laws. The saloon was the source of political power. It bred the gang, was the training-school of the boss. It gathered in tribute from the underworld and provided a club for the immigrant and the Irish leaders who ruled the city of New York. The saloon was the root of our political evils, that was clear. I must understand it; possibly I could aid in correcting its abuses if not in putting it out of business altogether.

I had a definite qualification for the rôle: I knew almost every saloon from the Battery to the old Hoffman House. For I walked to and from the law school, and the saloons gave free lunches, salads, fried oysters, and other delicacies that went with a five-cent glass of beer. The free food was much better than what we got at the boarding-house. Often when our room was cold or crowded with men out of work, I studied in the saloon across the street. It was the only friendly place in New York for me; it was my club, where I had a comfortable warm corner to myself. I could study there better than in the law library. The barkeeper, an Irish lad, listened patiently to everybody's troubles, including my own, and seemed to be really interested in them.

Pursuing my vigilance work, I talked with Jerry one night. I wanted him to see that he was disobeying the law.

"Tell me, Jerry," I said, "why don't you close on Sunday and at midnight? Why do you sell whiskey to women? Why do you have the hotel up-stairs?"

"Why?" he said reflectively; "because we can't get along any other way; because we have to pay two thousand dollars a year in taxes. We've got to sell bad whiskey, lots of it, just to pay the tax. Did you ever think how many five-cent glasses of beer we'd have to pass over the counter to make two thousand dollars?

"Eighty thousand," he went on, figuring it out and warming to his defense. "We couldn't keep open if we sold just beer. There isn't enough profit in it. When they put the tax up to two thousand, we either had to go out of business or make money in other ways. We rented the rooms up-stairs to women, and have gambling-wheels, and sell all the liquor we can to anybody who wants it, just to keep from going broke. Don't think we're doing all those

things because we like it. I wish to God we didn't
have to do them. The business was all right before
they began to pass the laws at Albany that got us
in bad with the police. A barkeeper used to be respectable; he could look people in the face. I used
to get home at midnight and I could stay at home
on Sunday. We didn't sell whiskey to women in
those days or have bedrooms up-stairs. But now
the laws have done for us. If we keep the laws, we
have to go out of business. If we break them, we
have to pay the police to let us do it."

"But if you can't observe the laws," I said, "you
ought to go out of business."

"That's what my old boss said," Jerry replied.
"He and a lot of other old Germans sold out when
the laws were passed. They kept good family saloons
where people got something to eat and drank with
their meals. They sold out to men who were willing
to take a chance. Of course," he added meditatively,
"there always are men who are willing to take a
chance."

He got up uneasily, and walked up and down the
room.

"There's one thing sure," he said—and I thought
he was puzzling the question out more for himself
than for me—"as taxes get higher, the saloon gets
worse and graft gets worse. There isn't any way
you can stop it. There isn't any way out."

Jerry was my first realist. He saw something
happen, he looked for the cause. His old German
employer had been a good man; he had no doubt
about his own goodness. When the saloons were
left alone, there had been good saloons; with high
taxes and regulation all saloons became bad. The
explanation was clear to him; he had to sell more
drinks and expensive drinks to pay the taxes. If
anybody was at fault it was the tax-collector; the

State asked no questions as to how he got his money; apparently it cared only for its share.

I went home to mull over Jerry's unexpected answers to my catechism, and a few weeks later I sent a report to Doctor Parkhurst, along with my resignation as captain of the Greenwich Village district of the Vigilance League.

It ran in part:

"I think we are after the wrong man. You and I are in partnership with the saloon. We get more out of the sale of whiskey than does the saloon-keeper. It costs forty cents a gallon to make; the government taxes it over a dollar a gallon. Then at Albany we tax the man who sells it two thousand dollars a year. If he fails to sell enough whiskey to women and children to pay our share, he opens a house of prostitution over his saloon. The laws make the police grafters. An honest policeman cannot keep his job. If a patrolman fails to come through to his sergeant at the end of the week, he is sent to the woods, to a lonely beat on the edge of town. If the sergeant fails to come through to the lieutenant, he too is sent to the woods. If the lieutenant fails to come through to somebody higher up, charges are framed against him and he follows the other two.

"And the people who make these laws and are responsible for the high taxes are our kind of people. They are in your congregation. They take millions out of the saloon-keeper, and he in turn takes these millions out of the poor. He ruins women and children. He ruins homes. Finally he corrupts the politics of the city as well. And you and I profit out of the ruin. We don't have to pay as much taxes as we otherwise would.

"I don't like to have my taxes paid by the saloon-keeper.

"It seems to me we are not on the level.

"The first thing for us to do is to get out of the saloon business.

"If we had started out to make the saloon as bad as it could be made, we could not have made a better job of it."

The report was never acknowledged. A fascinating little book by Frederic Bastiat that I read that winter confirmed my estimate of the correctness of Jerry's analysis of regulation. It was entitled *Economic Fallacies* and showed up the "seen and unseen effects" of sumptuary legislation. The way out of the saloon problem I came to feel was by taking off all the taxes. Taxation not only failed to reform the saloon, it produced by-products that were worse than the evils it sought to cure. By taxation we had destroyed the comfortable, friendly saloon, such as I had known in Baltimore around the university, where any one who drank too much or made himself a nuisance was put out. By taxation and regulation we made the saloon an evil, involved it in politics, associated it with graft. We tried with it, as with almost every problem of its kind, every solution except letting it alone.

And when we closed the saloon we lost something with a kindly side. The saloon was the poor man's club, as only the poor understood. A slum tenement with three, four, or five persons in a room, with cooking and washing, childbirth, sickness, outside boarders crowded into suffocating and sultry quarters, needs some escape. The saloon and the streets were the escapes the city had to offer. We decided for the poor that their vices and recreation should be suppressed. We feared graft and lawbreaking less than the vices of the poor.

Possibly my own poverty made me tolerant of the saloon; that and my liking for Jerry may have influenced my retirement from the Vigilance League.

Still my early judgments as to the stupidity of regulatory legislation have been strengthened with time, as has my contempt for the hypocrisy that is identified with it. We are not on the level in our moral crusades; worse still, of their hidden effects we are crudely ignorant. Possibly this is another by-product of the evangelical-mindedness that seeks a moralistic explanation of social problems and a religious solution for most of them.

CHAPTER VII

MY FRIENDS THE IRISH

Out of the Vigilance League, through with regulating my poor man's club, I continued to take refuge in the friendly saloon across the street. When the future looked dark and I had a sense of failure, Jerry's greetings were heartening. He too was insecure and unhappy underneath his blithe Irish manner, and we understood each other. I was often in need of encouragement, for my work at the law meant little to me and interested me not at all. I was trying to do two years' work in one and earn a living at the same time. The secretary of the law school had found me a job in a lawyer's office. There I worked from nine until three. Then I took lectures from three to six, and studied listlessly until midnight. I earned five dollars a week running errands, serving legal notices, making collections, and, with a second-hand typewriter, copying pleadings and briefs which I did not understand. The chief business of my employers seemed to be the collection of electric-light bills from saloon-keepers. This was intrusted to me. In making collections I had to sit around saloons with officers of the law carrying out writs of execution. I spent most of my time on the Bowery and the lower East Side.

My fall from dignity was complete. I felt mentally soiled by the work I was doing. I was compromising my university degree and I wondered if I could ever crawl back to a place among the men I revered. I had come to New York to do editorial work on a magazine or to rise rapidly on a metropolitan newspaper. Yet here I was, living in a cheap boarding-house, spending my days making collections in saloons, or pounding a typewriter in the office of a lawyer who knew nothing about jurisprudence, mediæval texts, or Roman law. And for some reason which I did not approve of I liked the work on the East Side better than the empty formulas I learned in the law school. I liked the Tammany officials better than the old English worthies whose opinions were quoted with so much veneration in the text-books.

And during that winter some of my political ideals suffered a collapse as complete as my dignity. I did not know they were going until they were gone. Politics I had believed was the business of a gentleman. It should be in the hands of good men —men who had succeeded in business, who observed the conventions of life, who had graduated from universities. Goodness would cure political ills. The scholar in politics was the ultimate ideal, the ideal of Plato, of James Bryce, of Woodrow Wilson. By disinterested service, by not wanting anything for ourselves, the state could be redeemed.

Equipped with this philosophy, I sat about saloons with officers of the law, and came across a view of life that I had not known before. Here was a world of political reality. Here politics was part of every-day life, part of the family, of religion, of race. Politics was daily work. My state was an abstraction. On the Bowery it was a real thing—a city block, a voting precinct, or a ward. To me politics meant disinterested service. To the people of the East Side it meant getting something for themselves and their friends. To me duty to the state was the important thing; to them the duty was to themselves. Government meant the district leader, the policeman, the local boss. They and the police court magistrates were the only officials the people had any interest in. The district leader had to be placated like a heathen idol, by service at primaries and elections and in other ways. He was good to those who served him and dangerous to those who did not. Faithfulness to him brought coal and food, outdoor relief, an annual outing to Coney Island at somebody's expense. It brought security in a strange land under strange laws which might get one into trouble. Faithfulness to the boss was the only civic idea. To the poor, politics meant bread and a circus. The idea of service was there but it was very different from my idealized abstraction. The God the priest talked about was nearer the people than the God I would have had them worship.

Politics was a hierarchy. The ward boss had precinct bosses under him. They were almost always saloon-keepers or contractors, and they had vassals who hoped to become petty bosses if they were faithful. There were jobs to be had as policemen or firemen, and at the start there was street-cleaning and work under city contractors. The East Side had an ethical code of rewards and punishments. Fealty was the first obligation. Betrayal of the boss or the clan was an unforgivable offense. Everybody understood it. The judge sympathized with it. The policeman was the creature of it. To be loyal to one's friends, to stand by the gang, to do as you were told, until you were in turn selected to tell others what to do, was all that the Constitution, the Bill of Rights, and the government of the United States meant to the average man in lower New York twenty-five years ago.

These practical East Side politicians, whose every act my code condemned, were Irish. They were kindly, tolerant; good companions. Their system was human and simple, something any one could understand. It took graft and gave graft. It took graft from the saloon-keepers, prostitutes, contractors, and big business interests as naturally as its members took help and gave help to neighbors when sick or in need.

It was the Irish clan transplanted to New York. As I watched its workings and remembered the praise lavished in the university on the English conception of government, I saw an age-long conflict between the Anglo-Saxon and the Celt. The Irish have wanted a state that did things for them; the Anglo-Saxons have wanted a state that did nothing. The English had no need of such a state. They were interested in making money, in getting on in the world. Business should do as it pleased; the state should own nothing and be nothing beyond a big policeman. Politics in England was a negative thing, aristocratic, distrustful of the people. My conception of politics as the business of gentlemen seemed now to have a shadow cast alongside it. It occurred to me that the British state, ruled by men of wealth and leisure, was ruled for them, not for the people; they unwillingly allowed others a share in it. I found myself leaning unaccountably to the Irish view of things. They warmed the state into a human thing, made frank demands on it for things they could not get for themselves. They provided an amalgam to extreme Anglo-Saxon individualism, which had an aversion to the state and a resentment of any extension of its activities beyond routine things. I began to think that perhaps politics had a human side, perhaps the state should do things for the happiness of its people instead of being merely a policeman. And perhaps things had to be gotten by the people who needed them most, not for them by some scholar or leader. I began to lose my distrust for the uneducated and the poor, who I had thought should hardly wield so sacred a thing as the ballot. I learned to take an interest in people. They had hardly existed for me before. Some priggishness I think went out of me, unwillingly, through my schooling on the streets of lower New York.

The Tammany politician was also a realist, a realist like Jerry the bartender. He was as ignorant as a child about my state, he knew nothing of the Constitution; his politics were quite unmoral. His instructor was the man above him. From top to bottom the state was something that served you, not something that you served. The sermons of Doctor Parkhurst, the Bulletins of the Reform Club and Civil Service Reform League never penetrated below Twenty-third Street. To these political realists the reformer was a queer bird; he talked bunk. He wanted something for himself as did they.

In the decades that have passed since that illuminating winter I have never ceased to like the Irish. I should not like to think of America with them left out. Because of their wanting things in New York we have playgrounds, public baths, Central Park, Riverside Drive. Their instinct for collectivity made the docks and the ferries public property. They have given us our water-supply and fire department, a wonderful library service, and as good a school system as is probably to be found in any large city. And under Tammany Hall a system of local taxation was created that is unsurpassed for honesty and efficiency in this country or abroad. Unconsciously aiming to shape the state to human ends, the Irish have made New York what it is.

I was unlearning again as I had unlearned at the university. There I had escaped from the opinions of neighbors, from the unquestioned authority of the Sunday-school and the church, the undoubted purity and respectability of the Republican Party. I had acquired new sanctions, the sanctions of educated men, teachers, scholars. The state should be governed by men trained as Plato would have them trained; by disinterested men, by men not moved by personal gains or identified with machine politics. These university dogmas were intellectual. Leaders were men who had achieved success in the realm of thought or in business. Their ideals of statesmanship were taken from England, from men who dedicated their lives without remuneration to the service of the state. I clung to these new sanctions of conduct. My confidence in my own kind was not impaired. I still believed that America would be aroused only through disinterested service. But this faith was strangely confused by new human equations, by the warmer point of view of the Tammany leader and his followers in the tenements of the lower East Side.

CHAPTER VIII

THE LAW

I GROUND away at my law-books through the winter and hoped to be admitted to the bar in June. One day in April the dean of the law school announced that the Board of Regents at Albany had made a ruling requiring at least two years' study as a condition for admission to the bar.

That made my position in New York untenable. I was quite broke; owed my landlady for many weeks' board and was becoming more deeply involved every day. I should have to accept my father's support, humiliating as it was to admit it; the more because his own business had gone from bad to worse during my years of preparation for a career. I told the landlady that I was going home and assured her that the board bill would be paid.

She was a kindly soul. "There now," she said, "don't let that worry you. You stay on. One more won't make any difference. Half the people in the house owe me money and you at least seem to want to pay. Perhaps, as you are a lawyer, you can help me collect my bills."

But I went home. It was a humiliating homecoming after my nine years of study. Some months later I was able to pay my landlady. My uncle was a lawyer and took me into his office, but at twenty-five, with no money, no profession, no outlook, and a disinclination for the law, the future seemed pretty hopeless. I had no liking for teaching, had failed at journalism, and was marooned in a small town where my university training was worse than useless. I was cheered somewhat by an Irish boy in the office by the name of Patsy Sheehan. He, too, was studying law, and his wit and humor relieved the dreary summer as I pored over dusty law-books that failed to awaken the slightest response in me. I envied his limited wants. Why had I eaten at the tree of knowledge? Most of the time I sat with my feet on the desk peering into a future that contained not a suggestion of hope or allurement.

Pat liked me. He took me back to the south ward school, to the old canal, to the things I had escaped from. He deferred to me; I had been to college. And he unconsciously carried on my education in politics.

"Remember Eddie Maddigan?" he asked me one day. "He went to the south ward school with us."

"Yes," I recalled, "he pulled me out of the canal when I was a kid."

"Well, said Pat, "Eddie wants to be clerk of the county commissioners. Two Democrats have just been elected; the Republican clerk is going out and Eddie wants the job. But the commissioners have appointed some one else. Let's you and I get Eddie appointed. You write the letters, and I'll stir up the Democratic wards."

I protested that I did not believe in that sort of thing; Maddigan was not the proper man for the position; the best man should have it.

"Oh hell," Pat said. "Didn't he pull you out of the canal?"

Unwilling to seem ungrateful, I agreed, insisting, however, there was nothing we two law students could do.

"You wait," said Pat. "Wait till I get tnem scared."

We got to work, Pat in the lower wards, I at my typewriter. A stream of letters poured in on the commissioners, signed by Pat's friends, telling them that the man appointed was not an organization man, and that members of the board would be defeated when they came up for renomination. Eddie Maddigan was the choice of the Democrats of the county, and should be appointed.

It was my first experience in making public opinion, in machine politics. To my astonishment something began to happen. The commissioners sent for Sheehan and asked him to do what he could to square them with the organization. Pat told them there was only one thing they could do, and that was to appoint the man the organization wanted. If they would select Eddie Maddigan there would be no further trouble. Eddie got the job.

Again I found there was something wrong with my system. The Bluntschli Library of Johns Hopkins University was bunk to my best friend. Maddigan was a nice boy; he was honest and was our friend. Why should we not get him a job? I felt rather proud of the threatening letters I had written, signed by prominent Democratic leaders of the fourth ward, who a few years earlier I had felt were very bad men. They drank beer in the saloons. They lived down by the canal; they were Democrats: and Democrats were outside of my pale.

One afternoon I was walking out into the country and passed a girl whom I had never seen before. I watched her until she disappeared. There was something about her that held me. I wanted to follow and speak with her. She did not live in Meadville. Perhaps she belonged to a theatrical company. She wore a wide, sweeping hat, her feet were unusually small, and her ankles were in keeping with her trim body. It was her eyes that held me. They were big and brown and warm.

That evening I asked my sisters about a strange

girl I had seen. They identified her at once. Everybody in town knew and wondered about her. She was Miss Marie Jenney, of Syracuse, and was attending the Unitarian Theological Seminary. There were other women studying at the school, but Miss Jenney was different. She was too beautiful to be a minister. People insisted that she could not be serious. They argued that there was probably a man at the seminary who had brought her there. Only a man could explain such a beautiful girl, with good clothes and evidences of wealth, at a theological seminary. Women did not go in for careers thirty years ago, and saving souls was a man's job.

A few days later I saw an announcement that the seminary students were to give a theatrical performance at the Unitarian church, and her name was in the cast. I slipped off to the church after supper and secured a front seat. There were three men in the play and I hated every one of them. Miss Jenney took the leading rôle. Her acting was extraordinary. As people passed out of the church they spoke about it, and said how strange it was that with such talent she was not on the stage. It seemed absurd for her to go into the ministry.

Nothing mattered but to find some way of meeting her. College would soon be over and she would probably not return. I waited about the Unitarian church the following Sunday and spoke with the people with whom she lived. They asked me to dinner. Miss Jenney came in late with her arms filled with flowers. I fell quite dumb at the introduction. But she scarcely noticed me. She ignored me during dinner. Why should such a woman want to be a minister, I thought; why should she be studying Hebrew, Greek, and the early church fathers? It was all very stupid. I had never heard of such a thing. She could not be serious. All girls got married if they could; certainly all good-looking girls did. I quoted a remark of Heine that every woman who did anything in the world had one eye on her work and the other eye on a man. The only exception was Countess Somebody or Other, but then she only had one eye. The joke failed miserably. I endeavored to bolster it up by saying that Johns Hopkins did not admit women and that I hoped it never would.

After dinner I tried to square myself. We talked about political economy, and I found she was interested, especially in Socialism and advanced ideas. Here was something I knew about and I tried to show my wisdom. But the afternoon was a dismal failure. She seemed quite willing to see me go.

There were some weeks left and I made the most of them. I arranged walks and picnics to the lake. I brought books on economics and we read together. But much of the time I was preoccupied and silent.

Books had taught me new things about economics and politics; they had taught me nothing about women. My beliefs about women were far deeper hidden in my mind than were even the moralities of the church. I had gotten them as a child, had taken them in from relatives, neighbors, family. Men and women fell in love, they married, had children; the wife cooked the meals, kept the house clean, entertained relatives and friends, spent as little as possible, asked for what she got on Saturday evening with the weekly expense-account in her hands. She cared for the family when sick, got the children ready for school and church, arranged the men's clothes, on Sundays went on a buggy ride, and during the winter made cakes and pies for the church sociables. She did not offend the opinions of neighbors or of her husband, she was careful of her conduct, and only had an opinion of her own in a whisper. In so far as I thought of it at all women were conveniences of men. Mothers were, sisters were, wives would be. Men were kind to them; they did not swear in their presence, they cleaned their boots before entering the house, gave them as good a home as they could, and were true to their marital vows. That was the most binding obligation of all. Men who failed in the latter regard were quite beyond the pale of the people I knew. Men whom I had discovered on questionable streets or who had been seen with women of doubtful morality I avoided; anything could be believed about them.

Some day I undoubtedly would have that kind of a wife. I had thought very little about it at college, for I had been completely absorbed in other things. At Johns Hopkins I had danced, gone to teas and dinners, had looked at girls from a distance, but they had not gotten in the way of my studies. In fact, I had never taken thought of my opinions about women; they had scarcely existed for me. I had a kind of fear of them; certainly a bashfulness that I had never outgrown. They were outside of my life, but when they entered they would enter on my terms, the terms of my boyhood conceptions as to the proprieties of things.

Miss Jenney was different from this picture. And I did not like to have my picture disturbed, especially as I was so greatly attracted to the disturber. I expected women to agree; she had ideas of her own; they were better than my own, more logical, more consistent too with my democratic ideas on other things. She believed that women should vote for the same reasons that men voted. I snorted at the idea. Women should go to college as did men and find their work in the world. This shattered my picture of her convenience in the home. Women, to her, should be economically independent, they should not be compelled to ask for money, they should have an allowance; they did their share of the common work, and marriage was a partnership. This destroyed my sense of masculine power, of noblesse oblige, of generosity. To her, life was not a man's thing, it was a human thing. It was to be enjoyed by women as it was by men; there should be equality in all things, not in the ballot alone but in the mind, in work, in a career. Men and women were different in some ways, they were alike in more.

Unlearning economics and politics had been an easy matter. I had given up a small-town authority for a more distinguished one. Giving up my masculine authority meant giving up of one eminence I felt sure of. We did not state these things; they broke into our talks about life, about ourselves. I tried to avoid them. They were disagreeable; when we were married there would be time enough to discuss such questions. But this independence of mind was one of the things that made me want this new woman who had come across my path and gripped me in a way that left no doubt in my mind as to what I desired. While she weakened my masculine authority, she gave me strength in other ways. I would get courage from a woman who saw things as she saw them; could rely on a woman who faced me when other women would have smiled assent.

She has courage as well as beauty, I thought. And we will have fine talks, endless discussions, for she was interested in all of the things that I had studied. And her mind assimilated them far more readily than my own had done. But I was never able to square my ideas of marriage with hers; I could not give up the belief that a woman's place was where other women were.

Then I heard about a job in Pittsburgh, and decided to try for it. It was not certain when I would get back. I was tortured with indecision. I could not go away without knowing about the other man. I had no right to be in love as I was, I had no money, no prospects, no chance apparently to get started inside of ten years at least. And I might never get started at all. The last day in town we walked out into the country. I wanted to go on and on. At each inviting spot I pushed on to the next. Then when we sat down I managed to say something. It was very incoherent, for I felt incoherent, but I seemed to be understood. There was no other man, and that lifted one cloud. But she wanted her career; she wanted to do something for the world. She loved her work and I hated mine. And I was twenty-five and was just where I had been four years before when I left Meadville with high hopes for the conquest of the world. We parted agreeing to write to each other. My letters alternated hope and despair; hers were full of the work she planned to do.

I had secured the position I had applied for as secretary of the Pennsylvania Tax Conference, and in the fall went to Pittsburgh to take the bar examinations. The tests were severe. I knew nothing of Pennsylvania law and very little of procedure. But my oral examiner chanced to be a man of learning. He inquired about my college training, and that seemed to satisfy him. He asked me two questions; the first was about equity jurisprudence, the second was to describe the feudal system.

I had studied these subjects at Johns Hopkins and was thoroughly at home with them. I traced equity jurisprudence in detail from the Greeks to the Romans; I showed how Greek philosophy had been woven into the Roman law and how later both had been appropriated by the church as a means of tempering the rigidity of the English common law. I talked about things and books the examiner had never heard of. I was equally familiar with the feudal system. I discussed its origin, dwelt on interesting obscurities. I killed as much time as possible. When the examiner who was to take me in the afternoon came to arrange for my other tests, the lawyer who had me in hand said:

"You don't need to bother about this man. He's all right. He knows more about the history of real property, about equity, than we do."

He little knew that this was about all I did know. I should have made a poor showing on any questions involving the technic of practice, the statutes of the State, or anything more recent than the eighteenth century. For the law was still a confused maze of irrelevant things to me. Legal axioms seemed to be arbitrary dicta rather than logical principles. My mind refused to assimilate what I read. Little impression was made upon it by the text-books or by leading cases. At the end of a day of study I often found myself just where I had been in the morning.

I passed the examinations and was admitted to the bar in Pittsburgh. There I remained for several weeks, trying to look on it as the best place for me to practise in. I had many college friends there and could have made advantageous connections. I knew of Senator Matthew Stanley Quay, who ruled Pennsylvania with a rod of iron. I had known his chief lieutenants, the Andrews brothers, since my boyhood, and might have received political recognition through relatives and friends. The corrupt political condition of the State had not shocked me or any one about me when I was a lad getting railroad passes from the Andrews brothers, but it had aroused my indignation when it was analyzed in the lecture-rooms of Johns Hopkins. I knew about it both theoretically and practically, knew that the most obscure township in the State was part of it. I had heard its history traced back to the Civil War, when iron and steel were back of the Republican Party. Together with the cotton and woollen mills of New England, they financed it. The steel industry, enthroned in power by the war, demanded a protective tariff. It got what it wanted, and the Republican Party became its political agent. Later the Pennsylvania Railroad and the Standard Oil Company joined in control of the State. Matthew Stanley Quay, who was the recognized State boss, later became United States senator. He welded the railroads, the iron and steel interests, oil, the coal-mining industry and manufactures into a political system. To these were added the saloons and commercialized vice. He perfected the spoils system and controlled practically all of the offices of the State. The least important township office-holder had his place and was expected to render unquestioning obedience. The saloons and houses of prostitution aided in keeping the cities corrupt and paid a great part of the costs of the machine; costs running into the millions, which big business interests were able to shift on to the underworld by protecting it through the local bosses.

Mr. Quay was the accomplished type of political boss. He was a real ruler, dictator of an economic soviet, made up of the big business interests of the State in league with the saloon and with vice. He was not responsible to the people and did not profess to represent them. He was an *imperium in imperio*. Courted by judges, senators, railroad presidents, bankers, and business men, he held a position preferable to any elective office. Along with other bosses he selected the candidate for the presidency. He was not personally venal; he made little money for himself. He made a god of his party, believed in it, slaved for it, and made others serve it with a devotion far more fervent than that which most of us have for the state or the church. Personally, Mr. Quay was a lovable sort of man. His followers were devoted to him. He had an extraordinary memory and knew men in every township. He prized his promises. The creed of the ward worker on the East Side of New York was *mutatis mutandis* his: that his word should be as good as a bond, that his promises should be kept at any cost, that he paid for what he got, and was loyal to those who were loyal to him. He controlled the press. Churches, saloons, and brothels worked with him. No voice was raised against the crime of selling out the State. Mr. Quay was the recognized broker of business interests and of offices as well. The only rebellions against the system were started by independent oil-producers, who had been put out of business by the Standard Oil Company. They were business revolts, in no way relating to better politics. There was nowhere an outcry over the evil thing of government by business, as represented by Mr. Quay. Apparently the people did not want to rule themselves. They preferred to have their officers selected by some one else. The State was pretty rotten, every one admitted, but a change—well, nobody knew what a change might do to business.

As secretary of the Tax Commission I saw things that confused what I had learned at the university. Members of the commission were educated, intelligent, well-to-do men; they went to church; they were respected in the community. Yet they saw no impropriety in taking passes from the railroads; they grew indignant at my statement that they were relieving the railroads of millions of taxes, or that the facts they used were not accurate. Everywhere there was indifference to political conditions and approval of Boss Quay. To speak critically of him was to invite disaster, professional ostracism. One could not hope for preferment if one's loyalty was questioned. In time I came to feel that the commission had been created with the object of bringing in a report favorable to the large corporations, and that my work was being distorted to that end. I needed the salary badly. I had earned little for over a year. But at the end of a few months I sent in my resignation, and reluctantly turned my attention to the law.

Pittsburgh seemed less and less inviting to me as I lingered on in it. I hated the dirt; one rarely saw the sun. The city was so corruptly governed that the streets were not well paved, there were no decent public buildings, and there was no concern over unsightly conditions. To question Boss Quay, the protective tariff, or the prevailing system was to be outcast. Liberal ideas were taboo, Unitarians ostracized, and the compensations of orthodox religion highly esteemed. One had to be a churchgoer to get on. On Sunday the heads of its respectable families talked about religion; after six o'clock on Sunday, and from then on until Saturday night, they talked business and baseball.

I decided that I was not willing to spend my life in Pittsburgh and that I would first find a place to live and then adjust my professional life to it. I visited Buffalo, Detroit, Chicago, and Cleveland, and liked Cleveland best. It had possibilities of beauty. It stretched for miles along the lake front and still kept some of the quality of a small town. I looked up a college friend who was practising law in Cleveland and told him my situation.

"You'll get along," he said. "Everybody does. Don't worry about it. You have to start at the bottom in the law, then some day you find an opening, and after that you have too much instead of too little to do. Come over and live in my apartment. I'll grub-stake you until you get started."

It was not in reason to refuse his friendly offer, so I moved into the apartment, on the edge of the red-light district, where half a dozen of us lived, sleeping two in a bed and knowing no privacy. Our clothes were common property. A colored woman cooked our meals, and one of the boys who was out of a job served as bartender. We drank and played cards; our amusements were boisterous and distasteful to me.

The first weeks in Cleveland were discouraging. I went from one lawyer's office to another, seeking employment, but without success. One day I walked into the offices of Garfield & Garfield, the eldest sons of the ex-President. I met Harry Garfield; told him that I had been to other offices but had found nothing to do. I said: "If you don't mind, I will sit in your outer office here and do anything you want done. I like this place better than any office in town and I want to stay."

"But we have no need of another clerk," he said. "We have only started at the law ourselves. There isn't anything for you to do."

"That's all right," I answered, "but if you don't mind, I would like very much to stay."

So I found a professional home. I sat for years rather idly around the outer office, picking up small collection fees, busied with unimportant matters. It was starting at the bottom, as my friend had said, but at least I had a place in Cleveland. I formed ties as the years went on; the friendship and hospitality of the Garfields and their families made the law tolerable to me. Ultimately I was taken into the firm.

CHAPTER IX

UPLIFTING

FOR two years I worked listlessly at the law during the day and played cards in the evenings. Never skilful at cards, and unable to see our drinking-parties to a finish without paying for it the following day, I sought escape by climbing nine flights of stairs to our law offices, where, high above the city, I sat looking out over Lake Erie far into the night. There I could be by myself. So far as I could see, my life was a failure. I disliked the law, had a fear of the judges, and most of all shrank from the experienced practitioners with whom I felt I could never cope. My university training gave me little comfort, it made me no friends, it did not aid me in trial work. At times it impeded me.

Apparently I had made a mistake in believing that I could escape from my small-town background, from business and farmer forebears. I should have remained with them, working in my father's store, possibly saving it and him from failure. But I had tasted of something at Johns Hopkins that made business commonplace. And I wanted to be back in the university library, where there was no conflict, no failure.

Thus I lived for two years. Then an opportunity came to move to a college settlement that was being opened. Settlements were the last word in social work at that time; they had been borrowed from London, they were the meeting-ground for college men and women willing to share their advantages with the poor. Here was my opportunity to justify my training, my sense of responsibility to the world;

75

here also was an escape from the life I was living in the crowded apartment on the lake front.

Residents at the settlement had good food and comfortable rooms; they enjoyed a certain distinction because of their good works. Having joined the group of young men and women who lived there, I soon found myself invited out to dinners, asked to make speeches about immigrants, on politics, on cleaning up the city. I acquired a standing I had not had before. I was climbing.

My activities at the settlement, as I recall them, were anything but fruitful. As a friendly visitor to the tenements, I was uncomfortable. When I organized clubs, I felt that I had little in common with the boys. I did not enjoy dancing with the heavy-footed mothers of many children who were lured from the tenements to our parties. When asked to teach politics, I remembered my experience on the East Side of New York, and felt that my philosophy was somehow out of joint. On the edge of the red-light district, the settlement was expected to investigate and see what could be done to improve the morals of the women who lived there. To that end I collaborated in making out meaningless charts which nobody read but which we exhibited from time to time at meetings of the board of trustees.

Living at the settlement brought me into contact with people who were identified with social work. I was invited to become one of the trustees of the Charity Organization Society, an institution of which its members were infinitely proud. It was putting charity on a new basis. It had scoured the country for an efficient secretary and was organized like a business corporation. Through it questionable private charities were being frozen out. Without credentials they found it difficult to collect funds; periodical accountings were demanded from them.

The society was stamping out indiscriminate giving.
Personal charity was out of date. Pleas for help
were subjected to an acid test before relief was given;
there must be no drinking, there must be evidence
of willingness to work. People were "cases." They
were card-indexed. The applicant had to prove himself worthy before he could receive any aid, and the
decision as to worthiness was left with a corps of
young girls trained in the profession, then just
emerging, of social work. Prominent business men
who sat on the board of trustees admired the efficiency of the society. Our monthly reports were
terse, matter of fact. There were no sob stories.
Our new secretary was a great success. He could
mix with business men; he could dine at the Union
Club with credit, and hold his own in argument as
to the proper way to handle impostors, weak women
who fell, and men who were out of work. He never
permitted sentiment to confuse his judgments and
showed an outstanding courage in opposing the president of the board, our most generous patron, who
had a tendency to be tolerant of human derelictions.

If doubts ever visited me as to the validity of the
rôle I played in charity work, I paid no attention to
them. I enjoyed the monthly meetings with men
and women whose names appeared in the papers
and who were known as the best people in the city.
But one day I received a letter from a certain Doctor
Tuckerman, an active member in one of the prominent evangelical churches. For no obvious reason
the letter was addressed to me instead of to the
secretary.

It ran as follows:

"You ask me to join the Charity Organization
Society and identify myself with its work. I do not
believe in the organization of charity. Charity cannot be organized like the Steel Trust, or run by paid

clerks. Charity means love; it is a personal thing, one of the beautiful things that Christ gave the world. When you do away with personal charity, you do away with love. You say that it is indiscriminate, that it impoverishes the poor. Can you picture Christ organizing love, card-indexing the good and the bad as you are doing on your basis of worthiness measured by business standards?

"Your society, with its board of trustees made up of steel magnates, coal operators, and employers is not really interested in charity. If it were, it would stop the twelve-hour day; it would increase wages and put an end to the cruel killing and maiming of men. It is interested in getting its own wreckage out of sight. It isn't pleasant to see it begging on the streets.

"You say that by giving to the society I can relieve myself of the burden of investigating cases. But I ought not to be relieved of this burden. The responsibility for poverty should not be taken from me. It were better if it were kept before our eyes. Nor do I like your thriftiness. Your circular tells me that I will receive a certain number of cards in return for my contribution. I may give them to people who apply to me for aid. They in turn present them at your office and an investigator is told off to ascertain whether the applicants are worthy. If they are discovered unworthy, you are elated, and the tickets are returned to me.

"I doubt, as I read my New Testament, whether the Twelve Disciples would have been able to qualify as worthy according to your system. And Christ himself might have been turned over by you to the police department as a 'vagrant without visible means of support.' "

The letter bothered me. Its phrases stuck in my mind. There was little talk of love, of kindness, of charity in our monthly meetings. They would have seemed out of place. It was our job to put an end to sentimental giving. I remembered my own protest against Doctor Parkhurst's vigilance work and my discovery that we were after the wrong man. Was this more of the same error? Was charity a business enterprise, designed to keep poverty out of sight and make life more comfortable for the rich? It seemed clear enough that more pay was one way to avoid poverty, yet my fellow members on the board of trustees talked with indignation of the demands of the workers in the steel-mills. Women who came to our monthly meetings in their carriages talked about the need of thrift, but the harassed mothers whom I saw now and then in the tenements gave every evidence of a thrift that needed no stimulus from us. I began to have a dislike for our complacent reports and statistics of unworthy cases. Investigations into men's habits irritated me. I knew quite well that if I put in twelve hours in the rolling-mills I should more likely than not drop into a saloon afterward. If I were down and out, I should live as other men had to live in the tumble-down shacks and lodging-houses under the hill, where the beds were kept warm twenty-four hours in the day by the turnover in the steel-mills on the flats.

Doctor Tuckerman made me feel uncomfortable in our weekly meetings; I felt dishonesty in our appeals for money. I could not forget his suggestion that organized charity was designed to get the poor out of sight, and that there would be no need of charity if the men who supported the society paid better wages and protected the workers by safety devices in the mills.

I ceased attending meetings of the trustees; then I resigned, and soon after left the settlement.

CHAPTER X

BEER AND SKITTLES

My next experience was to be a happier one. One night at a dance I met a fledgling lawyer like myself, a young Harvard graduate named Morris Black, of a prosperous and respected Hungarian family. We drifted into talk, told one another what we thought of our dirt-begrimed law-books, how we hated the petty things we were doing in the justice of the peace courts, laughed over the stupidities of our practice. We felt alike about life. He was emotional, moody, full of vital energy, a musician. I was reserved and undemonstrative. From our first meeting we were inseparable. We dined and drank and tramped together. His home became my own.

Out of memories of the comradeship of college *kneipes* we organized the Beer and Skittles Club, which rather by accident took on a serious purpose. Cleveland at that time was about to erect a city hall, the county was planning a new court-house, a public library and a new federal building were to be put up, and the old disgraceful Union passenger-station was to be replaced by a new, imposing one. Both Black and I had lived in Germany and we saw the possibility of combining these structures into a splendid group, as is done in many of the capitals of Europe. We invited the editorial writers of each of the Cleveland papers to join the club, and unfolded to them a plan of developing a great civic centre. We prepared illustrated stories of the grouping of public buildings in Vienna, Paris, Budapest, Dresden, and Munich, and printed them in the Sunday papers.

We induced the local chapter of the Institute of Architects to hold a competition for plans. Finally, when the subject had gotten well into people's minds, we went to Harry Garfield, who was then the president of the Chamber of Commerce, and asked him to appoint a committee to further the idea. From this time on the chamber made the plan one of its chief objectives. Yet nobody knew from what source the continued agitation was directed or that any particular group was keeping the subject alive.

The Beer and Skittles Club became known, but for other reasons. We met in an obscure restaurant down by the lake front, kept by Frau Wohl, a Hungarian. There we gave dinners once a week, which soon acquired a reputation. Even at resorts of *bon vivants* in Paris, Budapest, Vienna, and Copenhagen I have never eaten such dinners as this old Hungarian lady prepared for us. She was very proud of the club, and especially proud of Morris Black, whose family was of a higher caste in Hungary than her own. A drink that we concocted, known as Slivowitz punch, added to the fame of the club. It seemed as harmless as lemonade, but as the dinner progressed it worked wonders. It was our delight to invite men of substantial reputations to our dinners and later tuck them tenderly into a cab, with instructions to the driver to take them to their homes. However, we sometimes miscalculated, and one night Black and I cosily fell asleep on a bench in the public square where we had stopped to wait for a car. There we were awakened by a patrolman in the early morning and invited to come with him to the police station.

Such lapses, however, did not interfere with our plan for beautifying the city. Later, when I was in the city council, I introduced the legislation that committed the city to the project, and Cleveland has since carried through a monumental planning enterprise. It purchased a great stretch of land, running from the business centre to the lake front. The land was planned by an expert commission with sunken gardens and parking, with a wide mall running down the centre. Flanking the mall a city hall, county court-house, federal building, public library, and convention auditorium have been erected, with a Federal Reserve bank building not far distant. A uniform style of architecture and a uniform sky-line insured harmony and unity of effect in this splendid attempt at city-building.

One night, coming home from a dinner at Frau Wohl's, Black said:

"Fred, you or I have got to run for the city council. Let's clean up our district. It's a disgrace that it should be run by Bill Crawford, who claims to carry it in his vest-pocket. You run," he said, "and I'll work for you."

"No," I answered, "you'd better do it. I haven't any money. Nobody knows me. If either of us runs, it will have to be you."

We stopped under an electric light and flipped a coin to see who would make the race. It fell to him.

"Let's start to-night," he said. "There's going to be a Republican rally on Central Avenue; Crawford's announcing the organization candidate. Let's hear what they have to say."

We found the hall. It was packed to the doors with ward-heelers. Crawford was in the chair. He was a red-faced man, arrogant and overbearing, connected with some of the biggest business interests in the city. As we were entering, we heard him say:

"I shall now introduce you to the next council-man from the Fourth District. He has been selected by the organization. I want you to know him. I desire to present Mr.——"

He never finished the introduction. Black had grabbed me by the arm.

"Come on," he said, "I'm going to break through this crowd."

We had both played football at college and we went through the hall making a great commotion. Black, who had never made a speech, pulled himself on to the platform. His face was red from the rush; he was out of breath, and surprised at finding himself facing the crowd. His speech ran something like this:

"I am Morris Black. I'm a graduate of Harvard. You don't know me but you know my father, Joseph Black. Everybody knows that Joseph Black is an honest man. I'm going to run for the council. This district has been bossed by Bill Crawford long enough. It isn't going to be bossed any longer."

The meeting never recovered. We got out in some way, and the campaign started. We spent night after night on the streets and in saloons. We organized committees and called on people at their homes. We covered nearly every street in the district. We had to drink a good deal—or thought we did. Black's father was rich and he spent a good deal of money. The campaign was unconventional and spectacular; all the newspapers featured it.

Black was elected, and life began to be interesting. At last my Johns Hopkins creed was justifying itself. A scholar could break into politics. I had helped to elect one to office. Morris Black and I had made a beginning at providing democracy in Cleveland with the leadership of men who served not from hope of personal gain but from a desire to improve the world.

Morris Black had a meteoric career. He was always on his feet in the council chamber, delivering vitriolic attacks on Mayor McKisson, who to our minds typified the boss-ridden condition of the American city. Scarcely a session of the council passed without some spectacular fight between Black and McKisson. The community enjoyed it; the press displayed it. In a few months' time Black was a city-wide hero.

One night he was seized with an attack of appendicitis and died before morning. Thousands of people turned out for his funeral, packing the streets for blocks. There were no religious exercises. I delivered the funeral address.

My interest in life seemed pretty much ended with his death. When we were together, the law and its drudgery appeared unimportant, as did the odds we had to surmount before we could hope for success. Adventuring together, we had dethroned a city boss. Like a couple of Don Quixotes, we had attacked windmills, and the windmills fell. I grieved over the loss of a friend and over the closing of vistas of political possibilities.

CHAPTER XI

I ENTER POLITICS

THE year after Morris Black's death I was living at the University Club, listlessly engaged at the law and serving as secretary of the Municipal Association, which was active in unearthing corruption in the city administration and in attacking a group of councilmen known as the "notorious thirteen."

"Honest John" Farley, Democratic boss, was mayor of Cleveland. He was a big, raw-boned, profane Irishman of substantial wealth, who had made his money as a contractor. A fighting issue carried over from McKisson's administration into Farley's was the renewal of the street-railway franchises. Mayor McKisson, whom most of the people I knew considered corrupt, had been the target of Morris Black's attacks in the council. He was at war with Mark Hanna, and had kept himself in office by his fight against the renewal of the street-railway franchises. The newspapers opposed him, as did the Municipal Association, but somehow nothing was ever proved against him. John Farley had defeated McKisson two years before, pledging the Municipal Association in return for its support that he would oppose a renewal of the street-railway grants. Once elected, however, he had repudiated his promise and was doing everything in his power to jam an ordinance granting a very valuable franchise to the companies through the city council.

I had been bewildered the night of John Farley's election by a remark made to me in confidence by one of his supporters.

"Of course we were glad," he said, suspecting no indiscretion, "to have the support of the Municipal Association, but you know that didn't elect us. We should have been beaten but for Mark Hanna's contribution of twenty thousand dollars to the campaign."

This disclosure astounded me. Mark Hanna was a national Republican figure, by whom party regularity was the one thing insisted on. A man who would bolt his party was an outcast. Yet "Honest John" Farley had not been too honest to take money from a political foe, and Mark Hanna was not unwilling secretly himself to bolt the Republican nominee.

The Municipal Association had stuck to the fight against the franchise although some of the members were uncomfortable in doing so. It seemed to identify them with radicals and with the rather primitive methods that radicals employed, such as the spectacular "petitions in boots" which the people organized. Every Monday evening the petitioners came early to the council-chamber with clothes-lines in their hands, and taking front seats in the galleries they hung nooses over the heads of the councilmen under suspicion. They gathered round them as they left the council-chamber; even children were taught to cry shame at the children of suspected fathers and call them grafters.

I had written a pamphlet analyzing the proposed franchise and condemning its terms, which was printed and distributed broadcast by the association. It showed that the street-railway earnings were increasing at the rate of ten per cent a year and that in twenty-five years the franchise grant would be worth twenty million dollars. The pamphlet made a sensation when it appeared. Our office telephone was busy with protests. But Harry and James Garfield stood by me, as they did on all other questions involving freedom of opinion. Harry Garfield had joined in the protest.

The pamphlet helped to arouse public sentiment; the petitions in boots frightened the councilmen. And the franchise was temporarily defeated.

That was the political situation in Cleveland in the spring of 1901, when rumors began to circulate that Tom L. Johnson planned to return to Cleveland from New York to run for mayor on the Democratic ticket. I had heard about Tom Johnson ever since I had been in the city. He was a dramatic personality; every one had a story about him. I knew about his life what every one knew: that he had come to Cleveland as a young man with no capital and had bought out an old horse-car line of no particular value on the west side, thereby coming into conflict with Mark Hanna, who looked upon the west side of the city as his own. He and his brother Albert had driven their own cars and collected fares. When he wanted to extend his car-line into the public square, he went before a Republican council and promised to carry passengers over his entire system for a single fare. The extension was granted in the teeth of Mark Hanna's opposition. In time he was recognized by other street-railway magnates; and he induced them to form a consolidation, capitalized far in excess of the capitalization of the constituent companies. Then he sold out his holdings and went to Brooklyn, where he repeated the operation. He repeated it again in Detroit and Philadelphia. He acquired steel-mills in Johnstown, Pa., and Lorain, Ohio, and sold them out to the Steel Trust. He had made most of his money by stock manipulations of this kind and was reputed to be many times a millionaire. He had a palatial home on Euclid Avenue, where he entertained generously.

Although he was an intimate friend of many of the rich people of Cleveland, he was distrusted because of his unusual opinions and the apparent discrepancy between his social position and the things he advocated. He was a Democrat and an absolute free-trader. He had been elected to Congress by advocating free trade in a city in the heart of the iron and steel district. He had advocated it in Congress, protesting against a protective tariff on iron and steel, which he said would add new millions to his wealth for which others would have to pay. He advocated the public ownership of street railways, although he had made most of his fortune out of them. He had a devoted following wherever he went; many people loved him. Among the poor he was known for his generosity. Waiters, doorkeepers, cab-drivers knew him as the man whose smallest change was a dollar bill.

Odd among other oddities was the fact that Henry George had lived with him in Washington. *Protection and Free Trade* had been written by Henry George as a series of speeches which Mr. Johnson delivered in Congress. They were then reprinted in pamphlet form by the Government Printing Office, and a million copies distributed by Mr. Johnson under his congressional frank.

When I heard one day that this puzzling, contradictory, much-talked-of Tom Johnson had arrived and would announce his candidacy that evening at the Hollenden House, I freed myself from engagements and was there at eight o'clock. There was a stir outside and the crowd surged in. A short, pudgy man was pushed on to the cigar-stand above me. He stood round and smiling, hands in his pockets, he looked like a boy out for a lark. Politicians shouted like mad around him; evidently they expected a "barrel" campaign.

Surely, I thought, a man of wealth and position is not going to run for mayor in this undignified way. Politics is a serious business, a crusade against politicians and spoilsmen. Tom Johnson should have had a committee of prominent citizens to wait on him and ask him to run. He should have conferred with the Municipal Association and the Chamber of Commerce. That would have given dignity to his campaign.

When the crowd grew quiet Mr. Johnson began to speak. He started in the middle of things. He had permanently given up the making of money, he said, and had come back from New York to run for mayor. He had sold out all his railways and his iron and steel plants, and intended to devote the rest of his life to politics. He talked about the city. The steam railroads had gotten possession of the lake front and held it illegally. The lake-front land was worth millions of dollars. The city was contesting the railroad occupancy in the United States courts, where the case had lain for a dozen years. Mayor Farley was attempting to jam legislation through the council to validate these illegal holdings. In addition, he was doing everything he could to give the street railways a very valuable franchise; a franchise, Mr. Johnson said, worth many millions of dollars. He knew how much it was worth, because he had been in the street-railway business and had made millions out of just such franchise grants. He told how he had gone before the city council when seeking a grant for his company, and had said to the council that it was foolish for the city to give away such franchises. He had urged that the public should own the street railways and operate them, just as the water-works were operated, but if the city insisted on being foolish, he hoped it would be foolish to him. As a business man he had made money out of the city's stupidity. Now he intended to see to it that nobody got what he himself had gotten, without paying for it. Under municipal ownership the city could carry passengers for three cents, if the water was squeezed out of the capital stock. Much of this water, he admitted, had been put into the companies by himself.

It was all very simple, very winning. But I could see why my friends distrusted him. Was he as candid and honest as he seemed, or was he using his frankness merely as a political blind? I was at sea. Everybody said that the city needed a business man's administration, and Mr. Johnson was certainly an eminent business man. But he was not going at it the way I felt he should. He did not seem to be a reformer. He was not indignant enough. He said nothing about waste and extravagance; about bad men; about politicians; about the spoils system. He made no personal attacks on any one. He seemed not to have a high opinion of the kind of men on whom I counted to save democracy. He held a cigar in his hand while he spoke and went away with a crowd of riotous politicians. He was not at all like my picture of the business man who was to redeem politics.

I walked slowly homeward that night pondering on the enigma of Tom Johnson's personality, as I was to ponder on it for weeks to come. But a few days later something happened to divert my attention from him and centre it on my own affairs. One evening a group of men called on me at the University Club. Some of them I knew by name; they were residents of the brownstone ward in which the club was situated, the same ward that had sent Morris Black to the council. They came to ask me to run as Republican candidate for the council. They promised me support, management of my campaign, funds, everything needful. They spoke of the disclosures of corruption in the city government, of the "notorious thirteen." They reminded me that as secretary of the Municipal Association I had been appealing to other men to organize, to clean up the city, and hinted that there was a moral obligation on me not to refuse the candidacy offered. The situation, they implied, was one that demanded sacrifices.

I put them off for a day, talked to my law partners, reflected that I could not afford the expense or the distraction of campaigning, but waited eagerly for the gentlemen to reappear the next evening, and, when they came, consented to run. I liked being called from my law practice as Cincinnatus was called from the fields by the old Romans, liked being thought "a good citizen." And I was eager again to take part in the renaissance of politics which I felt was coming; the renaissance started by Morris Black and myself.

I plunged into the campaign whole-heartedly. Bill Crawford met Harry Garfield at the club at lunch one day and told him that he would wipe me off the earth. I sent word to him to go to it, we would have a good fight. And we did. I was out every night, making speeches in the saloons, visiting from house to house, as Black and I had done in his campaign. I spent more money than I could afford, but much more was being spent by some one else for my election. The other candidate spent more than we did, and that was comforting; moreover, I argued that one must beat the devil with his own tools. I had my photograph taken in a frock coat, and liked to see it on telegraph-poles, in shops, and in the windows of private homes. I looked thoroughly the good citizen. To my surprise, I found that many of the ward politicians were working for me. They distributed my literature, arranged meetings, and never called on me for money. I wondered at the time who had raised the money and gathered together such a motley array of workers. They don't realize that I am a civil-service reformer, I thought, at the same time disturbed and pleased by their assistance; and that what I stand for will put them out of business. For civil-service reform seemed very important to me; it would break the power of the boss, strip the mayor of power at the primaries, and make it possible to nominate good men for office. Although I took the support of the politicians, I did not disguise my opinions. In fact, I emphasized them. When I talked about these things, they smiled. I remembered that afterward.

The issue in the people's minds was the councilmanic scandal. The street-railway question made good campaign material, especially in the poorer sections of the district, which consisted of Euclid Avenue flanked by a strip of tenements on either side. It was known that I had taken a prominent part in the fight against the franchise. I urged the necessity of cleaning up the council, of electing a new sort of men to public office, of getting rid of the spoilsman. City administration, I said, should be taken out of party politics. The city was merely housekeeping, and housekeeping should be done on a business basis. In talking about the franchise, I denounced Mayor Farley's change of front; his "business men's settlement" with the street railways.

The principal issue in my mind, too, was corruption. The old gang should be cleaned out, a new kind of men put in. The kind of men I had in mind were business men, trained, university men. They were my friends. The others, the bad ones, lived principally down under the hill. They were immigrants. The Thirteenth Ward was the worst; it was

controlled by a Polish immigrant named Harry
Bernstein. He delivered, to a man, the number of
votes he promised to deliver, to whoever would purchase them. He was the city scandal. It was Bernsteinism that ruled the city and Bernsteinism that
must be wiped out. The risk of being dirtied by
politics had to be taken; the sacrifice involved in
running for office had to be made. And I was proud
to have been selected by my friends, by the good
people of my district, to make the sacrifice.

But the riddle of Tom Johnson remained. When
I could spare time from my own campaigning, I went
to his meetings. He would go to a Republican meeting and ask permission to talk from the same platform with the Republican candidate for mayor.
When permission was denied him, the crowd followed him out into the street, almost emptying the
hall. One night he talked about poverty, about how
to be rid of it. He said that society should be changed
not by getting good men into office, but by making
it possible for all men to be good. He said that most
men would be reasonably good if they had a chance.
We had evil in the world because people were poor.
The trouble was not with people, it was with poverty. Poverty was the cause of vice and crime. It
was social conditions that were bad rather than
people. These conditions could be changed only
through politics.

This bothered me, as did most of his speeches.
Surely some people were good, while others were bad.
My classifications were simple. Roughly, the members of the University Club and the Chamber of
Commerce were good; McKisson, Bernstein, and the
politician were bad. The bad were commonly in
power; they held offices and controlled elections.
They did not do their work well and were paid very
much more than they should receive. At the pri-

maries they elected their own kind to office. The way to change this vicious circle, I thought, was to get the good people to form committees in each ward as had been done in my own. If these committees nominated men who would go out and fight the politicians, if we gave enough thought to politics—as we were under a moral obligation to do—we should drive out the spoilsmen. It was all quite clear to me and very simple. It was the choice between the good and the bad.

But here was a man who said that bad people were not bad; they were merely poor and had to fight for a living. They got an easier living out of politics than they did working twelve hours a day in the steel-mills. So they went into politics. And being in the majority, they won out.

I resented what Mr. Johnson said, resented too the issues he ignored. He made my work in the Municipal Association seem false; made it seem as if we were trying to patch up something that ought not to be patched, that ought to be done away with entirely. I think there was a time when I might have turned against him. He was an enemy of my opinions, of my education, of my superior position. It hurt my ego, my self-respect, to be told that I was really not much better than the politician and that my class was not as important as I thought it was.

But I continued to go to his meetings while I listened to the criticisms of my friends who branded him as insincere. I could not understand why a man should make so much money out of business and then admit that the way he made it was wrong; why a rich man should advocate the things that he advocated, especially as what he proposed would take money away from his old friends. Still, much of what he said seemed true to me. Perhaps his personality was winning me; perhaps somewhere in the back of my mind there was approval of his ideas. I fluttered about him mentally, accepting, withdrawing, irresistibly attracted.

He often referred to *Progress and Poverty*, which I had read at the university. I had laid it aside, saying to myself: "That is the most interesting book on political economy I have ever read. What Henry George says seems to be true. But it must be false. Such a simple explanation of the wrongs of society and the way to correct them cannot be right. If it were, every one would have accepted the reform as soon as the book was published and we should have had the single tax long ago."

I finally called on Mr. Johnson at his office. I wanted to be assured of his sincerity. We talked a long time. Among other things, I told him about reading *Progress and Poverty*, of how I had been unable to answer the arguments but was convinced that it must be wrong.

He smiled and told me his own story.

"Years ago," he said, "when I was a young man just getting started in the street-railway business, I was coming up from Indianapolis to Cleveland on the Big Four Railroad. The "butcher"—as they called the man who sold books on the train—came along with a bundle of books on his arm. The conductor passed at the same moment, and taking a book from the pile, he said: 'Mr. Johnson, I think you would like this book. It is called *Social Problems*, by Henry George."

"I looked at the book and returned it. Thinking it was a treatise on prostitution, I said I was not interested in social problems.

"'It isn't that kind of book,' the conductor said. 'It deals with your kind of business—with street-railroads, steam-railroads, and the land question.'

"I bought the book and read it. I read it a second time. Then I took it to Arthur Moxham, my partner in the steel business, and asked him to read it. I said: 'Arthur, you know more about books than I do. I haven't read much. But if this book is right, then your business and mine are all wrong.'

"Some weeks after this, he told me he had read the book; it was interesting but quite wrong. He had marked the passages that were faulty. A short time afterward, I asked again about it. He said he had been rereading the book; it was wrong, but he had rubbed out some of his objections. Finally he came to me and said: 'Tom, I have read that book four times. I have had to rub out every one of my objections. The book is sound. Henry George is right.'

"In the meantime, I had read *Progress and Poverty*. I said to myself: 'If this book is really true, I shall have to give up business. It isn't right for me to make money out of protected industries, out of street-railway franchises, out of land speculation. I must get out of the business, or prove that this book is wrong.' I went to L. A. Russell, my attorney, and said to him:

" 'Here, Russell, is a retainer of five hundred dollars. I want you to read this book and give me your honest opinion on it, as you would on a legal question. Treat this retainer as you would a fee.'

"A few weeks later I got a memorandum from Mr. Russell pointing out the errors of Henry George. I was starting for New York on a business errand and asked Mr. Russell to go with me.

" 'We will talk this thing over in New York,' I said.

"In New York we met Mr. Du Pont, of Delaware, and Arthur Moxham. In the evening we all went to my rooms in the hotel. We took up Russell's ob-

jections one by one. We spent the whole night on
them. One question after another was disposed of,
and finally Russell threw up his hands and said:

"'I have to admit that I was wrong. The book is
sound. This man Henry George, whoever he is, is
a wonderful philosopher.'

"All four of us were content with the decision.
We were converted to an unnamed philosophy, by
an unknown prophet, an obscure man of whom we
had never before heard.

"The next day I began a search for Henry George.
I learned that he lived in Brooklyn, where I finally
found him in his study. I told him who I was and
how I had come to read his book, how I had proved
it to myself and to my friends. Then I said:

"'Mr. George, I see that no one has a right to
make money the way I have out of special privilege.
But making money is the easiest thing in the world
for me. I can make millions, but I can't write and
I can't make a speech. What am I to do?'

"Mr. George said: 'You go on and make money,
but you can learn to speak. You can speak if you
have something to say that you believe in. You can
go into politics. The land question is politics. Only
through politics can we bring the single tax to
pass.'

"Now you know," said Mr. Johnson, "why I am
running for mayor. I have been in Congress, but
there isn't much to be done there. The place to
begin is the city. If one city should adopt the single
tax, other cities would have to follow suit. If we are
the first to take taxes off houses, factories, and machinery, we will have a tremendous advantage.
Factories will be attracted to Cleveland; it will be
a cheap city to do business in, cheap to live in. Un-
taxing the things people use will cheapen them, it
will encourage production. And if we tax the land

heavily enough, we will discourage speculation. With cheap land on the one hand and cheap houses, factories, and goods on the other, Cleveland will be the most attractive city in America."

Mr. Johnson's sincerity was convincing. But I had one more question to put.

"Why don't you cut loose," I asked, "from Charlie Salen and the other politicians whom the people distrust? If you do that, you will make an appeal to all the people I know. You are a business man and we all want a business man's administration. Then you could get the young men of the east end, the business men, the educated classes, to support you."

"No," he replied, "they will never support me. They can't support me. There is nothing I could say and nothing I could do that would make it possible for the 'good people,' as you term them, to support me. This fight cuts too deep. It touches too many interests, banks, business, preachers, doctors, lawyers, clubs, newspapers. They have to be on one side. And it isn't my side. They will be against me. The only people who can be for me are the poor people and the politicians who will have to follow the poor people when they get started."

I had still a moment of hesitation. I did not see clearly enough what he wanted to do. I had never thought of ending poverty through politics. We should always have poverty. I did not believe in working with spoilsmen. I saw that Tom Johnson was fighting his friends, men of his own class, that he took pleasure in the companionship of common people. The people whom I trusted he found untrustworthy.

But suddenly I found myself saying:

"I think I will withdraw from the Republican ticket and come out and support you. I can't do it and remain a candidate. And you can do things I never could do."

"No," he said, "you get elected as a Republican. Parties don't matter. We will work together. If I am elected, I shan't be able to do anything without the council."

As we shook hands he looked at me closely. "You know you will have to pay," he said, "for siding with me."

He was wondering, he later confessed to me, if I would be willing to pay the price.

CHAPTER XII

A RUDE AWAKENING

TOM JOHNSON was elected mayor on the issue of municipal ownership and a three-cent fare on the street-railways. Along with a number of other men indorsed by the Municipal Association, I was returned to the council, which had enough independent members to be organized on a non-partisan basis. The beginning of the political renaissance had come. Spoilsmen, bosses, grafters would be driven out. Cleveland was to be America's pace-maker.

Mr. Johnson brought to the mayoralty extraordinary business talent and technical ability. He knew mathematics, electricity and power problems. He had been a shrewd monopolist and he knew every foot of the various street-car lines in the city. He had fought many legal battles around the obstacles placed in the laws of the State to shield the companies already in the field. Elected by a large majority, he would put his programme through, it seemed, with ease.

He did a characteristic thing by taking the oath of office as soon as the election returns were officially announced. Mayor Farley, he had discovered, was about to sign an ordinance granting the valuable lake-front property, which had been the subject of twelve years' litigation, to the railroads. To forestall this action Mr. Johnson walked into the mayor's office, and announced that he had been sworn in. In this way he entered dramatically on his ten years' administration.

The conservative press waited. It was puzzled. So were many of Mr. Johnson's old business associates. They were not yet convinced that he had abandoned his business past and had really dedicated himself to the public service.

Not as close to him while I held my Republican seat in the council as I came to be later, but enamored of the dream of a free city, with a master mind and a great idealist as its directing genius, I began to have a rough-and-tumble experience of city politics. Our first job was to clean house, to be rid of the spoilsmen, to drive out the "notorious thirteen." And we had made a beginning by our non-partisan organization of the council. A few weeks after the election I was asked by Mayor Johnson to introduce an ordinance making a grant to a natural-gas company, which proposed to provide light and fuel at thirty cents a thousand cubic feet. Cleveland was then paying eighty cents a thousand for artificial gas. I went over the ordinance with care, as did the city law department. When it was read in council meeting, bearing my name, I noticed that significant looks were exchanged among the notorious thirteen, and I suspected that they would be against it.

The following day a group of business men called on me to discuss the ordinance. Some of them were clients of our law firm. "Natural gas will ruin my business," said a coal merchant, as frankly as if it were obvious that a boon to three hundred thousand people could not be considered by reasonable persons in the face of his personal loss. The Chamber of Commerce came out against the ordinance. A new gas company meant tearing up the streets; it might kill the trees. And it would injure the existing company, which had twelve million dollars invested in the business. This was the nub of the situation. Soon a thoroughly organized campaign was started, backed by the press, the Chamber of Commerce, and

by many of my friends. As time went on it became
very bitter. I could not understand the opposition;
other cities had natural gas, it was safe, convenient,
and cheap. The arguments against it seemed trivial.
I expected the ordinance to pass by a substantial
majority. But it was defeated by one vote. To my
surprise a number of reform councilmen voted against
it. They gave no reasons; simply voted in the negative.

Immediately after the vote was announced a
councilman from the west side named Charlie Kohl
rose on a question of personal privilege. Drawing
from his inside coat-pocket a package of bank bills,
he addressed the president.

"Mr. President, on my way to the council-chamber this evening I was met by Dr. D——. He
asked me if I would vote against the gas ordinance.
When I told him I had not made up my mind, he
said:

" 'Charlie, I don't want this ordinance to pass.
It is a matter of great importance to the old gas
company. You and I have long been friends. I
helped you to be elected and I judge by what you
say that you may vote against the ordinance. Well,
here are two thousand dollars. Pay off the mortgage
on your house. I thought of giving it to one of the
other boys, but I prefer giving it to you.' "

He laid the roll of bills on the clerk's desk. The
atmosphere was charged with excitement. Reform
councilmen who had voted against the ordinance
were white in the face. The "thirteen" sat stolid.
The galleries were packed with men from the Chamber of Commerce who were there in opposition to
the ordinance and with city employees who favored
it. Friends of mine in the audience were opposed to
the ordinance. I expected them to protest, to make
some kind of demonstration over the disclosure.

But they did nothing. They were quiet, apparently unmoved.

I had heard of bribery, but it had never come close to me before. What could be done about it, I thought. Were we bound by a corrupt vote? Was it possible that the city should be denied the boon of cheap gas by such means?

In the suspense Mr. Johnson rose from his chair, apparently quite at ease. Pointing to Dr. D——, who was moving toward the door, he directed one of the policemen to arrest him and take him to his office. Some one moved a reconsideration of the vote. Here was a way out; the ordinance would surely pass now by an overwhelming vote. I had never made a sustained speech and did not know how to begin. But I got to my feet and blazed out my feelings. I was outraged, and assumed that everybody else was outraged. Here was proof of what the press had been saying, of what the Municipal Association had said, of what we all suspected. Here was proof of how city business was carried on. And the astounding thing was that bribery was not all done by paving contractors and ordinary grafters, but by men of another class. For obviously Dr. D—— was acting for some one higher up. He was acting for the existing gas company. The bills still bore the binders of the bank from which they had come. That shocked me most.

I concluded:

"I have heard complaints about the so-called anarchists who speak on the public square. Anarchy, as I understand it, means the destruction of organized government. What is bribery but the destruction of government? It means substituting money for honest discussion. It means an end to democracy. The anarchists on the public square, if such there be, merely talk about putting an end to government. Here are men who have substituted corruption for discussion, and ours," I said, "is a government by discussion. The real enemies of the State, the most dangerous of anarchists, are the men who have plotted this thing, to subvert the will of the elected representatives of the people."

On the vote the ordinance was adopted by a small majority. The "thirteen" said nothing. Some of the reform councilmen protested their honesty. Except my own, there was little indignation.

I left the council-chamber with a feeling of exaltation. Such disclosures as this would bring home to the people the necessity of putting good men in office, who would stand by the city's interest, men who had the courage to denounce corruption and bribery, no matter from what source it came.

As I went down the stairs I was roughly brushed by two members of the "thirteen." They had voted against the ordinance. I had noticed the expressions of astonishment on their faces when I spoke about the use of money and about the artificial-gas company. They were plainly very angry.

"What do you mean by double-crossing us this way?" they demanded.

"Double-crossing?" I asked. "What do you mean?"

"Oh, you know well enough," they said. "Why did you go back on the rest of us and leave us in the ditch? Why did you double-cross the gas company?"

I was in the dark. I protested that I did not know what they meant.

"Oh, you can't put that stuff over on us," said one. "You know you were nominated and elected by the old gas company in the Fourth District. What d'ye suppose they backed you for? Do you think they put two thousand dollars in your campaign just because you were beautiful? Come along, Mike, he double-crossed them just as he double-crossed us."

A chill of questionings went through me. Was this true? Were the members of the committee who urged me to run not the disinterested citizens I had supposed them to be? Had I been deceived about the moral awakening in my district? Had I been picked out in the belief that because I was a corporation lawyer I could be relied on to serve business interests and to do the bidding of the men who financed my campaign?

There had been no understanding on my part as to how I should vote on any question, and I did not know the business connections of the men who had called upon me. But I soon learned that what Mike and Johnny said was true. One member of my nominating committee was the son of the vice-president of the gas company, while the men who were with him were his associates in various business enterprises.

I was terribly confused. I began to understand much that had been mysterious. I understood where the army of men came from who had been set to work the day my name was entered in the primaries. They were gas-company employees. I understood the lavish expenditure of money and the mysterious smiles of members of the councilmanic ring when I had introduced the natural-gas ordinance. There was some trick in the whole thing, they said to themselves. Of that they were sure. Possibly it was a big shake-down that the old company understood but that they had not been taken in on. I understood the anger of Mike and Johnny as they left the council-chamber. We were all gas-company men. The same men that had financed them had financed me. They had delivered the goods, but I had not.

They had stuck to their friends, I had betrayed them. They had been faithful to the only political ideals they recognized, which was to keep your word no matter what it cost and to be loyal to those who were loyal to you. From their point of view I had been guilty of the one offense that could not be forgiven. I had double-crossed the men who had put me in office and who had financed my campaign.

And there was worse to come. The next day a group of business men and bankers called on me. With them was one of the trustees of the Charity Organization Society. He was a man whom I greatly respected, identified with almost every good movement in the city, one of the board of directors of the college settlement where I had lived.

"Fred," he began, "your friends are hurt by the things you said in the council last night. You compared the man who gives a bribe with the anarchists on the public square; you said that he was worse than the grafters in the council, for the grafters were poor and ignorant, some of them had to do what they were told. Of course no one can defend bribery. You know I wouldn't defend it. But you're a corporation lawyer, you ought to understand these things. Public-utility corporations are hounded by politicians; they have millions of dollars invested. They have to protect their investments, there are many widows and orphans. It is unfortunately true that they use money, but they can only get along by the means that you denounced. There isn't any other way for them to do business. They are always being subjected to some striking legislation. They can't get the things they ought to have with straightforward methods.

I was dumfounded. Here was a new angle of political morality held by respected friends, who had contributed to my election.

"Do you mean," I asked hesitatingly, "that a gas or electric lighting or street-railway company can live only by bribery and corruption? Can private individuals carry on businesses of this kind only by what we all know are criminal means?"

They did not like the way I put it, but they agreed that the situation was, unfortunately, just that. There was no other way, in the present instance, to carry on the gas business. It had to corrupt the government.

"Well," I said, "listen. I don't know whether what you say is true or not but you have all acted as though it were true. I have heard about the 'natural' way of getting a franchise. I know about the contributions made by public-utility corporations to political parties, and about the financial pressure that is brought to bear on councilmen. There's a saying over in the City Hall that the street-railways pick men out of the cradle and train them for the council. But I didn't expect to hear a defense of these practices from men like you.

"I think you have converted me to public ownership. When a private business can live only by bribery, then the logical conclusion is that we can't have that kind of private business. We can fight the spoils system, bad as it is, in the open; it is not nearly so dangerous to democracy as is corruption. For corruption"—I warmed to my theme of the night before—"will destroy responsible government. You gentlemen have made the most convincing argument that could be made for public ownership."

My speech in the council made a difference with some of my friends. That was the thing I was least prepared for. It was not that I had double-crossed my backers, for that was not generally known. It was something deeper than that. Apparently I had touched a herd instinct. The herd was not organized, but subconsciously all its members thought alike. It was afraid. I had justified my election pledges and I expected approval. I was rather eager for it. But I won no approval. Indeed, the reverse was true. I sustained myself by reflecting that some one had to pay in the cleaning-up process. It was rather fine that I was permitted to make the sacrifice. Still, it hurt me that my friends at the club did not come to me and say:

"Fred, that was a fine speech you made at the council meeting on the gas ordinance. Bribery is the worst of all crimes. You're right about its destroying responsible government."

These men had applauded my attacks on Mayor McKisson and the notorious thirteen. Why did they not applaud me when I attacked the men who did the bribing? Was not the giver as bad as the taker—worse, indeed, since he does not need money? Why should not every one see this?

Not long afterward I introduced for Mayor Johnson an ordinance providing for a three-cent fare on the street-railways. This involved bringing in another company and affected the interests of Senator Hanna, of the banks, of many of our clients and the men with whom I was associated. I was conscious of increasing social alienation. At the club I was made to feel uncomfortable. Most of the people I knew were opposed to everything I did. And I began to question my classification of people, which Mr. Johnson had questioned for me in his campaign speeches. Good people, my friends, were unconcerned over bribery; they were not outraged by it when it was done by people they knew. They would not stand by criminal proceedings instituted against bribe-givers. Why, I wondered, this palsy benumbing good people? When the way was pointed out, how could they fail to rise and save the city?

Subsequent experience on the city council increased these doubts. I was interested in playgrounds for children, in public baths and dance-halls, in the opening up of parks and providing recreation for the poor. Here, I thought, is something my friends will surely rally to. Here is a way to beat the saloon, to stop crime at the source, far more efficiently than by raids or regulation. I introduced legislation for these things, showed by the experience of other cities that crime had been reduced where children were taken from the streets and given a place to play, with trained instructors to help them do so.

But my friends did not rally to such measures. On the contrary, a committee of the Chamber of Commerce denounced public baths as socialistic. There was an outcry against the wider use of the parks, especially against taking down the "Keep-off-the-Grass" signs. Reform councilmen protested that these things would increase the popularity of Mayor Johnson and would add to the tax-rate. Such support as came to me came from the old gang. In time the measures came out of the committees where they had lain for weeks and were passed with the aid of the men whom I had previously denounced. The bad men in the council rallied to the children. They knew better than I did where the children lived and where they had to play. On measures where there was no money moving they voted right; while representatives from the east-end wards often voted wrong.

In the end, through the activity of Mr. Johnson, Cleveland acquired a city-wide system of parks, playgrounds, and public baths. On Saturday and Sunday the whole population played baseball in hundreds of parks laid out for that purpose. Cleveland became a play city, and this generous provision for play has declared dividends. Workmen like to live in Cleveland. Workmen are followed by factory-owners. The growth of Cleveland in the last decade is partly traceable to the policy of making the city an attractive place in which to live.

In spite of its initial confusion and in spite of disappointments my term on the city council was one of happy activity. I grew to love the city and the big problems it presented. I visited other cities to study police administration, methods of street-cleaning, the grouping of public buildings. The city appealed to me as a social agency of great possibilities; at an insignificant cost it could fill the lives of people with pleasure. It could protect the poor by more intelligent use of the police force. It could provide things at wholesale; could open playgrounds and public baths. It could develop the lake front into a beautiful, long esplanade. It could take over the charities and run them as public agencies. I no longer believed in private charity. It seemed unfair that men and women who had given their lives to industry should have to rely upon private benevolence when in need. I saw endless possibilities of beauty in Cleveland.

I was conscious, as time went on, of increasing isolation. True, it was partly of my own making, for I withdrew more and more into myself. I shrank from old friends who disapproved of me. I kept away from the clubs. What was the use, I said, of always inviting a row? It confused me that my friends did not see things as I did; that there was not generous approval of Tom Johnson when it became apparent that he was giving the city a clean, businesslike administration. I could understand the first questionings—I had had them myself—but they could not outlast a demonstration of his sincerity. But approval had not come from people I knew, from the Municipal Association, from the Chamber of Commerce, from young men who were open-minded on other things.

I was caught between two herds. I had come to like the politicians; I got on with them in the council, in ward meetings, in political conferences. They were human, generous, kindly, and for the most part did as Mr. Johnson told them to do. They were happy in his leadership; many of them turned out to be highly efficient in their jobs. But they were not my kind. With Mr. Johnson gone, they would follow any other leader. I could not be permanently identified with them anyway. And I missed friendliness, approval, a herd, that satisfied my university picture of the rôle I should play.

At the expiration of my term I was ready to run again as an independent candidate. It was obvious that I could not be nominated on the Republican ticket. The party had identified itself with the traction interests and was controlled by Senator Hanna and his associates. I could not stand on the Republican platform even if I were nominated, and I had alienated many friends who had been responsible for my nomination. I declined a place on the Democratic ticket that Mr. Johnson offered me, feeling confident that I could be elected as an independent candidate. The district was an intelligent one, the issues were clear, and the regular party candidates were obviously unfit.

But the ballots did not fall as I had expected. I was a bad third in the race. People were not voting as my pattern of politics led me to believe they would. I got scarcely any support from my own ward, the richest in the city. From that time on I was identified frankly with Mr. Johnson and with the Democratic party. I was appointed chairman of the finance commission of the city, and during the next six years devoted most of my free time to politics, to speaking campaigns, to daily conferences in the City Hall or with the mayor at his home, which became the headquarters of a group of young men attracted, as I had been attracted, by Tom Johnson's personality and programme.

CHAPTER XIII

A TEN YEARS' WAR

MR. JOHNSON called his ten years' fight against privilege a war for "A City on a Hill." To the young men in the movement, and to tens of thousands of the poor who gave it their support, it was a moral crusade rarely paralleled in American politics. The struggle involved the banks, the press, the Chamber of Commerce, the clubs, and the social life of the city. It divided families and destroyed friendships. You were either for Tom Johnson or against him. If for him, you were a disturber of business, a Socialist, to some an anarchist. Had the term "Red" been in vogue, you would have been called a communist in the pay of Soviet Russia. Every other political issue and almost every topic of conversation was subordinated to the struggle.

The possibility of a free, orderly, and beautiful city became to me an absorbing passion. Here were all of the elements necessary to a great experiment in democracy. Here was a rapidly growing city with great natural advantages and with few mistakes to correct. Here was a wonderful hinterland for the building of homes, a ten-mile water-front that could be developed for lake commerce, a population that had showed itself willing to follow an ideal, and, most important of all, a great leader.

I had an architectonic vision of what a city might be. I saw it as a picture. It was not economy, efficiency, and business methods that interested me so much as a city planned, built, and conducted as a community enterprise. I *saw* the city as an architect sees a skyscraper, as a commission of experts plans a world's fair exposition. It was a unit, a thing with a mind, with a conscious purpose, seeing far in advance of the present and taking precautions for the future. I had this picture of Cleveland long before the advent of city-planning proposals; it was just as instinctive as any mechanical talent. I saw cities in this way from the first lectures of Doctor Albert Shaw at Johns Hopkins; I went to Germany in the summers, especially to Munich, drawn there by orderliness, by the beauty of streets, concern for architecture, provision for parks, for gardens and museums, for the rich popular life of the people. And I studied cities as one might study art; I was interested in curbs, in sewers, in sky-lines. I wrote about cities—articles and books. I dreamed about them. The city was the enthusiasm of my life. And I saw cities as social agencies that would make life easier for people, full of pleasure, beauty, and opportunity. It could be done so easily and at such slight individual expense. Especially in a city like Cleveland that had few mistakes to correct, that was flanked on one side by a lake front which could be developed with breakwaters into parks and lagoons, and with natural parkways extending about it far back into the country.

I have never gotten over this enthusiasm. I never grow tired of city-building, of city enthusiasms, city ideals. And with all of its crudities and failures I have never lost faith that the American city will become a thing of beauty and an agency of social service as yet unplumbed.

The mad king of Bavaria dreamed no more ambitious dreams of city-building than did I of Cleveland. Here democracy would show its possibilities; the city would become our hope instead of our despair, and in a few years' time all America would respond to the movement. The crusade of my youth, the greatest adventure of my life, as great a training-school as a man could pass through—this the decade of struggle in Cleveland from 1901 to 1910 was to me.

The immediate struggle revolved about two main issues: the public ownership of public utilities, especially the street-railways and electric-lighting service, and the reduction of street-railway fares to three cents. Neither of them seemed adequate to explain the bitterness of the conflict and the power which reaction was able to organize to obstruct the movement. These issues mobilized the conservative forces of the city—banks, the Chamber of Commerce, lawyers, doctors, clubs, and churches. The press was partly owned by Mark Hanna, while advertisers were organized to bring pressure on editors and owners. Instinct held the propertied classes together no matter how detached they might be from the interests that were directly menaced. Before the expiration of the first two years of Mr. Johnson's term of mayoralty the city was divided into two camps along clearly defined economic lines. There was bitterness, hatred, abuse. Also social ostracism and business boycott. The press was unscrupulous in its attacks. On the one side were men of property and influence; on the other the politicians, immigrants, workers, and persons of small means. This line of cleavage continued to the end.

And I was not on the side where I would have chosen to be. The struggle brought me into conflict with friends, clients, my class. I preferred to be with them, I liked wealth and the things that went with wealth; I enjoyed dining out, dances, the lighter things of life. I suffered from the gibes of men with whom I had once been intimate, and fancied slights which did not in fact occur. I could not see why men would not treat political differences as natural; why my opinions on municipal ownership should make me any less desirable socially than I had been while living at the settlement engaged in uplift work.

Now, too, I was part of a political machine, was part of the spoils system, was apparently approving of things I had once thought to be the supreme evils in our politics; I was counselling with ward leaders, many of whom were saloon-keepers, none of whom were of my class or had any interest in politics beyond jobs, political power, and such distinction as came through the party organization.

This departure from former ideals did not disturb me as did the loss of old friends. I wanted to live with my class, to enjoy its approval, to exhibit the things I had learned at the university among people who lived in fine houses, who made the social and club life of the city.

Still, I was happy in the fight. It was always dramatic, and I had a passion for the things we were fighting for. I saw that the city must own its transportation system before it could begin to plan anything else; it ought to own its electricity supply; most important of all, it must end class war, which I was beginning to see was caused by the fight for franchise rights of great value involving most of the prominent men in the city. My passion for the city was also a passion for Tom Johnson. And I had come to love him as fervently as I loved the things he promised to achieve.

Street-railway franchises in Ohio were for twenty-five years. Many of them were expiring in Cleveland and the companies had been trying for years to secure their renewal. Mayor McKisson's opposition to Mark Hanna and the efforts of the Municipal Association had helped to balk the granting of the new franchises. Finally Mr. Johnson had been elected by a large majority on a perfectly clear issue of municipal ownership and immediate three-cent fares.

To me it seemed that his programme was one easy of achievement. He and the people were united. Democracy had spoken; it had chosen a natural leader, a business man known by every business man in the city to be a man of extraordinary talent and experience. "A million dollar mayor that Cleveland has gotten for five thousand dollars," was Albert Johnson's comment on his brother's election. "I would gladly give Tom a million dollars a year to work for my street-railways," he added.

But the city had no legal right to own and operate the street-railways. This prevented a direct attack on the situation. There were two alternatives, both almost impossible of execution. One was to negotiate with the companies and induce them to accept a new grant providing for a three-cent fare, with the right reserved to the city to buy the lines at their actual reproduction value. This Mr. Johnson said was impossible, because there were twenty millions of watered securities in the properties, much of it issued by the promoters to themselves. These securities would be wiped out under the mayor's plan. The second alternative was to find some one who would agree to build new lines on the city's terms, with a straight three-cent fare, and provision for the easy purchase of the lines by the city at their investment value. This seemed still more difficult of realization. Self-interest and herd interest would keep bankers and railway promoters out of such an enterprise.

Mr. Johnson chose, however, the latter line of action. Endless efforts were made to secure new lines of street-railways on streets which had not been occupied by the existing companies. Routes were laid out on unoccupied streets and bids invited,

The old company put in dummy bids at a low rate of fare, with no intention of building. These dummy bids had to be thrown out. New routes were planned and new bids secured. Finally a grant was made to Mr. Ermon du Pont, of Delaware, a friend of Mr. Johnson's. To get even so far had taken the greater part of two years.

When the grant was made to Mr. du Pont, I thought we had won the war. I supposed that the companies would negotiate, that they would not be able to stand the competition of three-cent fares. Moreover, some of the franchises had expired and they had no right in the streets. Mr. Johnson knew better. He said we had won only a skirmish. He knew the laws of the State and the skill with which they had been drawn to prevent competition by newcomers in the field. He knew that the grant to a new company simply meant a long legal battle.

He was quite right. The ordinance to the low-fare company was immediately attacked by an injunction issued by one of the Republican judges. The case had to be fought through the common-pleas court, then through the circuit court, then through the supreme court of Ohio, which was partisan, having been carefully hand-picked for such contingencies. After the supreme court of the State had disposed of the case, there was a further delay on appeal to the Supreme Court of the United States.

All this meant long delay. It meant that Mr. Johnson would have to stand for a second election on unfulfilled pledges. The companies planned to wear out the public as they had done for years until they should secure a pliant administration which would give them a franchise. In the meantime they were continuing to collect five-cent fares.

Nobody knew where the money to finance the low-fare company came from. Mr. Johnson did not

confide the secret even to his intimate friends.
Years later, when I went with him one day in New
York to call on August Lewis, I learned who the
good angel was. The two had long been friends,
brought together by a common affection for Henry
George. Outside on the street, after we had left,
Mr. Johnson said:

"August Lewis is the finest Jew since Christ.
You know it was he who put up the money to build
the first three-cent-fare line and to carry on the
legal fight. We could have done nothing without
his help. He never fully expected to get his money
back, and he only half expects it now."

As time went on the war widened out. Men were
selected for office, from city council to the supreme
bench, about this issue. President Roosevelt lent his
aid to defeat the enterprise by urging Congressman
Theodore Burton to run for mayor. Tom Johnson,
he said, must be defeated, otherwise he might
become a national figure. But the fight was carried
on for the most part in the courts, upon which the
opposition relied. All told, over fifty injunctions
were granted against the city, in its efforts to use
its own streets as it saw fit, to provide people with
cheaper fares, and to build a municipal electric-
lighting plant. To defeat the will of the community
the flimsiest of legal objections proved sufficient.
The sovereignty of a great city was far less important to the courts than that of the most insignificant property-owner who urged some damage to
himself, or some failure by the city to observe an
obscure provision of the laws.

Almost all of the best-known lawyers of the city
were retained by the companies. When the city
sought to employ outside legal assistance, the only
prominent lawyer who would accept its brief was
Mr. D. C. Westenhaver, then an associate of mine

in the law, and later appointed United States District Judge.

Mr. Johnson knew as much about the courts as did his opponents. He had been a street-railway operator and a shrewd monopolist, and he had no illusions about the blindfolded Goddess of Justice. He took such means as he could to get his cases tried before friendly judges. He nominated for the bench men in whom he had confidence, and in almost every instance he was able to say in advance what the outcome of the litigation would be; it depended on the judge who heard it.

"When I was in business," he said to me once, "and wanted my lawyers to both decide and write the decision of a case in the federal courts, I employed the firm of —— They represent most of the big corporations, and the federal judge is indebted to them for many favors, not the least of which is his nomination to the bench. When I wanted a fair and square fight in which the best man should win, I employed E. J. Blandin; for a rough-and-tumble fight and some one to rough-house a hostile judge, I chose L. A. Russell.

"Judges act like other men," he concluded. "If it is unpopular to side with me on a political issue, they will decide against me. They watch the election returns; they know who decides the nominations. They decide for their party and their class with their eyes open."

The long fight was featured by the press. Mr. Johnson had the support of the Cleveland *Plaindealer*, the most influential morning paper, and the Cleveland *Press*, a very powerful evening paper. *The Leader* and *The News*, papers owned by Senator Hanna and his associates, were bitter in their attacks, and especially in their innuendoes of personal dishonesty. Homer Davenport, the cartoonist of

the Hearst papers, was brought on from New York
by *The Leader*, while the Associated Press carried
cruelly unfair stories for the opposition. Mr. Johnson was charged with almost every conceivable
political crime, the most widely accepted one being
that he was trying to get possession of the street-
railways for himself.

One of the mayor's difficulties was to keep the
members of his own party in line, as defections were
always occurring in the council. It was necessary to
hold ward meetings, to bring pressure on councilmen who were weakening. The traction interests
spent money lavishly, and from long control of the
city they knew how to reach men through relatives,
contracts, bank influence, and other means.

Year by year some gain was made, some construction work completed. But the low-fare lines
could not get to the centre of the city. The central
part of the city was free territory; that is, existing
tracks could be used by any company on the payment of rental, and this free territory was our objective. One day the mayor called into his office
men on whom he could rely. Teamsters were engaged; rails and ties were assembled. One night on
the stroke of twelve the entire outfit was set in
motion. The plans worked perfectly. Rails were
laid along Superior Avenue on the top of the pave-
ment to the public square. Barrels filled with
cement were placed along the curbstones and in
them supporting poles were erected to carry the
electric current. Wires were strung and connections
were made with the tracks of the low-fare company
on the west side. The aim was to have the cars
running to the public square by morning, and in
that way escape another injunction. It would then
be possible to extend the lines out into the east side
of the city. But the old company routed a compla-

cent judge out of bed, who issued a blanket injunction against the operation of the cars. In the morning they were still halted on the farthermost side of
the square.

Year after year passed, with the controversy still
unsettled. Mr. Johnson had to face the people in
three separate elections. His methods of campaigning were spectacular. He purchased and equipped two
big circus-tents, capable of seating several thousand
people. The tents were set up in vacant lots about
the city, and the mayor with a group of supporters
would motor from tent to tent, making three or
four speeches an evening. Mr. Johnson drove his
own car, known as the "Red Devil," with reckless
speed. He had little respect for the law, and
the police winked at his violations of the speed
ordinances. After the meetings we would gather at
his home to outline the campaign for the following
day.

I had had no training in public speaking, but
standing before a crowd of people in the circus-tent,
many of them hostile and ready to hurl questions
at the speaker, taught me something of the art.
The opposition hired men to heckle us, and we had
to be ready with our answers or lose more than we
gained by a speech. There was always a campaign
on; there were endless referendum elections on ordinances or bond issues, as well as State campaigns, in
which the "Red Devil" and the tents were brought
into requisition for tours about the State. The opposition spared no money or effort to block every
measure sponsored by the mayor, or to thwart him
in the legislature and through the courts.

The cost of the long struggle was exhausting, and
might have worn out a man less resourceful than
Tom Johnson. At one time it looked as though the
whole enterprise might have to be abandoned for

lack of funds. As an experiment, Mr. Johnson appealed to the public to subscribe for stock in the low-fare company. The return on the stock was limited to six per cent, and at that time such lines as had been laid were buried two feet under the ground, as the courts would not permit the cars to be operated on them. Yet the people were so aroused that money poured in for stock, even though the subscribers questioned whether they would ever get their investment back. The subscriptions came in small sums like savings-bank deposits, and amounted to several hundred thousand dollars. Most of the subscribers were working people, many of them foreigners. Here was evidence that people believed in democracy, that they would make sacrifices for it, once an issue was presented that appealed to their deeper convictions. The poor loved Tom Johnson for the fight he was making, and his majorities were largest when the attacks on him were most virulent.

Our opponents at last, in 1908, put up the white flag. Many of their franchises had expired. Stock that had been sold as high as one hundred and fifteen dollars prior to 1901 had steadily fallen to less than seventy dollars a share. Finally, after every conceivable lawsuit had been exhausted, and bankers had become frightened over the collapse of securities, a settlement was reached. The old companies agreed to a valuation on their properties far below the capitalized valuation. On this valuation they were to receive a fixed return of six per cent and no more. The street-railway properties were to be leased to an operating company of five men, trustees of the city, selected by the mayor, who bound themselves to pay only operating costs and a six-per-cent return on the outstanding capital stock. All earnings in excess of these sums were to be used as the city might direct.

The rate of fare was to be on a sliding scale. It was to start at three cents and go up or down as the earnings of the company made it possible.

Mr. Ermon du Pont was made president of the company, I was vice-president and treasurer, and W. B. Colver was secretary.

The war over, we were ready to turn to the programme of city-building which Mr. Johnson had had in mind from the beginning. "The City on the Hill" would now become a reality. Something had already been done in breathing-spaces between the fighting. Fred Kohler, Mayor Johnson's brilliant young chief of police, had instituted a Golden Rule policy in his department that had shocked some ministers of Christian churches but had won admiring commendation from President Roosevelt. Harris R. Cooley, a lifelong friend of Mr. Johnson's and his director of Charities and Corrections, had one morning astounded the city by a wholesale workhouse delivery. "Imprisonment for debt," Mr. Cooley called the detention of men and women in the workhouse because they were unable to pay fines imposed by the police court. A hue and cry was raised against him, opposition papers said the city would be filled with criminals, but Mr. Cooley went on with his policy, and in time Cleveland became proud of its official humanity. A new workhouse, situated in a tract of two thousand acres laid out as a park, infirmaries, a boys' farm-school, outdoor work for prisoners, and the introduction of the honor system were some of Mr. Cooley's happiest achievements.

With a brilliant executive and the community behind us, we would make an experiment in democracy, in municipal ownership, in town-planning, and the taxation of land values. We were free at last to follow our ultimate ideals.

But we leaned too confidently on our success. We assumed that the officers of the old company were glad to see the controversy ended and that the stockholders preferred an assured income from their stock rather than a return to insecurity and speculation. We did not realize the sense of balked power, the latent hatred, or the nation-wide hostility on the part of financiers and street-railway owners to a three-cent-fare experiment, or to any advance toward municipal ownership. Nor did we dream of the things that could be done to make municipal ownership a failure.

A new line of attack was now adopted. The credit of the operating company was to be undermined. If the municipal company could be made to default in the payment of its guaranteed rental the contract would be forfeited and the properties would go back to the old owners, supported by a twenty-five-year franchise. This was one of the securities provided for when the properties were transferred to the municipal company. The industrial depression of 1907 and 1908 played havoc with our earnings. Thousands of men were out of work and did not use the cars. A disagreement arose with the employees. It was not very serious and might have been adjusted, but it offered a further opportunity to embarrass us. A strike was called. There was evidence that officers of the street-railway union had been paid large sums of money to bring it about. Certainly they received aid from the reactionary press that had never shown any sympathy for organized labor. Dynamite was used on the tracks. Car-riders were terrified, employees assaulted. There were threats that the power-houses would be blown up. Night after night we toured the city in police automobiles protecting the property or responding to calls from employees who remained loyal to us. Our earnings fell off. Finally word was passed around to the strikers to file referendum petitions against the ordinance upon which the settlement was based. The opposition papers supported the petitioners, and in a short time enough names to require the ordinance to be voted on by the people had been filed with the city clerk. We were in for another election. But for the first time we were on the defensive. We had to explain our failures. The community had stood by us when we were battling against an unpopular corporation, but now we were fighting organized labor. The forces of discontent were now against us. We received little support from the press. Our friends were overconfident and remained away from the polls. The evening of the election we followed the returns at the City Hall with every expectation of victory, but the issue hung in the balance all through the night, and in the morning it was still uncertain. We lost out by a few hundred votes.

The verdict could not be reviewed. There was no appeal to another test. The street-railway lines went back to the old companies. Their victory was an empty one, for their dividends were limited to six per cent and could not exceed a fixed amount, while the rate of fare started at three cents and rose or fell as earnings might determine. But the city had lost. A great movement was ended. The dream of municipal ownership, of a free and sovereign city, was set back indefinitely.

This defeat was Tom Johnson's death-blow. For eight years he had given every bit of intelligence, every ounce of energy he possessed to the city. When victory was in his hand the people turned against him. His health failed, his fortune was dissipated, and when he died, within two years, he questioned not the truth of his great economic vision but the value of his own effort, whether any good had come out of it all.

CHAPTER XIV

TOM JOHNSON

I HAD greater affection for Tom Johnson than for any man I have ever known. He was as dependent upon those he loved as he was indifferent to the hostility of his enemies. He had as much time for affection as he had for work, and he was greedy for both. He gathered his friends about him when developing plans, working on an invention, or at home in his big mansion on Euclid Avenue.

There was an enormous armchair in one corner of the fireplace. We called it the throne-chair. It was always reserved for Mr. Johnson.

It seems odd to be writing of him as Mr. Johnson. He wanted to be and he always was "Tom" to all of us. He was "Tom" to every one in Cleveland, and his appearance always gave rise to a chorus of "Hello Tom." Even the children on the streets greeted him as "Tom."

He was not fond of walking. His enormous bulk made rapid progress difficult and he was always in a hurry. One of his cars was waiting for him wherever he went, and it might almost be said of him that he never set foot on the ground.

His friends were young men, who were fascinated by his personality or his programme. A great part of his strength was his lovableness. He was open, frank, and joyous, like a big boy in his enthusiasms and in depressions, which he rarely showed.

The young men whom he drew about him always treated him as if he were of their own age. There was no reserve or awe. The men who formed this early group were Newton D. Baker, his law director, who succeeded him as mayor and was later secretary of war under President Wilson; Charles W. Stage, a brilliant young lawyer, who was the centre of any group, and whose gaiety and courage made him a universal favorite; John N. Stockwell, who took to any adventure like a duck to water; and W. B. Colver, an able newspaper man, who was later appointed chairman of the Federal Trade Commission by President Wilson.

With our wives we formed a group of our own, for the most part indifferent to the life outside. We had dinners and parties, went on picnics and took long motor-rides. Mr. Johnson's home on Euclid Avenue was the centre of our social life. We went there for breakfast, for luncheon, for dinner, as we chose. Sunday evenings found us around the big fireplace discussing politics, economics, philosophy, literature.

There were no jealousies and no friction. We were proud of Tom Johnson's confidence; happy in the prominence he gave us. We threw ourselves into his fight, but knew little of the political game we were playing. At most we were lieutenants, giving unstinted affection to a leader who needed little else from us. He had the resourcefulness of a Napoleon and unwearying courage. He gave us daily adventure, put us in the places where we could do our best work, and we worked under him like players in a football squad. Our friends at the east end spoke sorrowfully of us; we had been hypnotized by Tom Johnson's personality—we would find him out as others had done and return to our proper place in society. But there was nothing to find out in Tom Johnson except his greatness. We were never disillusioned; there were no disaffections, and for nearly ten years we worked and lived together in this way.

His home was a gathering-place for all sorts of men. He kept open house like a Southerner. William

Jennings Bryan stopped off to visit him when passing through Cleveland. Henry George, Jr., lived with him for months at a time, as his father had done. Devoted followers from other parts of the State, especially Daniel Kiefer and Herbert Bigelow, came to confer on local campaigns. Golden Rule Jones, Brand Whitlock, Clarence Darrow, Lincoln Steffens were frequently there; as were party leaders, political bosses, magazine writers, and business men.

Mr. Johnson was a challenging conversationalist. His family had been left destitute by the Civil War, and his life from childhood had been a series of adventures. Even as a boy he had tackled big jobs, had pitted himself against old men, and he knew business, politics, and banking like a scientist. He had made many profitable inventions, was a mathematician and electrician, and seemed to know the law almost as well as his attorneys. He knew the philosophy of Henry George in the same masterful way. He had lived with Henry George, whom he loved; had talked every phase of his philosophy through with him. He had its deeper social significances at his finger-tips. The single tax had come to him like Paul's vision on the road to Damascus, changing a monopolist into the most dangerous enemy that monopoly could have—an enemy not of men but of institutions. He was not a sectarian. His mind remained fertile. He had no pride about an idea proved to be false. He was as eager for a new point of view as most men are to retain an old one. His mind was a garden rather than a safe-deposit vault.

It was this that made him a dangerous antagonist, for he could see the other man's point of view. He made it a rule in business controversies to conduct them always alone, but to invite in all his adversaries. He knew exactly what he wanted; he knew he could convert some of them to his position. Then they would quarrel. When the Democratic organization got unruly he would not meet the trouble-makers; he would call in the entire organization, would listen to every one, then permit the organization to discipline its refractory members. To parry demands of job-hunters he filled vacancies before any one knew about them. Then he was sorry, but the appointment had been made.

His hardest work he always said was keeping the feet of his supporters warm. One of his sayings was: "Don't complain if your helpers betray you; don't complain of stupidity, desertion, or disloyalty. These are the obstacles that leaders of men have to encounter."

When some decision or action was followed by criticism, he would immediately divert attention by starting something new. "I always try to move so fast that the mud they throw will not hit me," he would explain. After a bitter attack on the part of the press, he would remark consolingly: "They never throw stones at a tree that bears no fruit."

For a time he kept up his old intimacies. I remember a dinner that he gave to Mr. Bryan, Myron T. Herrick, and Patrick Calhoun. This was before the political fight made such gatherings impossible. Mr. Johnson had supported Mr. Bryan for President in 1896, although he did not believe in free silver. He did, however, believe in the essential democracy of what Mr. Bryan stood for.

It would have been difficult to assemble four men more different from each other or more brilliant. All four were good story-tellers, self-confident, but appreciative listeners. Mr. Bryan was pre-eminently an evangelist. I have heard him say that if he were younger he would dedicate his life to foreign missions; the nations that knew not Christ were lost.

He was not a statesman, but would have been a
great Methodist bishop. He was at home in any company, and enlivened conversation with personal stories
and a sincerity for which he was not given credit.
He thought as the Middle West thought. More
than any one I have ever known, he represented the
moralist in politics. He wanted to change men. He
was a missionary; America was a missionary. Her
greatest contribution to the world would be her
righteousness—the righteousness which other peoples
did not possess. He was the *vox ex cathedra* of the
Western self-righteous missionary mind.

Myron T. Herrick had charm and an engaging
personality. He was opposed to Mr. Bryan on all
political questions. He had come to Cleveland as
a poor boy, had been admitted to the bar. He met
influential people, and rose rapidly. He became
chairman of the Society-for-Savings Bank, one of
the hundreds of mutual banks that the New England pioneers founded wherever they went. The
bank became a financial power; it had forty-odd
millions of deposits and gave its officials great
authority in the city and in the business world outside. It was banking power that gave Mr. Herrick
advancement in politics. Mr. Herrick was a good
conversationalist, a careful politician, an engaging
host. And he rose from the bank, first to the gov-
ernorship of the State and then to the ambassador-
ship to France.

Patrick Calhoun came from South Carolina, of
the old Calhoun stock. He was thoroughly the
Southern aristocrat. He termed himself a Jeffer-
sonian Democrat, and was opposed to almost everything that "Cousin Tom Johnson" believed in.
They quarrelled generously. The State, according to
Mr. Calhoun, should keep its hands off business. It
should permit men like him to exploit without stint

or control. Unhappily, he became involved in the corruption in the wake of the San Francisco fire and was ruined by the criminal prosecutions which followed.

This particular dinner turned into a sparring-match between Mr. Bryan and Mr. Johnson. Mr. Johnson led off.

"Suppose, Mr. Bryan," he said, "that you were President and Congress and the Supreme Court rolled into one. Suppose you had no one to consult but yourself and could put through your entire programme for regulating trusts and monopolies, as fast as your attorney-general could draft the bills. Tell us what laws you would pass and I will tell you how monopolists would defeat them."

Accepting the challenge, Mr. Bryan outlined the programme. He said: "I would make it a crime for men to organize monopolies. I would set the Department of Justice in motion and vigorously enforce the Sherman Anti-Trust Act. I would create commissions and give their members power to regulate business proceedings, fix prices, rates, and charges. The trouble is that the government does not use its power vigorously. It does not appoint the right kind of district attorneys."

Monopoly under his programme was to be made good. Bad men were at fault. They would either be led to see the evil of their ways or put in jail.

Mr. Johnson's eyes fairly sparkled at these proposals. He had been a conscious monopolist, knowing all the practices of monopoly; it had been an easy game for him. He had been cleverer than most of his associates. And he was far cleverer than the government could possibly be. Monopoly, he knew, could not be regulated. It was too powerful. Also too intelligent. Monopoly was on the job all the time. It employed the best attorneys. And it was in politics. Men like himself could always secure the appointment of commissioners or district attorneys or even judges favorable to the interests they were expected to regulate.

He showed the futility of the Sherman Anti-Trust law and of any attempt to put an end to monopoly by criminal proceedings. The corporation had to win only one trick, while the government had to win them all. The corporation had to find only one loophole, while the government had to block every one of them. Whether it was steam-railways, street-railways, gas or electric companies; whether coal-mines, the oil trust, or other monopolies, Mr. Johnson, through his own experience and knowledge, found an easy way to defeat the proposals made by Mr. Bryan to regulate monopoly by either civil or criminal proceedings. He took us into his personal experiences; told us of the pools he had helped to form in the iron and steel business, of the fixing of prices and the limitation of output. He told of meetings at midnight, in safety-deposit vaults on Wall Street, where men had met distrusting one another and had swapped securities behind locked doors.

Then he stated his own programme. It was economic, not moralistic. It consisted in taking away the special law-made privileges on which monopoly relied for power. Monopoly would collapse, he said, when its supports were taken away. His programme was almost automatic in its workings. Monopoly was born of a strangle-hold on natural resources; it was connected with transportation privileges and rebates, with the protective tariff, with patents. These were the four props on which it rested. Tax land values to the full, at a rate that would appropriate this unearned form of wealth, and monopolies dependent on coal, iron ore, oil, gas, or other natural resources would be forced to a competitive basis. Make transportation a public function, and rebates and discrimination, against which criminal proceedings were futile, would come to an end. Establish absolute free trade, and monopolies depending on the protective tariff would collapse. Abolish patent rights, by which commonly neither inventors nor invention profited, and monopolies based on patents would fall.

Mr. Johnson was in his favorite field, the field in which he was supremely competent. He had evaded regulation, escaped supervision, come out triumphant from criminal proceedings. For a quarter of a century he had been a conscious monopolist and he knew what it was that gave monopoly its power.

He was eager to share with Mr. Bryan his philosophy of freedom. "We ourselves have created monopoly by law. Take away special privilege, and competition will reappear. It is more responsive, more efficient, it will destroy monopoly and usher in a new society. There will be an end of poverty." It was Henry George's economic philosophy in a nutshell. Tom Johnson never wearied of restating it. This time, I remember, it failed utterly of penetrating Mr. Bryan's moralistic armor. He was left dissenting and unconvinced.

The single tax was a dividing-sword in Tom Johnson's own family. His children could not understand his philosophy. They protested against his going into politics. They wanted him to continue making money. And at times they were very angry that he did not do so. Yet I remember his saying to them that he would rather leave a world in which they would know no fear and their children would know no fear than to leave them with all the money in the world. There was no limit, he used to say, to the wealth that would be produced in a free society, in which law-made privileges were abolished. It would be ample enough for all. The fear of poverty would disappear and a new psychology of kindliness, generosity, and justice would take its place.

He divided wealth into two categories: that which was created by labor and that which was created by law. Wealth created by labor should be sacred even from the State. Mines and other natural resources, the ground-rent of cities and farms, the social values of railways and public-utility corporations, belonged by right to those that created them, to the people. This wealth was created by the needs of men, increasing with every increase in population, added to by every art and invention. All of these social values should be taken by the State in taxation. The single tax was the passion of his life—a passion for freedom, for a world of equal opportunity for all. For the promotion of this philosophy he had stopped making money. To that end he had entered politics. He had a vision of a new civilization free from poverty, free from fear, free from vice and crime; of a new society that would be born when the strangle-hold of special privilege was loosened.

Mr. Johnson's political philosophy was as clear and complete as his economic philosophy. He believed in a decentralized government. Government was efficient, he said, when it was close to the people; when the people knew their agents and selected them by the simplest possible means. Like Jefferson, he believed that power should be taken from the federal government and given to the States. Then he would take it from the States and give it to cities, which he would endow with full home rule. To secure highly decentralized government, he believed in direct primaries, the short ballot, the initiative and referendum, the recall and every political device that would make the State as simple, as easily understood, and as workable as a private corporation. He distrusted the courts and protested against their assumption of the right to declare laws unconstitutional.

I got the better part of my education from Tom Johnson. From him I acquired a simple, vivid picture of life. He cleaned up prejudices, swept away old habits of thought, old preconceptions. Political economy became a matter of a few principles which could be applied to any problem. The confusion of thinking which I had brought from the university was cleared up by his penetrating understanding, illustrated from his personal experience. My mind became receptive and retentive. History took on new meanings. I found myself able to make extemporaneous speeches on political questions with ease. My old embarrassment passed away.

There was deep, homely wisdom in Tom Johnson's daily talk, wisdom enriched by knowledge of the world. He was tolerant of everything, including conventional morals and religion. He judged no man, and so far as I recall had no hatreds. He saw men and institutions like a detached scientist; he was ready to learn from any one and to get what pleasure he could from every experience. His willingness to treat as friends men with whom he disagreed confused his enemies. He talked with antagonists with the ease that most men reserve for a circle of intimates. In the midst of a heated controversy with representatives of the street-railways he would stop to point out the differences between their philosophy and his own, or would go off into a discussion of history or of some recent book with an engaging and disarming intimacy.

Tom Johnson had wisdom as well as knowledge —the wisdom of deep understanding. I had known informed men, intellectual men; he was the first wise man I had known. Something in me wanted his wisdom. I was happy to throw up opportunities in other fields to be with him. My wife and I—the beautiful Miss Jenney of that disconsolate distant summer in Meadville had become my wife—lived in a little cottage lost in the centre of an estate in the heart of Cleveland. It was quiet and solitary. A stream ran through the grounds, there was a pond near the house. We had a room reserved for him, where Mr. Johnson would come in the afternoon to rest, to play a game of cards, or to think out his plans.

My wife had long been a suffragist and was a pioneer in Cleveland in that movement and in the organization of women's clubs. A remarkable speaker, she took an active part in our conferences and helped me in speaking and writing. The suffrage movement was then in its pioneer days and very few public men were willing to be identified with it. Mr. Johnson had never given any thought to it. He looked upon man as the protector and provider of woman, whose place was in the home. She was an ornament and should be given every opportunity to be as ornamental as possible.

One evening my wife said to him: "Mr. Johnson, you who are democratic in everything else, why are you not democratic about women? Why do you not believe in woman suffrage? Why do you think that men should decide questions for women?"

Mr. Johnson looked at her, apparently puzzled. "Perhaps I am wrong," he said. "I never thought of it that way. I come from the South, you know, and the women I have known have had the Southern point of view."

Other conversations on suffrage followed. A few weeks later there was an important convention at

Youngstown. Few men in the Democratic party were willing to advocate woman suffrage, and the mayor was always having trouble with men within the party organization, many of them saloon-keepers, who were a unit against it. Yet almost the first sentence in Mr. Johnson's opening speech to the convention was a declaration for the equal rights of women with men. From that time on, he lost no opportunity to speak for equal suffrage. When convinced of the rightness of an idea, he rarely weighed its expediency. Frankness was one of the elements of his strength.

On one occasion there was an important public hearing being held in the City Hall. The room was crowded with lawyers and real-estate men. The doorkeeper came in and whispered to the mayor that there was a woman outside who was raising a row. She said she intended to speak on the public square, but would probably be put in jail for her opinions. Mr. Johnson stopped the proceedings and had her admitted. She was belligerent. She launched at once into an attack on the police and on organized society generally. The mayor stopped her.

"What is your name?" he asked.

"I am Emma Goldman," she replied. "I intend to speak on the public square to-night and I came here to get a permit. I presume I shall be stopped or put in jail."

"No, Miss Goldman," the mayor replied, "you won't be stopped and you won't be put in jail. You do not need a permit to speak. The public square does not belong to me; it belongs to the people of Cleveland. I would not stop you if I had the power to do so, and nobody else has any such power. You have just as much right to your opinions as I have and just as much right to convert other people to them. That is what the 'Beehive' is for."

Emma Goldman looked nonplussed. But the mayor was not through.

"Can't we have a talk together?" he said. "I have always admired Prince Kropotkin, and I agree with a great deal of what he says."

Miss Goldman hesitated, found no answer. Then she turned and left the room. Her meeting was held without interruption.

After his death admirers of Mr. Johnson erected a statue of him on this spot on the public square that had been dedicated to free speech. There are rostrums at the four corners of the monument where speakers stand. To the north is the group of public buildings which began to take form during his administration and which was largely carried through by his insistence. Tom Johnson's belief in freedom is finely symbolized in this memorial.

To the group that surrounded Mr. Johnson each day provided some thrilling incident. For we worked under a leader who was always doing the unexpected thing, who was as resourceful as a great general in repairing his lines or developing new angles of attack. The City Hall was filled with newspaper men, and the opposition papers were venomous in innuendoes and charges against him, not sparing even his family. I once asked him if he did not mind the attacks on him.

"I have a number of axioms that I follow," he replied.

" 'Take your bumps on the bias.'

" 'Travel so fast that the stones don't reach you.'

" 'Make them forget what you did yesterday by what you do to-day.'

" 'When men hiss, remember there is only one kind of animal that makes that kind of noise.' "

To his intimate friends and followers his attitude

was: "You may be right or wrong, but whether right or wrong, I am for you."

Our group had differences as to policy, some of them radical, but there were no desertions, jealousies, or permanent misunderstandings. We felt much more important than we were. The opposition called Mr. Johnson the Democratic boss, which he frankly was. But he bossed his friends and followers by arguments and persuasion, as he did the employees in the City Hall.

Mr. Johnson played in a big way, just as he worked. At leisure he was a titan in search of amusement. A few miles outside of Cleveland he bought a piece of land containing a deep ravine, in which he laid out a trout-farm. He could not get sufficient water from the stream and was unable to buy more land, so he worked out a siphon that drained enough water for his needs from the surrounding farms.

On this playground he worked for weeks over a mechanical geyser like the geysers of Yellowstone Park. What Nature could do he could do. One day he called Mrs. Howe and me over the telephone and said that he had something to show us. He was in high feather, and drove us out to the trout-farm at more than his usual reckless speed. There, after some mysterious manœuvring with machinery, a stream of water gushed from the ground high into the air. It ran for a few minutes and then subsided. Then it started again. Its periodicity was perfect. The flow could be timed with a watch.

On another occasion Mrs. Johnson, much disturbed, called me to the house to intercede with her husband. Huge timbers, machines, electric contrivances, and steel rails were being hauled into the yard and pushed into the cellar. Workmen were coming and going mysteriously. Mrs. Johnson did not know what was going on and Tom would not tell her. When pressed for an explanation he would only smile. He spoke of it as "slip-slide" or "greased lightning," which increased Mrs. Johnson's alarm. Weeks later he invited us to dinner. The affair was staged like a birthday-party. After dinner we were taken to the cellar, which resembled a coal-mine. Big timbers were supported on posts. On the under side of the timbers were steel rails with wide flanges, from which hung a heavy car without wheels.

"This is a model for a railway without wheels," Mr. Johnson said. "I have had the idea in mind for years. If we can do away with wheels and eliminate friction, we can travel at a rate of hundreds of miles an hour. Great speed means getting rid of friction. The car floats. It sails through the air between the guide-rails.

"You'll see it move in a minute. It will be lifted into the air by one electric current and drawn forward by another. The problem is to synchronize the electric power so perfectly that the car will float without touching the rails."

Electric conduits carrying a powerful current were attached to the machinery. The current was turned on and we waited breathlessly. The car did not move. Instead there was a slow crunching noise. The entire structure crumbled before our eyes, under the terrific pressure to which it was subjected.

Mr. Johnson took the failure smilingly. The principle was sound, of that he was sure. The next day he set to work to build another model, and some months later we were invited to a second demonstration. This time the car started. It did not go far, but Mr. Johnson was satisfied. Wheels were not necessary. Friction could be eliminated. Passengers and freight could be moved through the air at great speed by synchronizing electric currents, the one lifting, the other pulling. There was theoretically no limit to the speed, while risk could be reduced to a minimum.

I do not know what Mr. Johnson hoped from this expensive experiment. He had thought about it for years and could not rest content until he had tested out the idea. The next time he went to New York he visited the officials of the General Electric Company at Schenectady. They were sceptical of the idea but finally sent two experts to Cleveland to study the model. They made a favorable report. Still sceptical, the company sent Mr. Charles Steinmetz to examine it. Steinmetz said that the idea was basically sound. Negotiations were opened for the building of a larger model, but they fell through because the company demanded control of the patents, which Mr. Johnson would not abandon.

That was the way Tom Johnson played. He loved to undertake the seemingly impossible, to conquer some problem, to solve some riddle. He could have made a fortune out of inventions had he devoted himself to scientific work.

He liked people with new ideas. One week we motored to East Aurora to see Elbert Hubbard. We found him in the fields with his shirt open at the neck, his hair flowing to the winds. He installed us in the Inn. There was music and talk and Hubbard was an engaging host. He impressed me as a very real person, courageous and honest in his personal interests, in spite of the fact that he commercialized his work. He drew to himself all kinds of people, who lived at the Inn, worked in his shops, found new contacts.

Mr. Johnson played with danger. He took all kinds of chances, some of which seemed foolhardy. He let himself into compromising situations, even when he knew that he was being watched by detectives employed to force, if they could, his retirement from politics. I occasionally went with him to New York. When we left the train, he would stop in the Grand Central Station and look searchingly around him. Then he would beckon to a group of men. He would look them in the eyes quite frankly, as if to say: "I know that you are detectives employed by the traction interests to watch me. I don't blame you for that. You have to make a living and this is your way." Then, having satisfied himself that he was right in his impression, he would say:

"Now, boys, I'm going down to the Equitable Building on lower Broadway to see my lawyers. I will be there for half an hour. After that I will call on my friend August Lewis on East Sixteenth Street. Then I will make some purchases on Fifth Avenue. I shall take lunch at the Manhattan Club about one o'clock. After that I don't want to be bothered. I expect to dine in the evening at the Hotel Brevoort. Now you have enough to make out a good report."

Then off he would go. He seemed to have complete confidence that the detectives would not follow him. He kept to his schedule up to one o'clock, and after that we followed our own devices. The detectives looked upon him as a good sport. They liked his understanding of the game and his tolerance of the work they had to do. They would rather protect than betray him. Possibly they felt that he was making their fight, and the least they could do was to be true to his confidence in them, even if untrue to their employers.

Tom Johnson was never through learning. At fifty he was as eager to know new things as he had been at twenty-five. He got up early in the morning to study. Mastering French seemed important to him. He practised it on his friends. He read and reread philosophy. He prized knowledge that he had had no opportunity to acquire. He wanted to know about art, and deferred to men who had had educational advantages that had been denied him. He set a childish valuation on things he did not know and did not have.

But when his own desires were involved he was a generous tyrant. At one time I was asked to fill in a semester as professor of politics at the University of Wisconsin for Professor Paul S. Reinsch, who was going to China. I accepted without telling Mr. Johnson of my plans. He protested that I should remain in Cleveland.

"But," I said, "I have accepted the offer from Madison."

"That makes no difference," he said. "You stay here. I will go to Wisconsin and arrange it. I want you here."

He followed me to Wisconsin. He had everything planned out. I must chuck the semester at the university and come back at once to Cleveland. Teaching boys was not important. He had found a house for us and we could return on the next train. He was hurt by my refusal.

He spent his fortune recklessly. He had done so from the beginning, even though his early life had been one of poverty. Money was something to be gotten rid of; its purpose was to give pleasure. He had many dependents that no one knew of. He gave to waiters, cab-drivers, door-men. But he gave nothing to organized charity. That meant a continuance of the system. Men would demand justice, he said, if they did not receive doles. He bought expensive cars, lived extravagantly, and lost a great part of his fortune in trying to save his brother Albert's street-railway ventures, of which he had been made trustee by his brother's will.

One day in the City Hall one of the opposition

lawyers served a notice on him that securities lodged
with a New York bank would be sold on a certain
day to satisfy a loan of $70,000. Tom listened. Finally
he said: "I hope you will be able to get more out of
them than I have. I can't sell them, possibly you
can."

When the attorney left I asked him what it meant.
"That's the end of my fortune," he said. "They can
sell these securities for any price and take a judgment
over against me for the balance. There is nothing
left but the Euclid Avenue home and that is in my
wife's name." Then he went about what he was
doing as though nothing unusual had happened.

He had told me the truth. In eight years' time
he had spent a fortune of from two to three million
dollars, invested for the most part in government
bonds. He faced the possibility of poverty with
apparently little concern.

Tom Johnson was, I think, one of the greatest
statesmen America has produced. He was an astute
politician, but he never compromised on important
measures, even when they were far in advance of
the time. He attacked institutions, not men. When
bribery or corruption was disclosed he made no
attempt to have men sent to jail. If society hung
great prizes in the form of franchises before men's
eyes, it must expect bribery. The thing to do was
to stop tempting people. He differed from most
reformers, as he once said, in that they would arrest
the burglar and compel him to give up a part of
what he had stolen, while he would put a policeman
in front of the bank and prevent the burglar from
entering.

CHAPTER XV

MARK HANNA

MARK HANNA once suggested to Tom Johnson that they go into partnership in the street-railway business. Mr. Johnson replied: "No, Mark, you and I are too much alike. We could not sit together on the same bench. Either you would push me off or I should push you off."

Mark Hanna and Tom Johnson were strangely alike. They were alike in their titanic mould. They were both men of big chest measurement, of stocky limbs, of physical power. They had big engines that gave them courage, directness, and power to command. They commanded easily, and received devoted service. They were alike in their instinct for monopoly. They kept away from competitive enterprises. They sought a strangle-hold; they wanted a cinch on society, something protected by law and made valuable by law. Something too that everybody had to use whether they wanted to or not—something for which a monopoly price could be charged.

Both men were lawless. They respected neither the law nor the courts. They knew how laws were made. They had used political power in the city council and in the State legislatures to tighten their grip on the community. They had made judges, and they knew that the judges they made would come to them again for support. They were lawless by temperament; they felt themselves above the law. That was part of their power. They had no reverence. They had supreme confidence in themselves.

146

An understanding study of these two men would tell us many things that are important to know. They had no fears. They stood squarely on their own feet. They leaned neither on religion, on the State, nor on the law. They were not hostile to religion—it did not interest them; they were not averse to approval—it was not necessary to them; they did not protest against the State—they ignored it. They had a quality of intelligence that was different from that of other men. They saw how to obtain wealth by other means than personal labor. And they unerringly pursued this kind of wealth. An explanation of Mark Hanna and Tom Johnson would furnish an explanation of personal power, of the ability to command. It would explain the Cæsars, the Napoleons, of history.

It was a strange coincidence that these two men lived their lives in the same city; and until Tom Johnson had his revelation they wanted the same things. Because they were alike in so many big ways they understood one another; they spoke of each other without hatred and with a certain respect.

Yet, alike as they were, they came to be as far apart as the poles in their political ideas. Mark Hanna had a feudal idea of society. "Some men must rule; the great mass of men must be ruled. Some men must own; the great mass of men must work for those who own." The men to do the ruling were the men who owned. The men to do the serving were those who worked. Life meant war to Mark Hanna. War on his business associates, on his employees, on the State itself. And he made war, not to bend men but to break them. He treated the State in the same way. It must be broken to his will. To get the things he wanted, Mark Hanna was willing to bring down the temple of government itself.

Tom Johnson was a maverick; Mark Hanna was the leader of his herd. In Cleveland he was back of the street-railways, the bankers, and the press. He had sensed the easy road to wealth through the tariff, through ore-mines, coal, natural resources, and franchise corporations. His street-railway interests involved him in politics first in his ward, then in the city, then in the State. And at a time when all America was indifferent to the value of such things, he had easily made himself master of Cleveland. This mastery Mayor McKisson challenged and Tom Johnson broke. But Senator Hanna along with Foraker, of Cincinnati, still ruled the State.

Ohio, like Pennsylvania, was corrupt and contented. Contented with its bosses. It believed in the necessity of a certain amount of corruption. And it hated any challenge, political, moral, or religious, to the system. Its two senators divided federal and State patronage. They frankly selected candidates for the supreme bench, for the legislature, for the governor's chair, for the federal judiciary. Boss Cox, of Cincinnati, and Walter Brown, of Toledo, helped them to rule the commonwealth. There was a pretense of popular government but no legislation in the interest of the people. Complaisant men were nominated for State offices; as long as they did as they were told they were able to look forward to a permanent career in politics. Mark Hanna could not return the councilman from his own ward in Cleveland, yet he had bound the city by a thousand thongs of State legislation.

With the nomination of Mr. Bryan in 1896, Mark Hanna became a national figure. His management of the McKinley campaign put the politics of America on a money basis and shocked ever so slightly the conscience of the nation. He made McKinley President and had himself appointed to the United States

Senate, Senator John Sherman being elevated to the
Cabinet to provide the opportunity. During McKinley's administration Mr. Hanna was a colossus astride
of the country. He decided important appointments.
He was consulted on legislation. He was the nearest
approach to a national boss the country had yet
known.

Tom Johnson was in the habit of saying that it
was unfair to make personal attacks on Mark
Hanna and men of his sort. They were what they
were because of the business they were in; because
of the business code of their class. Corruption was
impersonal. It sprang from the laws which invited
corruption. And Mr. Johnson was as good as his
word; he kept his criticisms of Mark Hanna to himself and the warfare between them impersonal.

I first met Mr. Hanna when Ralph W. Easley
came to Cleveland to organize the National Civic
Federation. The preliminary conference, which I
attended, was taken for a steamboat ride on Lake
Erie. There was plenty to eat, more to drink, and
wolves and lambs were herded together in apparently
peaceful fashion, the wolves being important business men, including Mr. Hanna, and the lambs
John Mitchell, president of the Anthracite Coal
Workers, Dan O'Keefe, of the Longshoremen's Union,
and other labor leaders. The federation was to
bring capital and labor together in a big committee,
where they could thrash out their difficulties. According to Mr. Easley, there was no real conflict
between capital and labor, and if they could be
brought together and kept together, strikes and
lockouts would be avoided. Mr. Hanna was to be
chairman of the committee.

I was suspicious of the idea from the start, and as
it turned out John Mitchell lost the confidence of
the Anthracite Coal Workers and his official po-

sition because of contact with the federation. And it was probably the intention of the promoters of the plan that just that sort of thing should happen; that labor men by sitting in with business men should lose their fighting courage; be weakened by respect for wealth. Opportunities were afforded them to make profitable investments; to buy in stocks on the stock exchange; to share in under-writing. There were dinners, conferences, and speeches. Labor leaders softened their utterances when speaking before such audiences. If member-ship in the federation was designed to weaken or destroy the moral fibre of labor men who accepted it, it was, in my opinion, thoroughly successful in achieving this end.

I had other opportunities to meet Mr. Hanna. I went to his house. I met him on various junkets. I went on a trip to Maine with him, in his private car, shortly after McKinley's assassination.

He was bullet-headed, cruel-lipped; dynamic in all his relations. Many of his associates loved him. I came to have affection for him. He suffered from newspaper attacks, particularly from the cartoons of Homer Davenport, which portrayed him as a bloated creature covered all over with wriggly dollar-marks. He was not content with the plaudits of his imme-diate associates; he wanted the approval of the crowd. He apparently loved William McKinley; talked to me on the trip that I took with him far into the morning about McKinley's personal qualities.

Mark Hanna wanted power. Money was the symbol of power in his world. It had no other symbol. Money controlled banks; it controlled public opinion; it controlled the State. So he sought money. Unerring instinct told him, as it told John D. Rockefeller and Tom Johnson, that the easy way to make huge sums of money was not through mills and factories, which were subject to competition, but through the seizure and protection by law of natural resources, railways, and public-utility corporations. Law-made wealth, he saw, was easy and sure. And he wanted money too much to be willing to risk battling on equal terms with other men for it. He believed in monopoly more honestly than most men believe in religion. Monopoly was his religion. He owned street-railways in Cleveland, iron-ore mines, and coal properties. When he wanted privileges from the State, he got them by political power; by personal control of men. He made public opinion by acquiring newspapers. Then he relied on the Chamber of Commerce, which was organized and officered by men of his opinions, if not his choosing. He subsidized and controlled men in the national grange to make the farmers obedient to his will, as he aided in organizing the National Civic Federation to control organized labor. He enriched himself without compunction, believing that the State was a business man's State. It existed for property. It had no other function. His rationalization was direct and complete. Great wealth was to be gained through monopoly, through using the State for private ends: it was axiomatic therefore that business men should run the government and run it for their personal profit. Men who questioned this idea were disturbers Socialists, anarchists, or worse.

His cult of power involved arrogance. For men whom he elevated to high positions he had a certain contempt, gave them orders as he did to his office employees. He expected loyalty from the men he made and saw no reason for their being loyal to the State. As for labor, in his own estimation he was its friend, he was a "work-giver."

Types like Mark Hanna recur through history. Lives of men of the Renaissance can be paralleled

152 THE CONFESSIONS OF A REFORMER

line by line with men of our own time. Mark Hanna
felt and acted as did Italian princes of the fourteenth and fifteenth centuries. In their attitude
toward the State, toward enemies, toward labor, an
analytical study of big business men of our time
would read very much like the lives of the despots
of an earlier age. Mark Hanna felt about the State
as did Louis XIV. He felt the same about men who
opposed him; about lesser feudal barons who got
in his way. His lordship over his associates was
scarcely concealed. They were vassals of a system,
but vassals of Mark Hanna as well.

He did not confer, he gave orders. He neither
understood nor brooked opposition. When he made
a decision, changing conditions could not change it.
It was this inflexibility that enabled Tom Johnson
to outwit him in their first street-railway controversy.
It was this that defeated him in the long-drawn-out
contest with the city. He had always had his way.
He would have his way. There was no alternative.

Personal contact with Mark Hanna and men of
his type made clearer to me the point of view of
business men whom I knew. In him the beliefs of
lesser men of his sort were blazoned in unmistakable
colors. I was habitually confused by estimable,
charitable gentlemen, some of them clients of our
law firm, whose opinions, grasped in a piecemeal
and haphazard way, I seemed to disagree with, yet
whom personally I warmly liked. They were the kind
of men I had hoped and expected would go into
politics as did my prototypes in all good statesmanship, the gentlemen of England. They had
made their pile, could afford to devote themselves
to other things. I was forever unwilling in the
earlier days of Cleveland to deprive these excellent
citizens of the rôle of saviors of the State, forever
unable to assign them to it. Mark Hanna clarified

them to me. In what he thought about himself and the government, I read what they thought. And wondered at what I read.

Business was the most important thing in the world to them. They had no other enthusiasms. They talked business, loved business, judged all men and all measures in business terms. The political state existed for their benefit. Lawyers, ministers, teachers were employees, vassals. Farmers and working men were a servile class. The fact that their property was often tainted with graft made little difference so long as the graft was not discovered or did not bring them into the courts. Bribery was not a two-edged sword. The man who took a bribe was a low person, to be abandoned if he was discovered; the man who gave a bribe was exempt from ignominy. He merely used money in a natural way to get what he wanted and he was working for everybody's good. The ethics of business was the same as the ethics of the East Side politicians of New York; whose psychology was the same. The ward politician looked upon the State as a thing from which he would get something for himself and his friends. He got political jobs, petty graft. The boss was his friend, and he and the boss shared in the spoils. Mark Hanna and his associates went into politics to get something for themselves and their friends.

The city and the State were enlarged precincts. The boss was part of the business system. He was an agent, a broker through whom they got what they wanted. They paid in cash for what they got just as the ward worker paid in personal services. The system at the top was the same as the system at the bottom. Business men, spoilsmen, grafters, all looked upon the government as a big Santa Claus. The poor got their graft; the business men got theirs. But the poor only got what the business men allotted to them. Hanna, Foraker, and their associates differed from the petty grafter in social standing and in the fact that the latter might be indicted and sent to the penitentiary for doing the things which Hanna and his associates, acting through impersonal corporations, ordered him to do.

The ethics of these men was clan ethics. They cared for the opinions of their particular herd. They craved the approval of members of the Union Club, of the Chamber of Commerce, and the board of directors of the bank. If the quickest way to do business was by bribery, then, since business demands results, that was the "natural," the businesslike, way to proceed. That street-corner orators denounced them as corrupt meant nothing to them unless that plain and ugly word got to their families, where it had to be explained. With the press under their control, district attorneys members of their clubs, and judges men of their selection, they had little fear of criminal proceedings. Difficult to initiate and easily suppressed, such proceedings were frowned down by public opinion, which counted them harmful to business and to the good name of the community.

The code of business in relation to labor ran something like this.

"By the superior intelligence of the employer a certain amount of wealth is produced, of which capital gets less if labor gets more. Without the employer labor would starve. Organized labor is the enemy of capital. Strike-leaders must be gotten out of the way, by bribery or otherwise.

"Free immigration provides a labor surplus. Immigrants can be worked twelve hours a day; by mixing nationalities they can be hindered from organizing; when they are maimed or worn out,

others take their places. They need not be supported during hard times; when injured they can be
sent to public hospitals for repair. Handled intelligently, ignorant men are cheaper than machines.
And out of a labor surplus come strike-breakers.

"Shorter hours in the factory mean longer hours
in the saloon. When men drink they come late to
work on Monday or do not come at all. They spend
less time in the wholesome atmosphere of the steel-
mill and the coal-mine. The saloon is a menace to
efficiency; therefore, it should be closed. The Anti-
Saloon League should be financed."

This was the code of many of the most distinguished business men of Cleveland. Industry was
war, with the employer and employee on opposite
sides of the trenches. The no man's land of this warfare was occupied by liberals and reformers, deserters
from their class, entitled, by its pitiless judgment,
not even to the rules of humane warfare.

The men whom I had wished to see in politics
were in politics. They contributed campaign funds,
supported bosses, controlled the press. They selected nominees, dictated platforms, controlled the
party organization. They organized citizens' committees to prosecute members of the council who
accepted bribes, and then organized public opinion
to stop prosecutions against their associates who
were involved in the bribe-giving. They talked of
the sabotage of the worker to reduce his output,
but saw no impropriety in organizing a monopoly to
keep up prices by reducing output. The lawyer who
took the case of a widow whose husband had been
killed in the steel-mills was an "ambulance-chaser,"
while the attorney who represented the corporation
responsible for the injury was elected president of
the Union Club. The ethics of business men was
economic. Their professed religious morals had

nothing to do with the code they practised. They were a herd.

I wanted to be part of this herd, even while I hated the things that it did. I wanted wealth, even though I knew that great wealth could only be gotten by means of which I disapproved. I wanted approval from my crowd and from myself as well. That was my conflict. It was for the most part subconscious. But it was always there. I do not know in which camp I should have landed had I been forced to make a choice between my living and my convictions. Largely by reason of the generosity of my law partners, the Garfields, I was never forced to make the choice.

CHAPTER XVI

MAKING LAWS AT COLUMBUS

THE struggle for "A City on the Hill" failed because the city was not free. It had only the shadow of self-government. It could not own or operate things, or control private property; it could not levy taxes as it willed. It could only borrow a limited amount of money and for limited uses; it could not control its own employees. The city was little more than a big policeman. Its people were bound like Gulliver by endless thongs written into the constitution and laws of the State. They were helpless before the bosses and business interests that controlled the government. Laws which crippled democracy were written by corporation lawyers. Privileged business defeated demands for home rule; it would not permit the city to own anything or to do anything that interfered with private property. The city could perform only perfunctory things and perform them only as the laws defined. It could give away things easily enough but could not own anything that was valuable, could not control property in the interest of all the people.

The mayor, council, and people were helpless. An injunction allowed by a pliant judge could balk their efforts. Tom Johnson's hands were tied for eight years by the constitution, the laws, and most of all by the courts. The city of Cleveland, like every other city in the State, was ruled by the legislature; the fight for good government had to be carried to the State capital.

Ohio at that time was managed like a private estate by Senators Hanna and Foraker. Senator

Foraker operated from Cincinnati, Mark Hanna from Cleveland, where he had his street-railways—"savings-banks," he called them. The two were in conflict over the control of the State but in complete accord as to the things they wanted protected.

An oligarchy of business bosses strangled Cleveland and every other city in Ohio. Two million city-dwellers were in servitude to three or four men who stood astride of the State, who filled the State offices, who selected members of the House of Representatives and candidates for the courts as they would select clerks in their offices. Cleveland, Toledo, and other progressive communities were made to stand still; worse, they were compelled to have their crooked bosses and their vice districts, because these conditions contributed to the continued supremacy of the interests that ruled the State. Cleveland could not achieve itself, because in doing so it menaced the private interests of Senator Hanna and Senator Foraker, of John R. McLean and lesser bosses.

Tom Johnson understood this system, having practised it from the inside for years without seeing anything wrong in it, and challenged it. Thwarted in Cleveland, he carried the fight to Columbus. He first elected a radical delegation to the State Democratic convention from Cleveland. He fought in the Resolutions Committee and for the nomination of progressive men for governor. When outvoted, he took his defeat smilingly and said:

"We have lost a skirmish but we will win the war."

He was nominated for governor on the Democratic ticket and carried on a whirlwind campaign. He took his big tent and hauled it by motor-car over the State. He drove his "Red Devil" from city to city, and talked in the streets. I marvelled at his carelessness in never preparing his speeches. And he was so winning in personality that many people distrusted him. They found it difficult to believe in the sincerity of a man so rich and so richly endowed. But he reached tens of thousands of people who never attended political meetings. He talked simply, about commonplace abuses, about taxation, about various forms of big graft, about bosses and the interests they represented. He learned about local conditions in advance. And he assailed Democratic crooks as vigorously as Republican ones. This novelty of attacks on men of his own party excited interest, inspired confidence.

Misrepresented by the press and in advance of his time in his economic programme, he was defeated for governor. His administration of Cleveland was misrepresented; the red herring of a wide-open town, which was the description given of Cleveland and Toledo, where Sam Jones was mayor, was drawn across his trail by the Anti-Saloon League, the churches, and reform organizations inspired to activity by the Republican leaders. Mr. Johnson was waging a long-visioned fight and he took his defeat philosophically, persevering year by year in his attacks on the boss system. He was always at Columbus, appearing before legislative committees and making speeches. He flooded the State with pamphlets. In time he broke the power of Boss McLean and came into control of the Democratic Party.

Largely as a result of his campaigns the State was awakened. Young men were inspired to enter politics. In 1905 a progressive Democrat was nominated for governor and elected. The Assembly was Republican by a small majority, while the Senate contained eighteen Republicans, eighteen Democrats, and one Independent. A group of progressive Republicans had been elected who were expected to co-operate in ushering in a new regime. There was elation throughout the State. Ohio was about to clean house.

To the men who had ruled Ohio for so many years Tom Johnson was anathema. He was rich as they were rich. He had made his money as they had made theirs. He had amassed a fortune and had then turned on his class. That offense could not be forgiven. He was an outlaw, hated for his desertion. And hated because he could not be ignored. He had been repeatedly elected mayor of Cleveland and was nationally recognized as one of the leading reformers in the country. He could not be disposed of as a demagogue as could lesser leaders. Tom Johnson had shattered the boss system. Ohio had become a doubtful State.

With three other men from Cleveland I was elected to the State Senate on the reform wave. The Democratic platform was clear-cut. It gave home rule to cities, gave them power to own and operate public-utility corporations, and do practically anything else that the people desired. It taxed railroads and public-utility corporations the same as other property. It committed us to a simple direct-primary law, to the initiative and referendum, and the recall.

I believed fervently in this platform. We would have great cities—the city was always my passion—in America if the people were given power. They had shown in Cleveland their willingness to follow a leader. But we had been thwarted by bad laws, an inflexible constitution, by out-of-date charters. We had failed because we were manacled by laws. Our first task was to get freed from the legislature. And I fully expected that we should succeed. We had a progressive governor, a progressive majority in the Senate, and the best Lower House that had been

elected for years. We had the support of the Scripps-
McRae papers. Apparently ours was a complete
mandate from the people. There was no reason
why our legislation should not go through in every
detail. I confided my expectations to Ed Doty, who
had long been the clerk of the House of Representatives. He laughed cynically.

"You'll be lucky," he said, "if you get one bill
through."

I looked at him uncomprehendingly and promptly
forgot what he said. I was all eagerness for the
session to begin. I sent letters to the Democratic
senators asking them to come to Columbus some
days prior to the opening of the legislature. I realized
that it was essential that we should control the
organization of the Senate, which included the clerk-
ship and the personnel of the committees which
shaped legislation and decided for or against the
favorable report of bills. All of the men responded,
and I made it my business to find out in advance
what each one of them most wanted. To my surprise they were not interested in legislation. Few of
them had read the platform. Many of them did
not know what was meant by home rule, direct
primaries, the initiative and referendum. They were
insurance agents, real-estate men, farmers—old men,
for the most part. And they were away from home
for a good time. They did not want to be bothered
about ideals. They would get their orders from the
county committee, the court-house crowd, whom
they did not wish to offend. What they wanted was
their share in the patronage—an insignificant job as
stenographer, assistant, clerk, or messenger for a
relative or friend.

The jobs were handed around to every one's
satisfaction. Then some one noticed that I had
nothing, and asked me what I wanted.

"To be chairman of the committee on committees," I said.

This seemed an empty wish, for there were no jobs connected with it. It was granted to me willingly. Controlling the committee on committees, I packed the Senate committees in which I was interested just as our adversaries would have done. I gave the reactionary senators unimportant assignments and put men who could be relied on in important positions.

The Assembly started out with a fine zeal, which lasted one day. A mandatory two-cents-a-mile passenger-railway-fare bill of a single paragraph was introduced into the Lower House; it was put on its second and third reading, and passed without being referred to a committee. It was immediately messaged over to the Senate, where it was given a second and third reading and adopted by a substantial majority. Fearing that the bill would be stolen or reconsidered, we suspended proceedings and had it engrossed, then got into a cab and drove to the governor's residence. It was signed and became a law before nightfall. The lobby had been careless. The first day was always given over to nominating speeches and to organization work, so many of the lobbyists had not taken the trouble to put in an appearance. This was the first two-cent railway-passenger bill enacted by any of the States. The law remained in operation until the outbreak of the war, and railroads made little effort to defeat it.

All of our measures were immediately introduced and referred to committees. Public hearings were called. I prepared what seemed to me conclusive briefs on railroad taxation and the initiative and referendum, expecting that early action would be taken on them. But the bills were not reported. They could not be gotten out of committees. We could not get a quorum. Postponements were granted on some pretext or other. The railway attorneys in the Senate seemed able to block anything they were opposed to.

When week after week slipped by without progress being made, we decided to start a fire behind the most reactionary members of the legislature. We found an intelligent street speaker named Billy Radcliffe and sent him out with a blackboard through the State. He would spend two or three days in a county and would show people in black and white, from the court-house steps, how little the railroads paid in taxes and how much the county would save under our proposal. He described the initiative and referendum in simple terms and explained how the Assembly was controlled by political bosses. It was effective campaigning. Members of the Senate began to come to me and say:

"Howe, I know you're behind this fellow Billy Radcliffe; he is talking about your measures. My neighbors want to know why I oppose them. My wife's bothered by what he says. If you'll call him off, I'll help get your bills out of committee and vote for them when they come up."

Still we made little headway. Our bills never came to a vote; they were blocked at some stage of the proceedings, either in the House or in the Senate.

One of the men elected to the Lower House from Cleveland was John N. Stockwell. He was a cheerful fighter, always making trouble, always on the job. Politics was an exhilarating game to him. Among other activities he began an investigation of the State treasurer's office to find out what was being done with the State funds, amounting to $15,000,000. By reason of the Republican majority in the House he was unable to make headway, and passed the job on to me in the Senate.

One Monday morning I went to the treasurer's office accompanied by a group of newspaper men. Under the law all of the State's money was required to be kept in vaults in the State House; it could not be deposited in banks. I asked the treasurer to be permitted to see the money. He refused. I then demanded the right to examine his ledgers. I demanded this as chairman of the finance committee and also as a citizen. The treasurer lost his temper.

"It's none of your damn business," he said, "either as a senator or as a citizen where I keep the money or how I run my office."

Within a few hours afternoon papers in Cleveland, Cincinnati, Toledo, and Columbus were carrying display head-lines quoting the State treasurer to the effect that it was "nobody's damn business where he kept the State's money or how he ran his office."

When the Senate convened at one o'clock I introduced a resolution for the appointment of a committee of three to investigate the treasurer's office. Through an understanding with the president of the Senate it was put on its passage immediately. The clerk read the resolution in a perfunctory way and it was passed without being noticed. Two reliable men were named with me on the committee. An instant later some one from the treasurer's office rushed in and told the Republican floor leader what was being done. But it was too late. The committee had been made up, and we immediately set to work.

The State treasurer refused to show us his books, so we seized his correspondence and found that money was being paid to him as interest on deposits for which he made no account to the State. Large sums were in a bank controlled by Boss Cox and

in which Republican leaders were stockholders. The
State treasurer and auditor-general rushed to the
supreme court and secured an injunction against
the investigation, on the ground that a Senate committee, though properly authorized, had no power
to make it. Then we followed other leads. Through
personal stock holdings in banks we dug into their
relations with the State treasurer. Millions of dollars were out on interest for which no accounting
was made. Legal proceedings were instituted against
the treasurer and the auditor-general, by which substantial sums were recovered. The State treasurer
left the country, dying a few months later. The
investigation aroused the hostility of bankers, but
it upset the State. Ohio gave its vote to Woodrow
Wilson in 1912, and has since elected a number of
Democratic governors.

I introduced many measures during my three
years in the legislature. Most of them never got out
of committees. When they did they were immediately
killed on the floor. The one exception was a bill for
removing the penitentiary from Columbus out on
to a big farm where the prisoners would work in the
open and where the honor system would prevail.
This the governor—the reform governor had died
and had been succeeded by a Republican lieutenant-
governor—vetoed on partisan grounds.

The last day of the session was Armistice Day.
The lobby went home at noon. Enmities were forgotten and by a tacit agreement each member was
permitted to call up some bill that bore his name
and if it was not too controversial it was permitted to
pass. Thus members had something to show to their
constituents. These last hours were pandemonium.
Many of the lawmakers were drunk. Nobody paid
any attention to what was going on. Scores of bills
went through by gentlemen's agreement. Nobody

knew what they contained and nobody cared. It had become bad form to enter any opposition.

I came away from the legislature with scant respect for the laws of the land. I had seen how they were made. Some were frankly bought and paid for. Many were passed the last day. Only occasionally were bills in the public interest forced through by the pressure of public opinion. And these were so crippled with amendments that they were of little value. A great part of the laws was so much rubbish.

CHAPTER XVII

I THROW AWAY BALLAST

IN spite of disappointments, work in the Senate, like work in the city council, fascinated me. During two long sessions of five months each I worked hard; evenings found me in the Senate-chamber grinding over bills, sitting on committees, or holding conferences. I dined and played cards with the lobbyists, found them much like other people, only more human and with no consciousness of disloyalty to the State. They were earning a living; if some one was willing to employ them, the moral responsibility was with their employers, not with them. They had the same psychology as the lawyer; they would use every device to win; the Assembly was the jury; it had to decide.

I liked the intimacy, the activity, the struggle. This was America. The legislature was a cross-section of the people. And I was so confident of the justice of our measures that I never lost hope.

But with the close of the last session I admitted defeat, not of our programme alone but of my political creed. I had been wrong and cynical, Ed Doty had been right. We had scarcely an item to our credit. We had spent hundreds of thousands of dollars of the people's money and had little to show for it. The legislature that had preceded ours had been known as the "garbage legislature." In commenting on our adjournment one of the newspapers said that we at least had not been that. But it was small satisfaction to know that we had not stolen everything "that was not nailed down."

The disturbing thing to me was that by all of the rules of popular government we should have won a sweeping victory. We should have carried through our entire programme, which would have democratized the State and made possible the city renaissance of which I had dreamed. We had good leadership and support from the press. There was no lack of intelligence; the legislature was far above the average. The two branches of the legislature were reasonably harmonious; our programme had been approved by the people. It should have been enacted into law. But for some reason or other the government would not work. It stalled, it did not function. Bosses remained unshaken in their power; our measures were buried in committees or crippled by amendment. Many of them were left hanging between the two houses. The supreme court had interfered to block inquiry and investigation. We could only win a skirmish, never a battle. We were defeated by the very instrument that was designed to insure popular government. The political machinery itself was at fault; that was the trouble.

Temporary defeat of our measures was one thing, failure of the government itself, another. And the government had failed. It was not designed to register the popular will.

I decided to take stock of my political philosophy. I had done this before in New York, when working for Doctor Parkhurst, and again when I left the Charity Organization Society in Cleveland. My early beliefs in the business man had been shattered by experience in the city council. The Constitution was the Ark of the Covenant in my eyes. Must that too be questioned?

I sat down with reluctance to examine my conception of the political state. It meant going back to the men whom I revered most, whose authority on the Constitution and on politics was infallible. It meant sitting in judgment on James Bryce and Woodrow Wilson and on their disciple—myself.

When I left Johns Hopkins I accepted without question the oft-quoted statement of Mr. Gladstone's, that the American Constitution was "the most wonderful work ever struck off at a given time by the brain and purpose of man." It was sacrosanct, near to being divinely inspired; it would remain unchanged for all time. To question its perfection or the disinterested motives of the men who framed it was sacrilege. And its chief distinction was that it distributed powers into three categories: the legislative, the executive, and the judiciary—this and the detachment of officials from popular clamor. These provisions were said to insure calm and dispassionate consideration. Passion was checked, judgment suspended, and intelligent action insured. Under this distribution there was discussion in the committees and then on the floor of the two houses. Before a measure passed beyond control it had to win the approval of the government. Then it had to be tested out in the courts. The co-operation of many minds was expected to bring forth the best possible results. This was "government by discussion," as described in the text-books. It was government by representatives of the people. It was assumed that men in public office wanted only to ascertain the public good and to act upon it; they were detached from private interests and sought by contemplative study to ascertain only the truth on public questions.

I cherished this belief in popular government, in the value of discussion, in the marvellous prevision of the makers of the Constitution. But I had been for three years a member of a legislative body in which no one listened to discussions. Members fled to the smoking-rooms during debate. When the time came to vote they did as they were told; they followed the floor leader or received instructions from elsewhere.

Business men and bosses showed no respect for the Constitution that I had been taught to revere. It had no sanctity in their eyes. The laws they wanted could be driven through it with a coach and four. It was only referred to when some labor measure was to be defeated. Liberal laws for the protection of women and children in industry were always discovered to be unconstitutional, while fifty-year grants to street-railways were upheld. Attempts to regulate tenements or to require safety devices in mines were held to violate sacred property rights, while monopoly powers assumed by private corporations were sustained as in line with progress. The courts constituted themselves judges of what was constitutional and what was not. Their decisions were in the interest of one class and against another. Cleveland could dispose of its water-front worth many millions for nothing, but could not build itself a public wharf. It could give up its streets for a generation, but it could not build a mile of street-car track for the convenience of its citizens. The State and the city could give things away without restraint, but when they attempted to own something that made money, or to do something for the welfare of the people, the hand of the court was raised against them.

Obviously the Constitution was not what I had believed it to be. It was an instrument that worked easily and well for one class and interest only. Government was something outside it.

The fact that bothered me most was that men from whom I had expected so much were opposed to progressive legislation. Good husbands and fathers, honest in their personal relations, many of them well educated, to a man they distrusted democracy—fought direct primaries, defeated home rule for cities, clung to the agencies that perpetuated the boss. They made a god of the party and shielded Republican office-holders from prosecution. Along with the Constitution my class had failed.

I learned all I could about members of the Senate. The leader on the Republican side was the county attorney for a steam-railroad. He was a powerful lawyer and a dangerous antagonist. He has since been appointed general counsel for one of the great transcontinental railroad systems. Generally speaking, the most capable members were county attorneys of steam-railroads, interurban railways, or banks. Another group were agents of insurance companies. They responded to instructions received from New York, Cleveland, or Cincinnati. The extent to which the Assembly was really governed from New York was astounding. These men seemed never to question the propriety of doing as they were ordered. They took pride in protecting their clients in the Assembly.

Then there were ignorant members, without opinions of their own, who did quite honestly and naturally as they were told. They wanted to be renominated. They took orders from the county organization or the local boss.

Back of the Assembly were bankers. They came near being the real rulers of the State. The county organization usually had a banker as its treasurer. He was often an official of the local street-railway, gas or electric-lighting company, and his bank had the deposits of one or all of these corporations. The county banker was a person of local distinction, active in the church, identified with good works. Members of the Assembly honestly relied on him for advice. To be sent for by him during the week-end was an honor.

Mark Hanna's law firm in Cleveland took a lion's share in lobbying. It was said that no bill was permitted to come out of committee until Mr. Hanna's lawyers had first examined and approved it.

There was little venality in the Assembly. Money was rarely used. It was not necessary. Some men were kept in line by being permitted to win substantial sums at poker. Others were compromised by prostitutes brought on from Cleveland and Cincinnati for that purpose. Indiscreet seekers after pleasure were made obedient by fear of exposure and blackmail.

Lobbyists were of every variety. Many of them had previously held State offices. The ex-clerk of the Senate was reputed to be the representative of the Standard Oil Company. The lobbyist of the steam-railroads was an elderly man, religious in demeanor, cynical in conversation, who knew everybody who had ever been in Columbus. He spent his time playing cards in hotels, and knew how members of the Assembly could be reached. Newspaper men were involved in the system, which was woven like a web in and out of the political and business life of the State. Mr. Warren G. Harding was often about the State House. At that time he was an inconspicuous editor in Marion, Ohio. We identified him in our minds with the things Senator Foraker was interested in. The party—by party he understood the Republican machine and particularly Senator Foraker's part of it—was his last word in authority. He would do almost anything in the name of party regularity —and do it with the rectitude of a religious zealot.

But the lobby was not the government. It was only needed on critical occasions. There was something behind the lobby that worked with clocklike precision and extended over the entire State. It included the local press and the press agencies, the Chambers of Commerce and the county rings. There was a replica of Mark Hanna in every county. He took orders and desired to be known as a man who carried them out without question. He had things to protect; he wanted to rise; he hoped with the turn of the wheel to find himself at Columbus, at Washington, or postmaster at home.

The thing that ruled the State was like the nervous system of the human body. It had filaments running into every township and every village. And the antennæ responded intelligently, not to the will of the people, but to the will of something quite outside my scheme of things.

Ohio, in short, was not ruled by the people. It was ruled by business. Not by all business, but by bankers, steam-railroads, public-utility corporations. Representative government did not represent the people; it represented a small group, whose private property it protected. Senator Hanna, Senator Foraker, and John R. McLean made a great part of their fortunes through the control of the political state. They legislated directly for themselves or they killed bills that would tax their property or regulate it. The Soviet of which they were the principal representatives needed relatively little direction. When crises arose, Senator Hanna marshalled his supporters, Senator Foraker marshalled his, and the Democratic bosses delivered a sufficient number of votes to insure the desired result. The bosses were quite non-partisan. When the things they owned or the power they enjoyed was menaced, party enmities were forgotten.

Continuing my inquiry into the Constitution, I went back to a study of the debates that preceded its adoption. I read the opinions of Alexander Hamilton and his associates and the proposals they made. They did not conceal their desire for an aristocratic form of government. They distrusted democracy and they did everything possible to make the government as undemocratic as possible. They made it complicated and difficult to understand; they introduced divided responsibility, checks and balances— confusion all along the line. That was their purpose. At the university I had thought of Hamilton as a great statesman—as the man who had saved the early government from bankruptcy, dissolution, and anarchy. I remembered now that he was a corporation lawyer. His ideas about property and the state were much the same as those of Mark Hanna. Alexander Hamilton feared democracy. He wanted to give the people an appearance of power, no more. To this end officials were made as irresponsible as possible. They were elected for different periods. An electoral college selected the President and Vice-President, while State legislatures elected members of the United States Senate. The system was so complex that people could not follow it. They could not register their will. Some one had to give all his time to politics just to make the machinery work. Hamilton urged these complications. He sought to create an even more aristocratic system. And what was created made the boss inevitable. He alone could follow the circuitous procedure involved in the election of many officials. The selection of assembly-men and State senators was supervised by the political machines. They sent the boss to the United States Senate. In Washington he could represent business interests and at the same time keep the State in hand. Even our cities were ruled from Washington. The boss and his business associates were the real government, outside the Constitution. They were scarcely mentioned in the text-books. In

the Bruntschli Library at Johns Hopkins, which contained thousands of treatises on politics, there was
only a suggestion of this state within the state, of
this system that had existed for the greater part of
a century. At the university we had studied the
writings of Aristotle and Plato, of Grotius, of Locke,
Hobbes, and Rousseau, of Alexander Hamilton and
Jefferson. We knew the theories of the state from
Greece to Washington, yet the actual political state
under which we lived and in the shadow of which
we had studied at Baltimore was referred to only
by muck-rakers, whom we held in contempt, and
in the yellow newspapers, which were not permitted
in the university library.

CHAPTER XVIII

RECASTING MY BELIEFS

My text-book government had to be discarded; my worship of the Constitution scrapped. The state that I had believed in with religious fervor was gone. Like the anthropomorphic God of my childhood, it had never existed. But crashing beliefs cleared the air. I saw that democracy had not failed; it had never been tried. We had created confusion and had called it democracy. Professors at the university and text-book writers had talked and written about something that did not exist. It could not exist. In politics we lived a continuous lie.

I set down for myself principles that would constitute democracy. I applied biological processes to it. From some source or other I had come to believe that Nature was very wise, and that her rules, by which billions upon billions of creatures were able to live, must be a reasonably good guide for the organized state. I took the private corporation as a guide. Business had succeeded in America and it worked with very simple machinery. It was not bothered by a constitution; it was not balked by checks and balances; it was not compelled to wait for years to achieve what it wanted. Its acts were not supervised by a distant supreme court. The freedom of a private corporation was close to license; what its officials wanted done was done. Mayors, governors, legislatures, city councils had no such power. In many ways the corporation that disposed of the city's garbage had more freedom of action than had the municipality that employed it. Here was a suggestion of machinery that worked well, even if it did not work in the interest of the public.

Business men had been given one instrument, the people another. The one was simple, direct, and powerful; the other confused, indirect, and helpless. We had freed the individual but imprisoned the community. We had given power to the corporation but not to the state. The text-books talked of political sovereignty, but what we really had was business sovereignty. And because the business corporation had power while the political corporation had not, the business corporation had become the state.

Nor had we followed what nature had to teach. We violated the instincts of man. Politics offered no returns to the man of talent, who wanted to see the fruit of his efforts. If business had been organized like the state, it would have been palsied. Business would have gone bankrupt under the confusion, the complexity, the endless delays which were demanded by the political state.

Taking the private corporation as a model, I evolved three basic principles; they were: Government should be easily understood and easily worked; it should respond immediately to the decision of the majority; the people should always rule.

Elaborated into a programme of constitutional change, these principles involved:

(1) The easy nomination of all candidates by petition. There should be no conventions. Direct primaries are the fountainhead of democracy.

(2) Candidates should print their platforms in a few lines on the election ballots. Voters would then know what a man stood for.

(3) The short ballot.

(4) The recall of all elective officials, including judges.

(5) The initiative and referendum on the Constitution, on laws, and on city ordinances.

(6) Complete home rule for cities. The city should be a state by itself, with power to do anything of a local nature that the people wanted done. A free city would be like the cities of ancient Greece, like the mediæval Italian republics, like the cities of Germany to-day. It would inspire patriotism. Able men would be attracted to the task of administering it.

(7) The State Assembly should consist of but one body of not more than fifty members. It should be in continuous session for a four-year term, the governor sitting with it and responsible to it for the exercise of wide powers.

(8) The courts should have merely civil and criminal jurisdiction. They should have no power to interfere with legislation. Congress and the State legislatures should be the sole judges of the constitutionality of their acts. The British Parliament and the legislative bodies of other countries are supreme. America alone has created a third assembly-chamber that has an absolute veto of the popular will.

Such a government would be democracy. It would be simple and easily understood. There would be no confusion, no delays. In such a state the people would be free. And they would be sovereign. Under the existing system they were neither sovereign nor free. We had stripped the state of sovereignty; the first thing to do was to restore it. Under such a system we could have a boss if we wanted one. Certainly we should have leaders. But we could hold the leader to responsibility. Things would be done in the open. We should not be living the lie of the existing system, which was not democracy but economic oligarchy.

Was this enough? Would people love, for example, the city because they could control it? I wanted cities to be loved. In Cleveland, when I was on the city council, I remembered that there had been men who not only served the city well but loved the public offices to which they had been selected. Members of the park boards had lobbied at Columbus to hold their positions. Members of the library and school boards performed their services honestly and efficiently without remuneration. The trustees of private clubs, of hospitals, of colleges, gave loyal and enthusiastic service to their organizations. But members of the city council and of the State Assembly did not. Public opinion in Cleveland could be aroused over the appointment of an unknown person to the park board. The people were jealous of their parks; they took pride in the public library and the schools, in the grouping of public buildings. But they took no pride in the city council or any of its works. They showed no concern over the election of a corrupt man to the city council or even to the mayoralty.

Why this anomaly?

It seemed that the only men who cared about politics were those who got something out of it. Some of them were at the top—they got privileges; others were at the bottom—they got jobs. There was no enthusiasm for the State or the city on the part of the great majority of voters.

I had studied municipal administration in England and Germany and had found there a new type of men in city politics and a burning interest in the city on the part of voters. Men of distinction, of irreproachable honesty served as mayors and councilmen. The cities owned and operated street-railways, gas, water, and electric-lighting services; they owned markets and other business agencies. The big municipal industries were owned by the city and operated on a high scale of efficiency. The city was the most important corporation in the community.

I talked to business men in England and asked them why they went into the council and gave a great part of their time to city business. They seemed as much at a loss as if I had asked them why they went to Parliament.

"Why," they said, "to be chairman of the tramways committee is one of the biggest jobs in the city." Or it might be the gas, electric-lighting, or water committee. "We were directors and stockholders when the enterprises were in private hands, and when the city took them over we followed them into the town hall. The voters wanted men of experience and honesty to run the enterprises in which their money was invested. We like big jobs and the distinction of doing them well. We want to have the best-managed city in the kingdom. There is rivalry between our cities about tramways and gas companies, just as there is about football. Cities are important; every one is interested in them, every one can take part in their affairs."

Here, possibly, was the clew that explained everything—concern and indifference, honesty and corruption, political dignity and debasement. In England and Germany voters were alert, because the city was a big thing, every one had to give attention to it. Because it was a big enterprise, men of ability wanted to run it, as they want to run banks, factories, business undertakings. They were able to do so because there were no more big profits to be gotten out of grants and franchises. Their purse was no longer at war with their patriotism. Tom Johnson was always saying that a street-railway franchise would corrupt the Twelve Apostles if they were councilmen. England had formerly invited corruption, as had we, by giving away colossal prizes in the form of franchises to men through the control of politics. Acting like an expert in hygiene, she went to the source of the disease: she took the profit herself. The same men who had previously profited by the gifts of the city were now anxious to serve it. They liked to do big things; they hungered for public places without other emolument than the distinction of important work well done.

Our business men were no whit different from Englishmen. The trouble was not with the American people, as Mr. Bryce had said, it was with American institutions. We had made the state so unimportant that the people were indifferent. They left it to bosses and to business because it did not serve them. Our failures were not traceable to too much democracy, but to too little. We had built our political system on distrust. The scientist who offers his life to discover the cause of yellow fever in the tropics differs less than we think from men who seem to want only to make their pile. They have not found his joy; they have not even perhaps the joy of white wings working in the street, who have some satisfaction in the consciousness that they are serving the public. Business men have bent the political state, cumbersome, unwieldy, unresponsive to its professed uses, to their private gain. But let the state be restored to sovereignty, let it become an important thing, and they would enter its service.

My philosophy was recast. Beginning with the sanctity of a document conceived in the past, it ended with a belief in democracy yet to be born.

CHAPTER XIX

PRE–WAR RADICALS

ONE day in 1903 Lincoln Steffens came into our offices. I had been reading his articles on "The Shame of the Cities" in *McClure's Magazine*, and was eager to meet him. I pictured him big, blond, and fierce, a militant reformer, hating corruption. The man who appeared had soft eyes and a quiet voice. Something unusual in the cut of his clothes, a pointed beard, and flowing tie suggested an artist. He seemed not to be hating any one or anything. I thought there must be some mistake—my visitor must be some one else. But he brought a letter from Ida M. Tarbell, whom I had known since my boyhood days in Meadville. And acquaintance furnished me the astonishing discovery that Lincoln Steffens was an artist rather than a reformer.

He was getting good copy, was seeing extraordinary men, bankers, bosses, grafters; he set down the things he saw and got more enjoyment than hatred out of the dishonor he uncovered. He paid little attention to the machinery of government, to the things other men thought important. He went back of charters, and dug into the real things that were responsible for the red-light district, for bosses like Croker of New York, Cox of Cincinnati, and Butler of St. Louis. He knew the "dirty" bosses personally; had gone to them and talked with them. They had liked him and he had liked them. They showed him their good as well as their bad side. He learned what these men thought about themselves; heard about the bosses who bossed them and the world of graft which we assumed that they had created. He found out that the "dirty" bosses took orders. They were scavengers, stokers, shovellers, who kept the machines going for the captains on the bridge. They organized the saloon; they took graft from prostitutes, bartered in contracts. But they did it not alone for themselves; there were others involved, men whom they only knew casually—bankers, clubmen, gentlemen, whose influence was so powerful that it protected them from exposure through the press.

Steffens disclosed what came to be known as the "invisible government." He coined phrases which stuck. He awakened us to shame—made it possible for us to understand what was the matter. He showed a more penetrating knowledge of politics than any writer in the country.

He came to Cleveland as a reporter. Tom Johnson, he thought, was different from other bosses only in that he was cleverer. He was playing the same game, cheating the people for some ulterior end, probably his private enrichment by getting possession of the street-railways. But Tom Johnson was elected by the people, and Steffens wanted to understand a city that brought its boss out into the open. He spent months in Ohio talking with all sorts of men. He went away convinced that there was something wrong, but that he could not find it. It would come out in time. Later he returned and continued the inquiry. My estimate of muck-raking rose greatly from seeing him at work. He was exact, painstaking, unflinchingly accurate. At last, almost reluctantly, he accepted Tom Johnson as a great leader. He described him as "the best mayor of the best-governed city in America."

Steffens changed after that. When he came to Cleveland he professed to be merely a reporter, who wrote political stories as brilliant as fiction and de-

lighted in his work. Under the influence of Tom
Johnson he came to believe in the single tax. Then
he studied Socialism and became a Socialist without
interest in Karl Marx, as he had been a single-taxer
without adherence to Henry George. He hated sects
and organization; organization, he said, would destroy the beauty of any movement. He was always
the psychologist, as he had been in his student days
at a German university. He outgrew Socialism.
Revolutions attracted him. He went to Mexico,
where he liked the thoroughness of the job. Then to
Russia, Germany, and Italy. Wherever a revolution
was threatening, there Steffens might be found, trying to understand it. He wrote little, sometimes
mere skits, but he worked on them as a sculptor
might work on a piece of marble. In his library I
have seen the floor littered with sheets of paper containing perhaps a single line, perhaps half a dozen
lines. Each was an attempt at perfection, each
breathed a desire for perfection half resented by his
friends, for it seemed to palsy his work for reform. He
remained the artist, observer, interpreter, trying to
understand the meaning and purpose of the organized state.

In the near-by city of Toledo, Sam Jones, a sucker-
rod manufacturer, had been picked out by business
men and Walter Brown, the Republican boss, for
mayor. He had been selected to aid the street-railways and electric-lighting corporations to secure a
franchise. But Sam Jones balked. He fell out with
the party organization, and the machine refused to
renominate him. Instead of retiring, he announced
that he would run for mayor anyway. He would run
without a party, without a committee, without help
from any organization. He would refuse to accept
campaign contributions. He would run as Sam
Jones. An independent candidacy seemed hopeless

at that time; people wanted things straight, they wanted a party prop to lean on, a business man who would give them things, not a person of uncertain opinions. But Jones was elected. His secretary, young Brand Whitlock, gave him Walt Whitman's poems to read and one of Tolstoy's novels. Then Sam Jones, sucker-rod manufacturer, ceased to be and "Golden Rule" Jones, a Tolstoyan anarchist, who took Christ as a quite literal model for living, began to function. He made public speeches in which he said little about himself, nothing about parties; he read from Walt Whitman and quoted Christ in a simple, unaffected way.

His office was filled with vagrants. People in trouble came to him freely. He went to the work-houses and talked with the prisoners, released them wholesale if they had been committed for drunkenness or vagrancy and were unable to pay their fines. As mayor he sat as magistrate in the police court. On Monday morning he would listen to the stories of drunkards, disorderly persons, and women picked up on the streets, and dismiss them with a sermon directed not at the prisoners, nor at churches or business men, but at society. His Monday-morning sermons shocked the city. He was a friend of gamblers and prostitutes. Gamblers were said to flourish in Toledo. The system that made them should be changed, according to Sam Jones; it was idle to punish its victims. It was the same with prostitutes: we had them because men wanted them. If they were to be punished, men should be punished as well. Especially since it was said that houses of prostitution protected society; they protected girls on the streets from insult, wives from assault. If this was true, prostitutes should not be punished; they should be treated as vicarious sacrifices to a bad social system.

Sam Jones made war on capital punishment and the inhumanity of prisons. He would have nothing to do with organized charity, with any of the conventions with which men fooled themselves. Organization he thought was unnecessary; conformity affronted him. He wanted men and women to be free in spirit. That was his message. The state should keep its hands off people. In his factory he paid good wages and shortened hours of labor. He built a working men's temple near the factory, where on Sunday afternoons the workers gathered to listen to speakers and music. His employees were devoted to him.

Good people shunned him. His quotations from Christ were a scandal to the churches. Preachers denounced him. The Chamber of Commerce opposed him. Every one was against him except the workers and the underworld. He was hated less for what he did than for what he said. His subversive thinking was worse than action. And in fact he did relatively little. That was not his job. People must do things, he believed, for themselves. When the people were right in their minds, politics would be right. And people would be right when they believed in the Golden Rule and followed it. Then bosses, party organizations, graft would disappear.

Sam Jones announced himself as a non-partisan candidate for governor. A party of us met him in the lobby of a hotel one evening when he came to Cleveland to speak. He was introduced to a group of women, some of whom were annoyed to observe that he did not remove his hat. A man from Toledo explained later that Mayor Jones had been laughed at for taking off his hat to a scrubwoman in the City Hall.

"If I should not take off my hat," he had said, "to a scrubwoman who does the dirty work that I don't want to do, then I will not take it off to any one."

Jones spoke that evening in the immigrant Thirteenth Ward, in a hall packed to the doors. His speech was as unconventional as the man himself. "I don't want to rule anybody," he said. "Nobody has a right to rule anybody else. Each individual must rule himself. He must decide for himself. I would be as bad as the party if I attempted to rule you or to make you 'Jonesites' as you are now 'Hannaites.'" His speech was free from cant, from assumption of superior virtue. People were pretty much all good, he said. It was conditions that made some of them bad. Men were not poor because they drank; they drank because they were poor. People were just people and he was one of them.

The vote from the Thirteenth Ward always came in as a Republican block of five hundred odd votes. It could be relied on by the machine. The night of the election the count was delayed. It did not come until morning. Sam Jones had swept the ward. The Republican candidate received only a scattering vote. For ten years the Municipal Association, good government clubs, and settlements had been trying to defeat Harry Bernstein and to clean up this ward. But we made no headway. Sam Jones had done by a single speech what we were unable to do. The immigrants and the poor had heard a gospel. It offered them nothing in particular, but it was free from cant. From that time on the Thirteenth Ward was uncertain. It could not be purchased. And it would not be bossed. It became increasingly radical as time went on.

Brand Whitlock, who started Golden Rule Jones on his way, was primarily an artist, like Steffens. His political life was an accident. I had the impression when we talked together—and I saw him often in Cleveland—that the office of mayor, to which he had been elected on the death of Sam Jones, distressed him. Brutality hurt him. The brutality of society to the criminal hurt him most. Society must protect itself, but the state, he believed, should help people, not hurt them. Personal liberty was a precious thing. He did away with third-degree methods, with solitary confinement and brutal jailers. Clubs and revolvers, that Sam Jones had taken away from policemen, Brand Whitlock kept away from them. He appeared at session after session of the State Assembly with bills for the repeal of capital punishment. His novel, *The Turn of the Balance*, was Tolstoyan in its indictment of inhumanity in prisons. The workhouses in Toledo were made as kindly as possible.

Brand Whitlock's real life was lived at home in his study, with his wife and friends, with books and ideas. He loved beautiful and delicate things. Since the little that was beautiful in Toledo was at war with him, he constructed a world of his own away from the public. There he was freely himself, intellectual radical and lover of literature that offered sure rewards to disinterested effort.

We saw a good deal of each other during these years. We felt about things in much the same way. I disliked the organization necessary to keep the political machine in good order; disliked compromise with spoilsmen, with ward leaders and the saloon. I could not make myself indifferent to being shunned by old friends. Reason about it as I would, explain to myself that when property was at stake men could not help thinking and acting as they did, I missed none the less the companionship of people I liked to associate with and suffered in the clubs when men rallied or shunned me. I felt close to Brand Whitlock. I too was writing—books idealizing a city that would be free from class war. I too wanted a free state, in which the individual would be important.

I saw Brand Whitlock again in Brussels after the war. Will Irwin and I were doing the devastated area with a French mission and we called at the embassy. It was filled with grateful memorials from towns and cities, from the King of Belgium and from foreign governments. There Whitlock seemed to me to be in his proper environment. We walked through the parks and talked about old days of struggle in Cleveland and Toledo. I saw that his thoughts still turned to literature. "I have gone through every political philosophy," he said. "I can see nothing in Socialism. The philosophy of Henry George of a free state in which the resources of the earth will be opened up to use is the only political philosophy that has ever commanded my adherence. But the world is not interested in such a simple reform. It wants too much government, too much regulation, too much policing. And it may never change."

Enfant terrible among radicals, Peter Witt was and still is an outstanding figure in Cleveland. He began life as a moulder, became a labor organizer, was blacklisted for organizing a strike, and turned to the street corner. He could be found almost any day on the corner of the public square dedicated to free speech. He respected no man because of his position. His language was vitriolic, his facts accurate, and his attacks cut to the quick. Some of his descriptions of prominent men are still quoted in Cleveland. He was the foe of all grafters and wrong-doers, big and little. A Democrat, he attacked grafters in the Democratic as well as in the Republican Party. He published in pamphlet form a record of tax-dodging and other misdemeanors that bore the title *Cleveland Before St. Peter*. In spite of his outlawry his integrity always commanded respect, and from a responsible municipal office, to which he has recently been elected, he continues his attacks on men and institutions.

Newton D. Baker, who had come on from his home in West Virginia to practise law in Cleveland, became Tom Johnson's solicitor in the city law department. The brilliant promise of Baker's student days at Johns Hopkins was more than fulfilled in these early years of his maturity. He was a splendid speaker, fluent, resourceful, and adaptable. Richly endowed mentally, he seemed never to know what it was to be tired. He did his work easily, mastered intricate legal subjects quickly, and had time for wide and carefully selected reading. He and I had lived together at Johns Hopkins and we set up housekeeping again in Cleveland. We were both absent-minded, absorbed in our work, indifferent to domestic comforts, but his mind was more orderly than mine, and I think that I was a trial to him now and then. I would forget to leave word that I was not coming home to the dinners that a negress cook, left to her own devices, prepared expeditiously for us out of canned foods; often I would neglect to say that I was leaving town for a day or two. Once intrusted with moving our goods from one apartment to another, I forgot to give the keys of the new apartment to the expressman, and when we arrived at night eager to fit up our new home, we found our household belongings, including books, out on the front lawn, soaked with rain.

Clarence Darrow was a frequent visitor in Cleveland. Personally, I never knew whether I admired or disliked him most. His realism hurt my illusions when it encountered them, and I hated having my illusions hurt. But he was an extraordinary personality—cynic and pessimist about politics and society.

Society could not be saved, he said, and it wasn't worth saving anyhow. He was a lover of books and supremely skilful in defending notorious criminal cases. He had an uncanny understanding of juries and the things that moved men to sympathy for his clients. To him the world was equally unmoral above as well as below. So why be squeamish about it in criminal cases?

Darrow was the star speaker at the opening of one of our most critical elections. The street-railway fight and the mayoralty were at stake. There was an immense crowd, mostly of working men. The Catholic bishop delivered the invocation. Then Darrow rose in a bored way, lounged to the centre of the stage, and looked over the crowd with something like a sneer.

"You are working men," he drawled, "most of you. You work twelve hours a day in the steel-mills. You work in the sewers. Work for the rest of us. You give us what we eat. You build our houses and keep us warm. You gave Tom Johnson and Mark Hanna their millions. Do you realize that you could make us earn our own living by our own sweat if you had the sense to do so? But you haven't. If you were not slaves, you would throw us off your backs. But what's the use of talking to you about your wrongs? There's only one thing for you to do, and that is to stop work. Then the mills would close; factories would close; everything would close. For once in our lives we should have to work for ourselves. But what's the use of telling you this? You haven't the sense to do the only thing that would do you any good."

Then he slouched back to his seat. We were all disturbed. The Catholic bishop would certainly send out word to the clergy next Sunday to defeat Tom Johnson. Mr. Johnson himself was uneasy. Clarence Darrow alone seemed unconcerned. What was the use of anything? Why bother about municipal ownership, about the ballot, about electing Tom Johnson or anybody else mayor in a rotten world?

During these years I was studying cities, writing about them for *Scribner's Magazine* and for Walter H. Page, then editor of *The World's Work*. I visited Joseph W. Folk, of St. Louis, who was in the midst of his graft prosecutions.

"Do you get any support," I asked Mr. Folk, "from the press and the well-to-do classes in your fight?"

"I did," he said, after a moment's thought. "For a time I had the whole-hearted support of the press, the Chamber of Commerce, and the business men of the city. As long as I was after Boss Butler and the grafters in the city council, I was a hero. But when I started to prosecute bankers who were involved in a city franchise, the press turned against me. The prosecutions were bad for business, people began to say; they gave St. Louis a bad name; they should be dropped. I have had little encouragement since then and the only financial help that came to me was from a man by the name of Charles R. Crane, of Chicago. He sent me a check for five hundred dollars. I don't even know who he is."

I had been hearing of Mr. Crane in other cities. He was a millionaire, had been president of the Municipal Voters' League of Chicago, and had backed it in its long fight against grafters. His philanthropies, if they could be called philanthropies, were very unusual. They went to individual men here and there, often to men whom he did not know, who were making some kind of lone fight that interested him. He supported Francis J. Heney in San Francisco. He liked a good fight and took this way of encouraging it. He was later appointed minister to

China by President Wilson, whose enthusiastic supporter he was.

I later came to know Mr. Crane personally; was always meeting him in strange places and always hearing of his unusual kindnesses. One evening at a dinner, while I was Commissioner of Immigration, I told a story of a mother and three little girls who had been ordered deported. The following day I received a substantial check from his secretary to be used for their needs. He gave almost secretly, seemed to expect no gratitude, and not to be concerned over the uses to which his money was put. As a young man he had become interested in the Far East, in Russia and Turkey. In these countries he spends much of his time to-day. Prerevolutionary liberal Russia was his enthusiasm; he supports many Russian causes and aids many old Russian friends. He is the head of a woman's college in Constantinople, to which he contributes generously. His time and fortune are devoted to men, movements, and institutions, from the Woods Hole biological laboratory to the Slavic University in the city of Prague. Mr. Crane's enthusiasms are as original as his generosity is modest. His leisure and wealth have been put to discriminating and admirable uses.

I went to San Francisco and found conditions that astounded me. In a riot of corruption following the earthquake the city council had bartered with contractors and public-utility corporations. Fremont Older, editor of the San Francisco *Bulletin*, had unearthed some of the scandals; Francis J. Heney was employed as special counsel to conduct prosecutions. Abe Ruef, the city boss, had gone to the penitentiary; Patrick Calhoun, my old acquaintance from Cleveland, had been indicted as president of the local street-railway corporation and was being tried. San Francisco was like an armed camp. The ballot was in the discard, men were resorting to force. A house had been dynamited to destroy evidence and a number of people killed. Heney had been shot through the face in open court.

Calling on Fremont Older in his office, I sat down before a window opening on Market Street. Older, who was a big, powerful man, seized me by the shoulder and threw me on the floor.

"Don't sit there," he said. "Something might happen to you by mistake. Last night, when I was leaving the office, a jailbird friend told me that a man with a gun had been planted in the skyscraper that is going up across the street. Under cover of the racket from the steel riveters he is to pick me off and nobody be the wiser."

That was my introduction to conditions in San Francisco. Mr. Older told me that not long before he had been kidnapped in plain day on the street and rushed from the city in an automobile, with a gun at his back. He had been locked in a Pullman compartment. His captors, one of them a prominent attorney, had gotten drunk and talked about the plans to dispose of him. He was to be taken from the train at midnight, carried to the mountains, and shot. A man who overheard the conversation telegraphed to a judge for a writ of habeas corpus, and when the train stopped he was released. His captors escaped without identification.

I met Rudolph Spreckels, president of the First National Bank, who had been active in the prosecutions. When he stopped to talk on the street, he backed against the wall of a building.

"It's not safe to stand in the open," he explained. "It's better to see what's going on around you."

And coming back with Francis Heney from the "High Jinks" of the Bohemian Club in the big woods of California, I saw him stiffen as we stood at the

top of the companionway on the ferry-boat crossing
from Sausalito to San Francisco. He swung slowly
around on his heel watching two men who passed us
to descend to the main deck.

"That may have been a close shave, Fred," he
said, "for you too. You see that young cub? He's
just back from Harvard. His father is under indictment for bribery, and he announced in the club the
other day that he would shoot me on sight. I'm not
slow on the trigger myself and I had my hand in my
side pocket."

That was San Francisco during the graft prosecutions after the earthquake. Arson, murder, dynamit-
ing, abduction—all were traceable to the attempt of
a few men to secure and hold a street-railway franchise which they had gotten by bribery. Bankers,
business men, editors were involved. Social lines
were drawn as in Washington or Baltimore during
the Civil War. And well-to-do people were almost a
unit in protesting against the criminal prosecution
which followed.

Heartening all of these liberals and reporting their
doings was a weekly publication in Chicago, *The
Public*, edited by Louis F. Post. Fearlessly honest in
opinion, keenly understanding in its reporting, it
gave form and direction to the liberal movement and
charted the lines of its progress. It was the best mir-
ror of pre-war liberalism that we had; a reading of
its pages discloses the fineness, the intellectuality,
the hopefulness of that movement which was the
last protest of the democracy of the pioneer period
still under the influence of the free land of the West.

What has become of this movement that promised
so much twenty years ago? What has become of the
pre-war radicals? They had a large following; their
voices inspired America during the years that preceded the war. They gave themselves without stint,

they fought for the most part alone, and they felt that a change was impending that would end the abuses that had come with the rise of great wealth, based for the most part on the unparalleled resources of America.

Lincoln Steffens spends most of his time in Europe. To my question when I last saw him as to what he was doing, he answered smilingly: "I am learning to be an intelligent father." Brand Whitlock has gone back to literature, Newton Baker to the law. Fremont Older edits the San Francisco *Call*. Joseph W. Folk is dead. Most of the radicals of pre-war days have laid down their arms. Was the fight too hard? Did youth burn itself out? Has the movement become a class struggle, finding its leaders among the farmers and workers? May it be—as some of them feel—that there is little for liberals to do? Though the old order decays, the new order cannot be rushed. It must come in its own way. There must be the frosts of winter before there can be an awakening of spring.

Robert M. LaFollette persisted almost alone in the fight. For a quarter of a century he did at least two men's work, fighting special interests, assailing the trusts and the protective tariff in the Senate, and attempting to hold the railroads in leash. Between sessions he toured the country reading the roll-call on his associates until they were one by one defeated, and a statement made in his maiden speech in the Senate came true. He predicted then, when the Senate emptied itself to show disapproval of him, that "he would live to see the day when the seats now vacated temporarily would be permanently vacated of their present possessors."

He fought in Wisconsin to preserve the gains that were made there; was recognized in the Senate as a scrupulous and tireless worker, never content with a statement until it had been verified, loading his speeches with statistics and supporting material which make them authoritative; his voice has carried the progressive cause from one end of the country to the other. During the war he was ridiculed, misrepresented, cruelly handled by the press. A phrase in one of his speeches, "We have grounds of complaint against Germany," was distorted by the press agencies to read: "We have no grounds of complaint against Germany." He was assailed by the President as a "wilful" man, was all but abandoned by his friends, and for years lived under the shadow of proceedings to oust him from the Senate. Threatened by disease and harassed financially, he bore his isolation without complaint; accepted no friendship which impaired his freedom, never compromised with a conviction, and displayed unflinching courage of the kind that enables men to go to the stake.

I travelled with him through the West on his last campaign, saw the devotion of throngs of farmers and workers that gathered to hear him and came to believe that he was probably the best-loved man in America.

CHAPTER XX

CONFLICT AND COMPROMISE

MY early years at the law had been made tolerable to me only through intimate association with Harry and James R. Garfield. They had the kind of moral distinction that the Romans described as manliness — *virtus*. It was tolerant, kindly, scrupulous. To them I was a liberal, even a radical. I became identified with things they did not believe in. I left the Republican Party, turned Democrat and free-trader, and was closely associated with Tom Johnson. The causes that I espoused were bad for our business. I undoubtedly offended substantial clients, yet my partners never protested against my choices; they never sought to dissuade me from any decision, and never in an association of a dozen years alluded to financial considerations as a reason for keeping silent or changing my course. I realized at the time how generous this was. And I have realized it more fully since. For the herd instinct is strong in all of us. It is jealous of departure from creeds and punishes deserters from the ranks more severely than it does those who have never been admitted.

When James R. Garfield was elected to the State Senate I left the comparative idleness of the outer office and was taken into the firm, which, as Garfield, Garfield & Howe, lasted for a dozen years. Then James R. Garfield went into President Roosevelt's Cabinet, and Harry Garfield was called to Princeton as professor of politics, to become later president of Williams College.

The law was my mistress for fifteen years. Not a very jealous or exacting one, it is true, for I gave a good deal of time to politics, to writing, and to travel. Nor much cherished. I never overcame my dislike for the profession and got little enjoyment out of such success as I achieved. Trial work was distasteful to me. In jury cases I was less skilful than rough practitioners for whom I had little respect, and the lack of finality and long delays annoyed me. Cases wore on for years; nothing was ever finished. Personal-injury cases, in which our firm represented corporations sued for death or injury claims arising out of the hazards of employment, I found particularly disagreeable. There were no workmen's compensation laws at that time and corporations were able to avoid responsibility for neglect by pleading the defenses of contributory negligence, the assumption of risk, or the negligence of a fellow employee. These defenses were dug up by judges from mediæval times, when there was no great aggregation of capital, when masters worked close beside their men, when neither steam nor electricity had come into existence. It seemed incredible that a learned profession should countenance the absurdity of applying rules of bygone days to modern industrial conditions.

I remember one case of the death of a worker in the steel-mill. He had been ordered to repair something at the top of a blast-furnace. Protesting that the place was dangerous, the scaffolding insecure, and the heat unbearable, he had been ordered again to do as he was told, and had fallen, in accordance with his own just and terrible prevision, into the mass of blazing iron. The defense was that the man had known the danger and had voluntarily gone into it. He had assumed the risk when he accepted employment. Furthermore, some other employee, and not the corporation, was alleged to be responsible for the defective scaffolding. The workman himself, or one of his fellows, was guilty of the negligence that caused his death.

I still remember the faces of the widow and children, the plaintiffs in the case, who were left penniless. The policy of corporations was to wear out plaintiffs by keeping the cases in the courts. This was cheaper than settlement, and as cases could not be gotten through the Supreme Court inside of three or four years, it meant an all but complete denial of justice. The attitude of corporation lawyers was that claimants for personal injuries were "strikers," and that the lawyers who took their claims on a contingent fee were "ambulance-chasers."

I got a certain compensation from occasional criminal cases. I liked the personal problems involved, liked to go back into the life and experiences of men and women and find the thing that had started them wrong. Then having found the cause—it might be parental neglect, a chance escapade, some trouble with the police that marked them as suspect—I would make this the crux of my argument before the jury. I had considerable success in such criminal work as came to me and got satisfaction and pleasure out of it.

But there was a deep and fundamental protest within me against the law as an institution. I liked change, fluidity, movement. Anything that balked freedom irked me. The law was opposed to change, it thwarted the free movement of life. It was not responsive to changing conditions. The law was in fact a dead man's philosophy. It went back for its leading cases to the distant past. It found its guiding principles in the opinions of men long since dead rather than in the needs and conditions of to-day. The common law was developed into a system of jurisprudence at the hands of mediæval lawyers who were paid retainers of the old aristocracy. It was custom developed into law for the convenience of the ruling class. The American colonists brought the common law to America, and here, as in England, it has resisted change. Only under protest does it adjust itself to present-day conditions. The law is not only static, it takes pride in the fact that it is static. It glories in the past, in the opinions of Coke, Littleton, and Marshall. The common law is almost the only body of human thought that is guided by the opinions and ideas of the past. Science, engineering, medicine are perennially new. They reach out to the future and invite the imagination of men.

It is for this reason, among others, that lawyers are peculiarly unfitted for public office. They resist change. They are instinctively hostile to anything new. They are inexperienced in constructive things. Their professional life and training is associated with the past. They want the past preserved.

I found the procedure of litigation stupid and costly. It required months to bring a case to trial, years to reach a final decision. The rules of evidence were technical. There were endless delays and adjournments. There was no finality. One of the classical bits of humor of the legal profession was that "law is the last guess of the Supreme Court." More than half of the cases overruled by the higher courts were overruled because of some immaterial error that did not affect the equities of the case. Yet I could not fail to see that it would be a comparatively simple thing to strip the law of its technical stupidities, if lawyers really desired it. The delays and absurdities of practice could be swept away by a few statutory changes, which would enable cases to be brought to issue and disposed of in a few months' time. The law, it was evident, remained confused and costly because it was to the interest of lawyers to keep it so. They did not want simple, inexpensive procedure.

I was critical of my profession, alive to its falsities above as well as below. Mr. Johnson would have nominated me for the bench, had I wished it, but I had no desire to be a judge. I wanted to take part in the affairs of the community. To be denied the right to express my own opinions was to be a man without a country. I resented the elevation of the courts above the people, their freedom from criticism, and the sanctity with which judges enveloped themselves. I felt that a judge should be criticised as freely as any other public official. He was merely an agent and as such no more sacrosanct than the mayor. The courts were agencies for administering one kind of justice, the city and the State agencies for administering another kind. I came to see that judges had been enveloped with sanctity for a purpose. Sanctity had come with their usefulness to corporate interests; with their interference with the legislature and Congress, with use of the injunction in labor disputes and their concern for property. It was to the advantage of the interests so protected to bestow upon judges immunity from criticism. It added weight to their opinions.

Lawyers had none of that reverence for the courts which they insisted on others having. They had no reverence for the administration of justice. I had seen how judges were nominated for the State courts by Mr. Hanna on the one hand and Mr. Johnson on the other. They were selected not because of their legal abilities, but because of their known opinions, prejudices, bias. I saw a number of vacancies in the federal judiciary filled while I was practising law. Lawyers who represented the large corporations, the Standard Oil Company, the Pennsylvania and Lake Shore Railroads, and the mining interests knew of the prospective vacancies before any one else; they held conferences about them to which members of our firm were invited. They canvassed the names of men who might be induced to accept the position, and who should be presented to Senator Hanna or President McKinley. Lawyers who were independent-minded were dismissed from consideration, no matter what their legal qualifications were. When satisfactory nominees had been decided on, a committee went to Washington to confer with the President or with the senators from the State. If some unsatisfactory person was said to be under consideration, the leading members of the bar rushed to Washington to protest. I do not remember a vacancy on the federal bench to have been filled without consultation with the leading corporation lawyers of the city, and almost always the nominee was of their choosing. The same concern was shown in making up the slates for the State bench. To business interests the judge was a most important public official. Rarely did a liberal mind find a place on the ticket.

This concern over the judiciary was not, as these men said, a desire to keep it out of politics, to elevate its character. For very inferior men were often nominated. The real reason was that the courts were in politics. They had the final say as to legislation. They decided on the constitutionality of city ordinances, State laws, and federal legislation. They had great power in labor disputes. And this power made them invaluable allies to business interests, especially to the railroads and public-utility corporations, whose contracts with the city or whose rights in the street were subject to regulation. During the street-railway war in Cleveland over fifty injunction suits were allowed against the city. This meant costly struggle, years of delay; it meant that the street-railways could continue to collect fares that had been reduced by the city until the cases were finally disposed of. It meant millions of profit to the corporation. The attempt of the city of Cleveland to oust the railroads from possession of the lake front was held by a federal judge for twelve years without decision.

This assumption of legislative power on the part of the courts pushed me to a study of the debates on the federal Constitution. I could find in them no provision and apparently no intent on the part of its framers to make the courts the final arbiters in the legislative field. The reverse seemed to be true. On reading the debates of the convention, I found that several proposals had been made to lodge such power with the courts, and on each occasion the proposal had been voted down. Interference of the judiciary with legislation was a part of the real government that was outside of and indifferent to the Constitution.

My disapproval of judges extended to their adoption, about that time, of the wearing of gowns. Gowns were traditional, copied from England. Black was the symbol of secrecy, of mystery and fear. And as courts arrogated power to themselves they needed adventitious aids to security. I disapproved of judicial dignity that did not come from justice. If decisions of the courts were wise the people would respect them; if they were unwise or unjust the people should protest. Courts needed artificial aids to dignity no more than did mayors, governors, or members of Congress.

And I realized that a very poor lawyer might be a very good judge. To be a good judge required relatively little ability, especially in the supreme courts, which reviewed cases on appeal and error. Ample time was given for the study of cases; most of a judge's work was done for him by the contending lawyers. Reasons for supporting a decision were to be found in the brief of the successful lawyer. More ability was required of a first-class trial judge, who had to be well informed in the law, had to know the rules of evidence and to be able to decide questions quickly and wisely. Otherwise he would be reversed by the superior courts on error. The alleged wisdom of appellate courts was a fiction which the courts themselves created. Right or wrong, there was no one to question the wisdom of appellate court judges; their decision was final.

Nor did the law impress me as a learned profession. It was a business, a trade. I had little reverence for the leaders of the bar and found no inspiration in the philosophy on which the law was built and the absurdities to which it clung. The "sublimity of human reason" lawyers called it at banquets. Voltaire had certainly named it better the "conservator of ancient abuses."

The lawyer, like the business man, had a code of ethics of his own. It was flexible; it lowered rather than elevated the ethics of the community. By it a lawyer was enabled to defend a known criminal, to promote monopolies in defiance of law, to accept any retainer if it was not too obviously bad. The code ran as follows:

An attorney is an official of the court, a part of the machinery for the administration of justice. There are four participants in the administration of justice—the judge, the jury, and the counsel for the contending parties. It is the duty of the judge to know and expound the law; of the jury to ascertain the facts. It is the duty of opposing counsel to represent their clients to the best of their ability, no matter what the equities of their case may be. The lawyer owes but one duty, and that is to his client. It is not his business to see that exact justice is done, to be concerned over guilt or innocence. That is the business of the judge and the jury. And the lawyer is under moral obligation to render legal services to any one who presents himself. He can be assigned to that duty by the court when a criminal is without counsel.

But lawyers only applied this code as it fitted in with their interests to do so. They would defend a big corporation or a rich criminal, but did not defend the poor. They would accept a retainer from a corporation for an injunction case against the city of Cleveland, but could not be induced to accept its brief when the city was contesting the street-railways. They expressed indignation against "ambulance-chasers" who took the cases of widows and children left desolate by death or injury, and utilized every technicality of the law and every means of delay to defeat such contestants in the courts. They saw no impropriety in getting their cases before friendly judges or in filling the federal and State courts with men who were sympathetic to their point of view. For years a mysterious stranger went around among the prominent lawyers of Cleveland and collected substantial sums of money annually for which he gave no account. He did not even explain what the money was for. But every one knew that this money went to some one in the court-house who made up the jury lists and who saw to it that men friendly to the corporations were placed on the panel when contributing corporations were the litigants.

I sensed these things at the time, but I kept silence. I was part of the system. It was not safe to talk too much about the things one knew. To challenge the purity of the bench meant challenging the foundations of society, offending a code of ethics that I was expected to believe in. But I was personally involved and I had to work out a compromise with my conscience. The compromise was never logical. It was rarely satisfactory. And I presume it cost me heavily. For I found each succeeding compromise easier to make than the one preceding.

The legal work from which I got the greatest satisfaction dealt with the reorganization and financing of railroads and public-utility corporations, work which I knew was not in the public interest. Among our clients were bankers and trust companies in New York and Boston, on whose petition a number of railroads had been put in the hands of receivers because of default in interest payments on their bonds. The railroads were then operated under the jurisdiction of the United States Court, and were put in good condition out of earnings. When they had been rehabilitated they were sold under order of the court and purchased by the same interests that had thrown them into the receivers' hands. In this process the previous owners were squeezed out; they lost their investments. The new owners, operating through powerful trust companies, put no money into the property, yet they received new issues of securities running into the millions. These securities, worth little at the time, would acquire a market value as railroad rates were advanced and earnings increased.

Cases like these led me to study the history of railroad-building and reorganization. I found that almost all of the railroads west of New England had gone through this process, some of them over and over again. Often a railroad would be intentionally wrecked by the men who operated it, in order to throw it into the hands of receivers. Small railroads would be destroyed by various devices and then secured in the same way. In these proceedings judges were selected who could be relied on to carry the programme through as planned. Sometimes the process of wreckage would begin again as soon as the new management stepped in. Bankers made big profits out of the reorganization. They were not interested in the operation of the railroads; they were only interested in the flotation of securities, the taking of bankers' commissions, and in the exploitation of the system.

These proceedings were doubly reprehensible. Many people were needlessly robbed of their investments through foreclosure proceedings that might easily have been avoided had the courts shown any concern for the original owners or made an attempt to operate the properties so that they could be returned to them after they had been put on their feet. In addition, the public had to pay dividends on watered securities, which represented no actual investment, but which were used as a basis for demanding increased rates. Legal ethics justified the participation of lawyers in such proceedings; it was the duty of the lawyer to give counsel to whoever requested it, justice being the courts' responsibility. As a matter of fact, lawyers never thought of defending such participation. They were happy to be let in on the proceedings. For their fees were fixed by the court and were always generous.

It happened that I was appointed receiver of a private water company in a good-sized city not far from Cleveland. The company was in bad repute with the city council; it refused to have any further dealings with the manager, whose policy seemed to be "the public be damned."

I believed in municipal ownership of all public utilities, as a matter of political morality. Yet here I found myself bound by professional ethics to carry out the orders of the court and to act in the interest of the bondholders of a public-service corporation. One thing was clear to me. I would run the corporation scrupulously. People were entitled to pure water and they should have it. I determined to run the water plant as if it were a dry-goods store, and every consumer could go into a store next door if he were not suited with the service received. Pure water could only be obtained by heavy expenditures. I had a tunnel built out into the lake, and installed mechanical filtration plants. I studied the subject of rates and charges and proceeded to reduce the rates and improve the service. As a result earnings began to increase. Soon the operating deficit disappeared. In a few years the corporation was paying substantial dividends, and the plant almost ran itself. Because it was a monopoly relatively little intelligence was required to operate it. The people had to take what it offered or go without. Engineering problems were solved by employing good engineers. Labor problems were not harassing, for wages were not a material element in the cost. A dry-goods store could not have been run as easily.

When the question of a franchise came up my moral adjustment was difficult. Opposition to the company had practically disappeared. I knew the local boss and was on friendly terms with members of the council. The boss was an Irishman, a wholesale liquor dealer, whose sympathy had gone out to me because of difficulties I sometimes had with radical members of the council. Our contract with the city had expired and it was necessary to negotiate for a new franchise that would give us security and a monopoly of the water-supply for twenty or twenty-five years. Franchises were usually obtained by bribery and improper influence. I had made no attempts to placate the press, had not contributed to campaign funds, nor had I used any personal political influence. Ordinarily this would have been fatal. But the public and the council had come to trust me and that made my problem the harder. I believed in municipal ownership; my clients wanted a long-term franchise that would prevent municipal ownership. Obviously I could not serve them and the community at the same time. For they needed different things. I had to make a compromise. It was unsatisfactory, as usual, but it offered a way out.

I arranged for the use of a public hall and made an address on public ownership. I showed that publicly owned water plants were better built, that they gave better service and provided water at lower rates than did the private plants. I made as good a speech as I could for the public ownership of water companies.

That seemed to put me straight with the city. And my clients could not complain, for they knew that I believed in municipal ownership. Then I went before the council.

"Gentlemen," I said, "I have told you that the city ought to buy the water plant. It is on a paying basis and is in good condition. It will become more valuable as time goes on. But I cannot represent your interests and the interests of my clients at the same time. I must negotiate for them. We have no rights in the streets. We need a contract in order to obtain credit with which to develop the property. We want a new franchise."

After months of negotiations the city awarded us a franchise. It was liberal in its terms, and gave us all or more than we were entitled to. True to the nature of franchises, within a few years it became very valuable.

After the matter was disposed of, members of the council asked me whether I would accept a franchise for supplying the city with gas. A group of men had applied for one, but the council, they said, would prefer to give it to me.

"No," I replied, "I am not sure but that one franchise has already corrupted me. A second one surely would."

During twenty years of operating this water plant I repeatedly urged municipal ownership, but found that my advocacy had the effect of defeating agitation for it. Suspicion was immediately aroused when I suggested that the city acquire the property. People argued:

"If the company wants to sell the plant, then we don't want to buy it, for the company would not give up a good thing willingly."

There was apparently no angle from which the subject could be approached. To oppose public ownership might speed up purchase by the city, but it would violate my convictions. To advocate it aroused public distrust. I had given good service, had kept out of politics, the public trusted me and members of the council liked me; yet as far as the community was concerned, the result was almost as bad as if I had corrupted the council, the local bosses, and the press in the "natural way." Apparently it was not possible to operate a private corporation of this kind and be true to the stockholders on the one hand and to convictions like mine on the other. I had succeeded only in protecting the rights of my clients, who in the end were far better served by my methods than they would have been by the usual management of a public-utility enterprise.

My professional relations warred indubitably with my convictions. So did the enterprises with which I was connected. I was constantly required to make some adjustment between the things I believed in and the things I did. Always there was the conflict involved in getting on, in standing by the game from which I got my living, a living that was constantly increasing with my own needs. Of the men I had known when I came to Cleveland those had risen the fastest and farthest who asked no questions of their clients, who had the most skill in devising means to defeat the law, especially in taking advantage of some business reorganization or foreclosure. To raise a moral question with a client was the surest way to lose him. He did not hire a conscience; he hired a lawyer. And he wanted a lawyer to sense his wants and devise means to satisfy them. Most lawyers made more money out of business than from the law. They were let in on enterprises, they participated in underwritings, they were looked upon as an anchorage by men who felt that they could afford to pay in this way for additional protection.

Constant dilemmas of compromise brought me face to face with the problem of wealth without labor.

CHAPTER XXI

WEALTH WITHOUT LABOR

THE clients of our law firm were for the most part railroads, bankers, manufacturers, business men, and individuals with trust funds to administer. I noticed that they fell into two quite distinct groups. Some of them had a great deal of litigation; some years they prospered, other years not. They had not the best of credit with the banks, enjoyed no social distinction, and sometimes went through insolvency.

The second group seemed free from business worries. Its legal work was consultative; its wealth increased from year to year. These men took life easily, were socially eminent. They officered the clubs, were prominent in the Chamber of Commerce, were deferred to in conventions. The men in the first group were quite as intelligent as those in the second; they worked harder. Yet they were harassed, uncertain, and struggling.

Why, I asked myself, are some men easily and permanently rich, while others, at times equally well-to-do, have an uncertain status? Why is one group prominent in the affairs of the community and distinguished in its social life, while the other, quite as able, has no such financial or social power? What is the key to social and financial success? I set myself to discovering it.

Obviously it was not hard work. One could not get very rich by using his hands or his brains. Hard work did not guarantee success. Nor did thrift and saving. These were virtues of the poor, inculcated by banks, by employers, and by the Charity Organization Society. Rich people did not save, they spent; the more they spent the more they insisted that other people should save. They urged their employees to be sober, to work hard, to come early and stay late, but they did not do the things they taught. There was one philosophy for rich men and their families, another for other people.

I took the directory of directors of Cleveland corporations. I studied the family histories of the city, of its early settlers, and the holdings of our clients in various corporations. I worked out a tabulation of prominent men and of the kinds of business enterprises with which they were connected. I found that I was making an investors' guide. It indicated where one should invest his money and what he should avoid. It showed how some men got rich easily; how others toiled unprofitably. It was a guide to social distinction; to family permanence; to identification with the aristocracy. For the most obvious thing to be deduced from it was that the aristocracy of Cleveland was found among those who owned city land which their families had secured as early grants from Connecticut, and which they had held on to during the intervening years. The table ran like this:

GROUP ONE

Names of men of financial and social power whose wealth had permanence and increased from year to year.

What they own or are and the business they are connected with.

The land on which Cleveland is built.

Iron-ore mines of Lake Superior district.

Coal-mines, oil, and gas.

Industries protected by the tariff, especially iron and steel.

Directors of banks.

Stockholders of street-railways, electric-light, gas, and other public utilities.

GROUP TWO

Men of apparently equal talent whose wealth was subject to business vicissitudes.

What they own or are and the business they are connected with.

Competitive manufacturing establishments.

Wholesale and supply houses.

Retail business houses.

Brokers of all kinds.

Men without banking connections.

Lawyers, doctors, and professional men.

The most distinguished group lived on Euclid Avenue, where their families had lived for generations. The land on which Cleveland was built was part of the Western Reserve. It had been settled by a group of New England families, who had received a grant of land from the State of Connecticut, known as the Connecticut Land Grant. Late in the eighteenth century the colony had founded the city of Cleveland at the mouth of the Cuyahoga River. Many of the families had held on to their original grants and permitted the city to grow up around them. Their residential sites on Euclid Avenue were broad and deep and suggestive of old English estates. They bore imposing homes set far back from the street. Cleveland had grown slowly for seventy years; when I came there in 1894 it had a population of three hundred thousand people, which doubled within a few years. About 1900 old homesteads in the heart of the city and along lower Euclid Avenue were being torn down and skyscrapers erected. Instead of selling the land to builders, the old families leased it on long-term leases, as is done in London and by the Astors in New York, and collected ground-rent. The amount of the rent was reappraised every ten years. In fifteen years' time the annual rental of certain parcels was almost equal to their purchase price when I first went to Cleveland. The land shot up in value from a few hundred dollars a front foot to a thousand dollars, then to two thousand dollars; some of it was selling at six thousand dollars before I left the city.

The families that owned these sites received substantial fortunes every year from ground-rentals. Much of their wealth was accidental. They had resented the intrusion of business, had fought the laying of street-car tracks on the avenue, or had insisted on living in the homesteads of their fathers in the face of encroaching industry. Many of these families bore old New England names. They controlled the banks and the social life of Cleveland. Ownership of land was the hall-mark of power and of caste. No other kind of wealth gave the same kind of standing.

One day a young man named Van Sweringen came into my office selling real estate. He and his brother had acquired options on a large estate on Euclid Heights, about ten miles from the centre of the city. He offered to sell me a building lot. I was not interested.

"That property will not be built on in my lifetime," I said. "It's an afternoon's journey to get there. I prefer to live in town."

Van Sweringen called several times. He was never intrusive, never urged the matter, but merely laid the suggestion before me. The offer was always the same—a good-sized building lot and a participating interest in a syndicate made up of my friends which was to own several thousand feet of land on the boulevard.

"You can pay anything you want to," he remarked the last time he came. "A few hundred dollars will do. You may never have to pay the balance."

I did not go into the venture. Instead I invested in a manufacturing enterprise and lost my money. The young men who went into the Van Sweringen syndicate made but one small payment and were never called on for further assessments. Each of them secured a home site worth from five to ten thousand dollars, and cleared as much again on the rise in the value of land in which they had a participating interest, at that time grown up in underbrush. Euclid Heights became the home of the wealthy population of the East End. Laid out by expert landscape-planners with parks and playgrounds, connected by a rapid-transit railway with the heart of the city, it is one of the beautiful suburban developments of the United States.

This was the beginning of the Van Sweringen wealth. These two young men who came to the city poor have since become a power in the United States. In Cleveland they own some of the best down-town property, a rapid-transit railway, a great terminal depot, and a palatial hotel. They purchased the Nickel Plate Railway, then the Chesapeake & Ohio, and the Erie, and have developed a great consolidated railroad system. The beginning of their wealth was land lying about Cleveland, poor farming-land in the early nineties, so far from the city that it failed to attract the attention of local real-estate speculators.

After this building development started I wanted the city to share in it. German cities, I knew, acquired land in advance of their growth, laid out transit lines, developed their suburban allotments themselves, and profited on the transaction. I laid my idea before Mayor Johnson, with more urgency than Van Sweringen had used with me.

"The city ought to buy land about the heights," I said. "It ought to buy every foot it can get at the present price of about two hundred dollars an acre. Let us reduce the appropriations for other departments, if necessary. Let us buy land for parks, for the infirmary, for the workhouse, for anything the law will allow us to buy it for. We can pay off the city's debt merely by buying this land and permitting it to ripen on the market."

But the city could not buy land freely. The laws of the State would not permit it. A tract of two thousand acres that it did acquire for the infirmary and workhouse is worth to-day at least ten times what it cost.

Other men in the group of the permanently rich owned iron-ore deposits in the Lake Superior districts. I had heard stories of these purchases when I first came to Cleveland. The land had been cut over by timber kings, who, if they knew of its hidden wealth, had given it little thought. A speculator from Milwaukee secured options on the tracts, which he hawked about for years trying to find a purchaser. Finally a part of the land was sold to the Carnegie Steel Company. When the United States Steel Corporation was formed it became a part of that organization. I remember reading the testimony of Mr. Charles Schwab before a congressional committee, in which he stated that these iron-ore holdings of the Steel Corporation were carried in its capitalization at eight hundred million dollars. A few years before this land was practically worthless. It had no buyers. A number of Cleveland men had acquired similar iron-ore holdings, from which they derived fabulous wealth.

These iron-ore deposits are the key to the power of the Steel Trust. They make it an almost complete monopoly. When I was a boy hundreds of men were amassing fortunes out of iron and steel in Cleveland, Youngstown, Sharon, and Pittsburgh. Steel rails were selling at sixteen dollars a ton. To-day it is dangerous for independent producers to enter the iron and steel business. They dare not do so because of the control of raw materials by the trust. They have to buy from a competitor in whose hands are the natural resources.

After the trust was formed prices went up. They have been kept up ever since. Yet the mining of iron ore is a very simple process. The surface of the land is stripped of a layer of earth. Huge steam-shovels gather up ten or twenty tons of ore at a single scoop and dump them into an open freight-car. The car is hauled a few miles; then the bottom is opened and the ore falls by gravity into the hold of a lake freighter. In Cleveland, Ashtabula, or Conneaut it is unloaded by great electric "clams" that go down into the vessel and bring out ten or fifteen tons of ore by the mere pressure of an electric switch. Again loaded on open cars, it is hauled to Pittsburgh to be converted into the finished product. The hand of man scarcely touches the ore from northern Minnesota until it is dumped into a blast-furnace a thousand miles away.

Why, I said to myself, with these great deposits of wealth and with engines that do the work of a hundred men, have the gains gone neither to labor nor to the public? Civilization could be remade by cheap iron and steel. Steel is king. It controls water and rail transportation, forms the skeleton work of cities; the conduits that carry gas, water, and electricity issue from steel-mills. We live in a steel age. A hundred discoveries and the opening up of unparalleled deposits should have made it possible to produce iron and steel far more cheaply to-day than in the early days of the Bessemer process. But prices have not gone down. They have gone steadily up. The gains have gone to a few individuals who own something they did not create.

The Standard Oil Company had its modest beginning in Cleveland. It was one of a dozen oil-refineries in Ohio, and of hundreds in northwestern Pennsylvania, where I had grown up as a boy. Oil, too, was a gift of nature; it had been deposited in the earth, and along with natural gas delivered itself to those who tapped the soil. Railway favoritism had given Standard Oil its strangle-hold on the industry; railroad rebates had ruined scores of our neighbors when I was a boy, and in time had made the Standard Oil Company dominant not only in oil but in transportation, in banking, in related industries, and in international affairs as well. There were families rich from coal; others from timber and mining ventures. Nature herself had endowed these men with wealth; labor had contributed little to it. Such wealth meant hereditary power; it grew with each passing year; it enabled its possessors to levy tribute, to shape civilization, to control the development of America and the destinies of the world.

Other men, closely associated with the landed group, owned street-railways, gas, and electric-lighting companies. Among them were Tom Johnson and Mark Hanna. Tom Johnson had acquired a worthless street-railway in Cleveland and had cleaned up millions, in his early forties, by the sale of such properties. In public-utility corporations men were able to capitalize something that they could not capitalize in other businesses; they capitalized population, growth, sanitary demands, and then sold out the capitalized value to the public.

Woven into these interests were the banks and the trust companies. Our law firm had them for clients. I studied their methods. The banks gathered in the people's money. They carried advertisements showing that the deposits of the people were many times as much as the money invested by the stockholders in the capital stock. The directors controlled these deposits, amounting to from eight to ten dollars of other people's money for every dollar of their own. As directors they could borrow without fear. They knew where new lines of street-railways were to be built and were able to speculate in land in advance of railway extensions. They knew of coal-mines that were being projected. They knew the business of every other man in town. They participated in underwritings and were courted by other business men.

Here was another source of power and of wealth.

This group of men held the money and the credit resources of Cleveland in their hands. They could build skyscrapers and hold them until they were filled. They could underwrite issues of securities, put on the market by New York banks. In a hundred ways the directors of the banks were able to make profits which were not available to other people.

The control of other people's money was next in importance to the ownership of land. Organize a bank and your own dollar grew to ten. The pennies, dimes, and dollars of the millions created millions for the few. All told, the deposits of the people of Cleveland amounted to two hundred million dollars, or thirty times the amount of the city's debt, yet a handful of men closely associated, socially intimate, members of the same club, were able to use this money as they saw fit. They could lend it to their friends, or to syndicates which they organized. They could use it in New York. They could do pretty much as they willed with the business life of the city. They influenced the press. They were closely identified with both political parties. The banker was a political power, as he was an industrial power, through the use of other people's money.

Here again I found that the way to get rich was to have other people trust you, work for you, save for you. If you could use the money of other people, you need not have much money of your own.

The title-page of my manual for investors read as follows:

"Avoid competition—become a monopolist.
   Great wealth comes from what the community, not the individual, creates.
The road to wealth and distinction is through control of the gifts of nature.
Make society work for you.
Everybody works for those who own the land.

Don't save—spend.

Thrift, humility, and sacrifice are virtues for the poor.

Temperance is a virtue not intended for club consumption.

Aristocracy is not a matter of birth. It is a matter of ownership of the earth."

These business maxims violated all of my early teachings. "Take care of the pennies and the dollars will take care of themselves" did not figure here. Thrift had been a household word in my childhood, a primary virtue inculcated by all. If I was industrious and honest; if I worked hard and diligently; if I did things that were distasteful; if I respected my superiors, I should become rich and respected, my life would be crowned with success. The rich men I knew were not thrifty; they asked others to be thrifty for them. They did not save; others saved for them. They admonished others to virtues of meekness, humility, and duty, but they observed none of their own admonitions.

They got an underhold on society, got it through monopoly and made other people work for them. They capitalized something that every one had to have or controlled a service that every one had to use. They got rich easily, often quickly, and kept the wealth they had acquired. It did not take much intelligence to secure this kind of wealth, or, once secured, to hold on to it. Many men who got rich out of land had done so against their will, or by accident. Millions were made out of public-utility corporations by bribing public officials or contributing to one or both of the political parties, in consideration of a franchise grant, while hundreds of millions had come from iron ore, oil, and coal.

Men who worked the hardest and who had often the greatest ability received the smallest returns.

Those who contributed most to the community by building up industry, producing useful things, for some reason or other did not rise. But year after year the other group grew richer and acquired social and political power.

My manual of investments showed me clearly how money could be made. Then a problem confronted me. What was I to do about it? Almost everything that offered substantial profit was related to an underhold on the people. Mankind, according to my social philosophy, was being mortgaged by the private ownership of natural resources, by watered securities of steam-railroads, by franchises to public-utility corporations, and by the protective tariff. I saw also that other people had to pay. A privilege to me meant sacrifice to some one else. Otherwise the privilege would have no value. Some one had to labor that I should live without labor. There was no escape from that.

Was there any compromise that justified me in enjoying privilege in the world in which I found myself? I wanted wealth, wanted the comforts and conveniences that wealth brings. I wanted to make a living as easily as possible. But there was no field of activity in which I could acquire wealth without violating some of my convictions. I believed in the public ownership of public-utility corporations. Yet the community insisted on giving away franchises. Railroads should be agencies of public service, but they were operated for private profit. The protective tariff I held to be an immoral thing; it increased prices, was a mother of monopoly. Speculation in land was unsocial. Individuals should not be permitted to enjoy increased land values created by the community.

Must I refuse, I thought, to accept anything I did not myself produce? I might betake myself to the woods with a rod and gun, but my abstention would not change conditions. Change could only come through political action. It involved education, agitation, possibly control of the government by new groups.

I worked out a compromise. I followed the manual in making investments, and kept away from competitive enterprises. Some money that I put into land cleared several hundred per cent in a short time. A railroad and coal underwriting cleared immense profits. Securities in a public-utility corporation that cost me little sold later for one hundred and seventy dollars a share. Industries protected by patent rights yielded fertile returns on investment. "The world," I said to myself, "is topsyturvy; there is no personal wrong in taking advantage of its topsy-turviness to make such money as one can. But I will keep my opinions straight. I will advocate municipal ownership, will be honest about the tariff, about land speculation, about special privileges of all kinds. I cannot escape the world into which I am born, but I will do what I can to change it."

CHAPTER XXII

SINGLE-TAXING A CITY

An opportunity came to put my philosophy of the single tax to the test, but it came inopportunely. The Municipal Traction Company had failed, my experience in the Senate had closed a chapter in politics, my law business had suffered, and I wanted to leave Cleveland. I had a small income and could do as I chose. I felt a sense of guilt at leaving Tom Johnson, for he was my best friend; he had been the centre of my life for eight years. And he urged me to remain. We would take up the fight again, he said, it had been longer than he anticipated, the people were more wedded to reaction than he thought, they had to be educated—we could not leave the job half done. But I wanted to be doing work of my own and wished to get away from the hatreds, the conflict, the ostracism which I professed not to mind. And I felt that Mr. Johnson only half believed that the fight could be renewed.

I went to Europe in the summer to think things out. When I returned in the fall I had decided for New York. I arrived in Cleveland on the day of the primaries and went directly to the voting-booth. There I discovered that I had been nominated by Mr. Johnson for the Tax Commission. The work of the commission included the appraisal of every piece of real property in the city and required six months for its accomplishment. The other nominees were men with whom Mr. Johnson had great influence, the majority of them single-taxers. Election meant that I should be arbitrarily turned away from my own purpose, but it meant also a chance to do a piece of constructive work. It meant that I could try out our theories in practice.

Mr. Johnson's nominees were approved by the people, and I acquiesced in the work that he had laid out for me. The task of the commission was an appalling one, for real estate in Cleveland had not been appraised for ten years. Previous appraisals had been done badly, if not corruptly, and there was universal inequality. The constitution of the State required that property should be appraised for taxation at its full value, a rule that had never been followed, and apparently nobody expected that it ever would be followed. The poor were unjustly discriminated against, their homes being often assessed at full value, while valuable down-town property was assessed at as low as ten per cent of its value. Home-owners were paying millions of dollars a year in taxes that should have been paid by some one else. The opportunity was before the commission not only of correcting the inequalities of assessments, but of taking the first step toward the single tax by increasing the valuation of the land and reducing the valuation placed on improvements. This meant a complete reversal of the policy pursued by previous assessors, who had put a low value on land and a high value on buildings. Their rule had been that the more defenseless the taxpayer, the heavier his taxes; and that the more men contributed to the upbuilding of the community the more they should be taxed for their well-doing.

The commission elected as chairman Mr. Arthur May, a prominent business man, liberal in his opinions and sympathetic to Mr. Johnson. At our first sitting we determined to do the job thoroughly, and put an end to the injustice that had prevailed. We would place all property on the tax-list at its full

value as required by the constitution; we would see
if it were not possible to assess real property by scientific rules that could not be challenged; when our
work was completed we would publish the valuations
determined on in such a way that every property-
owner could compare his valuations with his neighbors'. Favoritism should end and wealthy taxpayers
should be assessed on the same basis as the poorest
home-owners.

All this was revolutionary. Such a procedure had
never been heard of. Every county in the State violated the provision of the constitution, and apparently everybody, including the courts, approved of it.
New York City was the only community that had
made an attempt to assess its property at its full
value, and by a defensible system. Before we began
our work, members of the commission went to New
York to confer with Mr. Lawson Purdy, who had
been for many years chairman of the Board of Commissioners of Taxes and Assessments. The most corrupt Tammany governments of New York had retained Mr. Purdy and given him a free hand in working out an honest and equitable assessment of real
property on a basis of its market value and according
to a uniform rule. No city in England or on the continent, as far as I know, approximated New York at
that time in the honesty of its tax system, and Mr.
Purdy, in my opinion, has made one of the most distinguished contributions to municipal politics of any
man in this country or abroad. The New York plan
of assessing land at its full market value compelled
owners to improve their property. They had to build
high-class structures in competition with others. It
put a penalty on idle landholding, and compelled
shacks and tax-earners to be razed. Compulsion on
landowners to improve their property led indirectly
to the fine architectural development of the city.

We studied the work of the New York commission for some days and decided to employ an expert land-valuer as secretary and bring him on to Cleveland. This caused outcry from the opposition press, to which we turned a deaf ear. Our secretary was given a free hand; aided by Mr. Purdy, we proceeded to organize a corps of valuers taken for the most part from Case College and Western Reserve University.

The commission prepared a large map showing lot lines of valuable down-town property. Then we invited in the owners to aid us in making our preliminary valuations. We asked them to select the most valuable site in the business section. About this there was little disagreement: it was on Euclid Avenue, not far from the public square. Then the commission fixed the valuation of this piece of property at its actual selling price and announced it to the assembled property-owners. There was immediate protest; the valuation increased assessments from three to ten times what they had been before. The commission's reply was that any one who was dissatisfied with his valuation could post an offer to sell at the appraised value; if the commission was not able to dispose of the property at the valuation placed on it, it would reduce the assessment. This effectually closed all protests; no one took advantage of the offer.

We continued this procedure in different sections of the city, values being fixed largely by the people themselves in public meetings called for the purpose. When our work was finished, valuations were printed in pamphlets by streets and numbers, so that every property-owner could compare his assessment with that of his neighbor. There were fewer appeals than had ever been made in the record of Cleveland or in that of the State. Our assessments of over a hundred thousand pieces of real property remained practically unchallenged; we had secured an approximation to exact equality in their values.

Another rule adopted by the commission reversed the principle that had previously obtained. We decided that men should be taxed on their *opportunity* rather than on their *efforts*. Our idea was that the dog in the manger who held his land idle or retarded the city's development was a public nuisance and should not be encouraged in being a nuisance. He should be forced to do his share in the upbuilding of the city. "Payne's cow-pastures" were a case in point—a big tract of land near the centre of the city held out of use by one of the old families, who waited for the ripening of values before thev should place it on the market.

We listened willingly to the pleas of men who had recently constructed fine office-buildings.

"Is it just," they said, "that we should be punished for improving the city? We tear down shacks and put up fine buildings. On land next to ours tumble-down buildings disfigure the city and retard its growth; yet this adjoining land has been greatly increased in value by our buildings. Is it just that we should be punished by a high valuation on our building while the man who refuses to build reaps a profit which he did not create?

People interested in better houses had similar arguments. The city was growing rapidly, rents were rising. Great stretches of land in the suburbs were held out of use by speculators. The commission could encourage the erection of houses by placing a relatively low valuation on improvements and a high valuation on land.

We went as far in our application of the reasonings as the constitution permitted. Logically we would have relieved all buildings of taxation. But we were bound by the constitution to assess improvements.

We met the situation by depreciating buildings in a variety of ways, and materially reduced the valuation upon them. As a result of our work a great part of the city's taxes were assessed against land rather than against betterments. They were shifted from labor on to opportunity. They penalized speculation and encouraged effort. The home-owner and the poor were relieved of millions of dollars of taxes that were placed on down-town property, manufacturing sites, railroad rights of way, and the water-front.

The work of the Tax Commission was the most satisfactory experience of my political life. It confirmed my belief in the results that would follow the taxation of land values and the exemption of improvements from taxation. We were only able to make a beginning, but the years that followed witnessed a building development in Cleveland that has made it one of the finest cities of the Middle West. Vacant land has been forced into use, tax-earners have been replaced by commercial buildings, Euclid Avenue has been developed into a business street for five miles flanked with splendid structures. Suburban land has been laid out by expert planners with broad boulevards, parks, and playgrounds. For miles about the city development work has been going on and the population has been dispersed over a wide area. Cleveland bids fair to become one of the beautiful cities of America. It has grown with astounding rapidity and a great part of this development is due, in my opinion, to the automatic operation of high taxes on land values and relative low taxes on buildings; one penalized the speculator, the other gave a premium to the builder. Cleveland has followed one of the natural laws in the social state.

CHAPTER XXIII

LEISURE

WHEN the work of the Tax Commission was completed and the last record of assessments signed, sealed, and delivered to the county officials, I was at last free. I could leave Cleveland, could keep the promise I had made to myself when I entered the New York Law School, that I would quit the law at forty. If I had been successful, well and good. If not, there was no need of further trying. Success there had been of a kind, but it had given me little enjoyment. The law had been my Leah; I had served fourteen years, like Jacob for Rachel—now I would enter into the reward of freedom and devote myself to writing. That desire was stronger than the associations of years in Cleveland.

My wife encouraged me to begin the new adventure, and we were ready to go to New York. But the break was halted by an invitation to edit the Cleveland edition of *Ridgway's Weekly*, an ambitious enterprise launched by E. J. Ridgway, then editor and owner of *Everybody's Magazine*. The new combination newspaper and magazine was dedicated "To God and Country." Simultaneous publications were to issue from New York, Washington, Pittsburgh, Cleveland, Chicago, New Orleans, Denver, and San Francisco. It was to carry telegraphic news, the best of fiction, and twelve local pages gotten up by the local editor; to be printed on a newspaper press and devoted to progressive ideas. The whole thing was on a novel and extravagant scale. The magazine was advertised widely and we anticipated a great success.

For weeks I worked over my edition and for two days before the first issue appeared I hardly left the printing-office. When the magazine was laid on the press I fell asleep, contented, on a pile of white paper. I was awakened in the morning by a man standing over me holding a copy of the magazine in his hands. He had bought it on the street and had called to pay his respects. "Are you the editor of this sheet?" he asked. I proudly admitted that I was. "Well, look at it," he said. "I could get out a better-looking thing than that down in Bucyrus." I looked at the magazine. The first page was a blur. The second, third, and fourth pages were no better. It could hardly be read. The promoters in New York had failed to try out the idea of printing a magazine on a high-power newspaper press. As the day wore on I heard from other cities. Their results had been the same. Their editors were in sloughs of discomfiture, as was I. Cheery notes from New York ordered us to proceed with the next issue, but the blurring continued, and in six weeks the magazine was dead. It cost the promoters over half a million dollars and might have succeeded had a single printing been tried out before the enterprise was launched.

The failure of *Ridgway's Weekly* left us free to go to New York. We found a comfortable home in the old Chelsea Hotel on West 23d Street and soon made agreeable contacts with people we wanted to know. My wife threw herself into the suffrage movement, which was then beginning to command attention, and in which she had been one of the pioneers in Cleveland. She organized the Twenty-fifth District of the Woman Suffrage Party and gathered around her a brilliant group of workers.

After graduating from the Meadville Theological Seminary, my wife had gone to Iowa, where she became the "Little Minister" in the pulpit of the Unitarian church in Des Moines. The church grew, she had a devoted following; when we married there was a loud protest from her friends. I had ended her career. Her achievements when she came to Cleveland were greater than my own; she was widely known as a speaker, as a leader in the suffrage movement, and in social activities. She was eager to continue her work, work which was life to her. But I wanted my old-fashioned picture of a wife rather than an equal partner. Women did not take part in things in Cleveland; only a few had gone to college at that time; there were but few activities open to women. They did not earn their own living. That was a public admission of failure by the husband. I found reasons for deciding against each suggested activity in turn.

It did not occur to me that there was anything illogical in my position, anything unjust in it or out of keeping with what I believed in. My mind simply held fast to assumptions of my boyhood, which social prejudices seemed to justify. And as I look back over those years I realize that I never honestly faced what I was doing or the rightfulness of my wife's claims. It was not until we came to New York, where the suffrage movement was claiming women of distinction, where no more notice was taken of a woman in work than a man, that I recast my prejudices. My mind did not do it, new standards did. Then I was as eager for her to find her work as I had been loath to have her do so in Cleveland. And she rapidly found opportunities to her liking. She arranged meetings at Cooper Union on various subjects, she developed dramatic activities in connection with her work as chairman of the Twenty-fifth District, and rose rapidly in the many activities with which women were connected. But I had taken many years out of her life, had denied her the opportunity to pioneer, which she feared rather less than did I, and many of the enthusiasms that had been denied her in Cleveland could not be warmed into life again.

She had aided me greatly in public speaking and writing and gave me generous freedom to do as I chose with my life. She had consented to the abandonment of the law for the uncertainties of literature, the assured life of Cleveland for the hazards of the metropolis. All this fitted in quite naturally with my domestic picture at the time.

As I reflect on this evolution in my opinions, I see again the resistance of the mind to facts that involve sacrifice or personal discomfort, that involve disapproval by one's class or the society in which one lives. There was every reason why I should have allowed my wife any right which I enjoyed, should have given her every freedom which I took for myself, should have encouraged her to express her talents, which I recognized were of an unusual sort. I was proud of these qualities, and my belief in freedom should have made me the first to insist that she use them as she willed. Instead, I discouraged them, because I preferred my early picture of a wife, a picture that fell in with the current assumption of the period that a woman should quite literally "serve," quite literally "obey," her husband. Property rights die hard. Up to very recently a woman was property. Social *mores* die harder. They relate to the herd in which one lives. And social standing is as much prized as property. As to women, I followed the changing *mores*. I spoke for women's suffrage without much wanting it. And I urged freedom for women without liking it. My mind gave way, but not my instincts. One can be a hard-boiled monopolist in personal relations, just as in property; and as unwilling to permit individuals to change as the

Constitution of the land. I hated privilege in the world of economics; I chose it in my own home.

And I have sometimes doubted whether many of the men who spoke and worked for the equality of women really desired it. Intellectually yes, but instinctively no; they clung as did I to the propertied instinct, to economic supremacy, to the old idea of marriage, in which all that a woman got she got through petitioning for it. There is something so jagged about our convictions; they do not run a hundred per cent true. My own unwillingness to abdicate masculine power made me better understand men's unwillingness to abdicate economic power.

And in the woman movement, as in other social movements, equality had to be seized by the class that had it not. I remember a saying of Tolstoy's that the "rich would do anything for the poor but get off their backs." That seemed to be true in the relation of sexes as it was in the relations of classes.

With our life adjusted to new friends, with leisure and freedom from economic fears, I could now write as I had not written before. For years I had been planning in detail the writing of a series of ten books on the general subject of democracy. It was to occupy the rest of my life. Though some of my early illusions were gone, my enthusiasm for democracy remained. Democracy had never been synthetically studied. It had only been partially tried. Endless books on the subject of government were concerned with the Constitution, with city charters, with the machinery of government. Academic in form and substance, they did not portray the invisible government that lay back of the shadows with which we were familiar; they left us still in the dark as to what was the matter with the city and the state. They did not deal with the economic foundations of politics, with its social possibilities, or suggest what the city and the state might become if they used their powers to serve the people.

I had dreams of social democracy. What we needed were facts. I would assemble the achievements of Germany, England, Switzerland, and Denmark, and present them as a demonstration of constructive democracy, of the kind of a society we might have if we but saw the state as an agency of service.

My plan was ambitious. It included first a volume on the city, then a study of the American State, then one on the federal government. These books were to be illumined with comparisons from Europe, with studies of public ownership, social insurance, co-operation, city-planning. One volume was to be a survey of contemporary civilization, followed, I hoped, by a history of the world, interpreted in economic rather than political or personal terms.

America seemed to me a country so much absorbed in elementary activities, in wholly individual efforts to get on in the world, that it had not had the time to think of anything else. Only yesterday we were pioneers, homesteaders, home-builders. We had quite naturally left politics to any one who would relieve us of the responsibility. We were not only business-minded, we were parish-minded. We did not know what was going on outside of our own environment. But we were practical—facts were important to us; all that was needed was to show the way and we would follow it. The right kind of books, written from experience, factual in presentation and popular in form, would bring to America the one thing needed. Albert Shaw had inspired me with an interest in the city at Johns Hopkins. The city was the place where we had to begin. It was close to the people, it touched them in many ways. The time had come when, having built our own homes, we were ready to build a city like a home. When I wrote *The City, the Hope of Democracy*, the first book of my series, I felt that it would be a manual of reform; it would hearten people and point out the steps to be taken. I put into it all my faith in the future of American cities, in the certainty of their redemption.

I sent the manuscript to Charles Scribner's Sons, confident of its value, certain of its success. It was accepted and the proofs came back to me interlined with helpful suggestions and humorous queries as to facts or arrangement. They were initialled W. C. B. My sense of literary form was not commensurate with my zeal for the subject. There were exaggerations; I was frankly a propagandist disposed to repetition as a means of emphasis. I fancy that I am one of a large number of writers who owe an unexpressed debt to Mr. W. C. Brownell, one of America's distinguished critics, as he is certainly one of her kindest. He gave me continued encouragement, along with illuminating suggestions as to style and manner of treatment that were never dogmatic and were always right.

A second book, *Wisconsin: An Experiment in Democracy*, had followed as the fruit of two winters that I spent at the University of Wisconsin lecturing on European and American politics. I utilized the opportunity to make a study of an American State that had used its powers under the liberalizing legislation inspired by Robert M. LaFollette. I wrote about Wisconsin as an example of what the American State might be; of the dignity that it might enjoy, not unlike that of the smaller countries of Europe. The close identification of the State university with the State government I found admirable; admirable, too, the aid that the agricultural college had been in up-building farm life. Through social legislation, education, and the expansion of State activities, Wisconsin was making itself an invaluable experiment in democracy.

I was always planning books in my mind, sometimes two or three at a time. I had a mental affinity for facts and ideas that fortified my belief in democracy and my pictures of a society that would come in through the adoption of relatively few reforms. I remembered everything that furnished material for such writing. When I went abroad I spent my time studying cities, states, and institutions. They became photographic in my mind, they took the form of models; they had psychological significances. I was never weary of reading about the Athens of Pericles, the Florence of the Medici. I had a passionate belief that people could and would build as great states as ever rulers had built. But everywhere I found the conflict that balked democracy in its work. I found it especially in America and analyzed it in a book entitled *Privilege and Democracy*. It was a diagnosis of the America of my generation, of the ascendancy of business and our indifference to an organized, well-ordered state. In England and Germany I saw democracy coming into being in cities rather than in Parliament; I described it in three books— *The British City : The Beginnings of Democracy, European Cities at Work,* and *The Modern City and Its Problems.*

Socialized Germany, published in 1914, contained parts of an ambitious work that I had long had in mind, to be called *The Peaceful Revolution.* During the war I wrote *Why War?, The Only Possible Peace,* and *The High Cost of Living.* Later *Denmark : A Co-operative Commonwealth Ruled by Farmers* marked a return to the original series on political and industrial democracy.

But I anticipate by years the winter of 1910 in the old Chelsea Hotel. I went to New York with the idea of devoting the rest of my life to writing. But with leisure to write books, I could not write. I had won the prize of complete freedom from uncongenial work, and for some reason or other I could not use it. The spur of contact with life was lacking. Apparently I needed to earn my freedom from day to day.

I got that contact partly through magazine writing —for *Scribner's*, for *Everybody's*, then under the editorship of John O'Hara Cosgrave, finally for Benjamin B. Hampton, who had gotten control of the *Broadway Magazine*, renamed it *Hampton's*, and started it on its rapidly rising career of brilliant editorship and militant reform. Hampton handled me with more brutal kindness than any man I ever had anything to do with. His criticisms, delivered with crushing directness, destroyed any comfort I took in myself as a writer. Before my first article was published I rewrote it half a dozen times; each time I admitted that it was greatly improved, and each time it came back blue-pencilled almost beyond recognition, with contemptuous marginal notes on my workmanship.

Hampton drove me to work hard. He made me more direct. He tried to cure me of my tendency to repetition; to staccato sentences intended, willy-nilly, to dent the reader's mind. He insisted that I tell a story and be done with it. He trained editors, and built up a powerful magazine. But the monthly magazine was becoming a nuisance to business, and *Hampton's*, along with *McClure's*, the *American*, *Everybody's*, and a number of lesser publications, were either purchased, starved of advertising, or pushed to the wall. I got a race-course training in language from Hampton, along with an abiding respect and love for a potential genius and an inspiring fellow craftsman.

CHAPTER XXIV

THE PEOPLE'S INSTITUTE

ONE day I was invited to speak at the City Club of New York at a meeting where the guest of honor was Count von Bernsdorff, the German ambassador. The subject was municipal administration in Germany. Some one liked what I had to say, and a short time after I was asked to become director of the People's Institute, a kind of popular university, which conducted a public forum at Cooper Union and carried on various educational activities south of Fourteenth Street. Its founder, Charles Sprague Smith, had been the moving spirit in many progressive political ideas. The director organized and presided at three meetings a week in Cooper Union, was chairman of the Board of Review of Motion Pictures, and had charge of the organization of concerts, dramatics, and various neighborhood activities. Here was contact with life and with liberal movements in the city. I gladly accepted the invitation.

We moved down to West Twelfth Street, on the edge of Greenwich Village, and began in earnest our New York life. Brilliant young people, full of vitality, ardent about saving the world, floated in and out of our apartment. The Hotel Brevoort was our neighborhood club. Socialism was the vogue, also woman suffrage. Graduates of Harvard, Columbia, and Vassar, concerned for the well-being of society but not for its conventions, formed an American youth movement. They protested against industrial conditions, suffered vicariously with the poor, hated injustice. Greenwich Village was a Mecca that called to itself poets, budding novelists, newspaper men. Girls exchanged the dulness of social work in the settlements for something more fundamental. Young men challenged the stagnation of home and university. There was a splendid enthusiasm among these emotional rebels, a generous willingness to make sacrifices. And a demand for immediate change. They started radical periodicals for the expression of their ideas. Muck-rakers, it seemed, had had their day. Mere uplift was inadequate. Constructive change was demanded.

There were leaders among these leaders. Max Eastman, handsome, eloquent, winning, was associate professor of philosophy at Columbia. Poet and dreamer of better conditions, he was drawn from the university into life. Crystal Eastman, a graduate of Vassar and later admitted to the bar, held an important position as secretary of the Workmen's Compensation Commission, to which she had been appointed by Governor Hughes as the result of a brilliant investigation of housing and industrial conditions in Pittsburgh. This brother and sister became the centre of a group of writers, artists, and poets, who started *The Masses* in 1912 and carried on its publication until 1917, when it was discontinued as a result of the war. Art Young, the cartoonist, loved for his genial personality, appeared from no one knew where and disappeared, and seemed as much at home in one place as another. Floyd Dell came on from Chicago, where he had been literary editor of the Chicago *Evening Post*. Jack Reed, recently from Harvard, was beginning that tempestuous career as poet, magazine writer, war reporter, and finally revolutionary agitator which led him first to Mexico with Villa and then to Russia, where he died, honored by a monument erected by the revolutionists. Boardman Robinson and John Sloan, the artists, Mary

Heaton Vorce and Inez Haynes Irwin, the well-known fiction-writers, formed part of the group that contributed to *The Masses* as a forum for the expression of their ideas in art and literature.

Inez Milholland stood out in the group of women as a beautiful and commanding personality. Educated at Vassar, with the widest social opportunities, easily first in every field, she chose to give her wonderful vitality to the neediest claimants on her sympathy. For distress arising from the miscarriage of justice she was willing to make any personal sacrifice. We were neighbors in the country and I have known her to leave home on a moment's notice to rush about the State, following up some clew that might lead to the reprieve of a criminal whom she believed to have been unjustly condemned to the chair. She would stand by the telephone for hours appealing to the governor, to judges, to persons of influence to aid in the release of some one she thought innocent. Few people whom I have known controlled their lives as completely as did she; few lived in more complete indifference to public opinion, and none gave themselves more joyously to friends and the things they believed in. Persistence in a speaking campaign for suffrage when her strength was not equal to it cost Inez Milholland her life.

The great hall of Cooper Union, the centre of the activities of the People's Institute, was a free forum for the discussion of questions of the day. Socialism and feminism were presented from its platform. Prominent foreigners coming to this country spoke there. Protest meetings were organized to defeat obnoxious measures before the Assembly at Albany, and the defense of Thomas Mott Osborne, warden of Sing Sing, was carried on from it. At the Osborne meeting, presided over by Mr. Adolf Lewisohn, the banker, there was an immense crowd, mostly from the East Side. The highly respectable committee that had organized the meeting occupied the platform. Toward the close of the evening a man stood up in the centre of the hall and began pushing his way toward the platform. There was a curious hush in the audience. Some one whispered that it was Alexander Berkman. When he drew himself up over the footlights and walked over to Mr. Lewisohn, I think more than one person on the platform suspected violence. I was not sure myself of his intention. But he merely announced his name, said that he had been in prison ten years, knew more about prison conditions than any one in the audience, and wanted the platform. Apparently undisturbed, Mr. Lewisohn gave it to him and the discussion went on.

Emma Goldman, deported to Russia in 1920, took part in discussions in those more confident days from the floor of Cooper Union. She presented her ideas with a brutal frankness and disregard for conventions that suggested the advocacy of force. Had she been staged in some more conventional activity she might easily have been recognized as a remarkable person. She was an excellent dramatic critic and gave lectures in up-town halls before sympathetic audiences. A trained nurse, she would work under an assumed name at her profession until she had money enough to pay for the cost of printing her magazine, *Mother Earth*. She was indifferent to material comfort, generous to the last degree. Tolerant of people, but intolerant of institutions, she denounced the latter unsparingly, and dramatized her own radicalism, partly to secure a hearing, partly because she felt the necessity of becoming a martyr to her beliefs, as were other revolutionists in Russia. It was her ideas quite as much as herself that she insisted on exhibiting. And her ideas were always unusual and unashamed.

On one occasion the speaker was Burkhart Du

Bois, the editor of *The Crisis*. His manner was modest and dispassionate, without the slightest incitement to antagonism. At the close of his address a hot-headed Southerner arose from the audience, and, shaking his fist at the speaker, shouted: "Have you the effrontery to assume that the day may come when a negro might hope to be elected the President of these United States?"

There was a long pause, a tension was felt in the audience, and everybody got ready for a good race row.

Mr. Du Bois waited for perfect silence, and then quietly, almost sweetly, he let fall one little word:

"Yes," he said casually, and added promptly:

"Are there any other questions?"

There were other questions, but they were friendly. I have always remembered this incident as a masterly example of poise and self-control.

During these years my life was less conditioned than I had ever thought possible. The People's Institute was an unusual institution; the trustees, and especially Henry de Forest Baldwin, the chairman of the Board of Trustees, were unusual men. A substantial budget was assured, a proper environment for work provided, the director was then free to do pretty much as he pleased. The idea seemed to be that there should be a clearing-house for new ideas in New York, and a forum where promising men could give them free expression. If a contributor withdrew his support—well, that was to be expected. When the trustees of Cooper Union took exception to meetings staged in the great auditorium, they were confronted with the deed of gift of Peter Cooper; and if they still insisted on the right to censor the meeting, the Institute declared it would discontinue its work. It insisted on being free; rather it insisted that the director should be free. I confess that I took this freedom very literally. When the subway contracts were being put through by the Gaynor administration, I organized a campaign for their rejection; they were a betrayal of the city's interests and the pledges on which the administration had been elected. Meetings were held, the Institute took the lead in opposing the contracts. One of my friends, a financier of standing, called me to his office and smilingly asked me if I realized that I was fighting all of the banks, the public-utility corporations, the railroads, the real-estate groups, and almost all of the big interests of the city, and that it would cost the Institute the support of many of its big contributors. But the trustees, some of whom did not believe in the position taken, made no effort to dissuade me from my course.

The Institute had always taken a lead in reform movements, and I was a member of the committee of citizens that nominated John Purroy Mitchel for mayor. I had known him as president of the Board of Aldermen, had co-operated with him in the fight he made against the subway settlement, and had been appointed by him, along with Professor Frank Goodnow, of Columbia University, later president of Johns Hopkins, to make an exhaustive study of the school administration of the city. The report which we submitted suggested the lines of charter changes that have since been adopted. As mayor Mr. Mitchel drifted away from his early militancy, he lost interest in the things he had stood for, and alienated the great mass of the people who had previously supported him. When renominated for mayor, he was badly defeated.

The fight over the subway contracts brought me into contact with William Randolph Hearst. He was different from any other man I had ever met. He was inscrutable, Buddha-like in his detachment. His mind seemed absent from his body. As a host he paid little attention to his guests; at dinners he scarcely spoke with his neighbors. Only once did I ever see him rouse himself. After a dinner he got up from the table and began to talk. Then his speech became a torrent. It rolled hatred of the wrongs he saw in the world; hatred of corruption and unscrupulous power.

I could never make out whether he suffered from the abuse to which he was subjected and whether he missed the companionship of men of his class. It was obvious that he had extraordinary ability, that he knew and controlled every one of his enterprises in detail. I could not classify him. He evaded understanding. There seemed to be something Oriental in his mentality; a kind of unsocial quality that freed him from the influences that were usually important to men.

Several times I went to Detroit to try to persuade Henry Ford to contribute to radical movements. I was never able to enlist his interest. He, too, mystified me; perhaps the very simplicity of the man bewildered me. He did not fit in with my formulas, either. Once I spent several days at the plant waiting for an opportunity to discuss my mission. But his mind seemed never to leave his car, or tractor. He would go away abruptly and be found standing over some obscure part of the car, beside a workman performing some routine function, or before the motion-picture screen that was exhibiting the tractor which was then being perfected. I have never seen more complete absorption: he listened to his attorney listlessly, to his superintendent with irritation, to guests without interest. He left his luncheon untouched, abandoned visitors who had come half-way across the continent to discuss something with him; but when he did talk on some public question it was with an understanding of cause and effect that was quite out of keeping with his apparent ignorance of the essential facts. His mind leaped from starting-point to conclusion. Intermediate factors were as though they did not exist.

He saw the labor problem in personal terms. He had no faith in labor-unions, apparently little faith in the experts whom he employed. He had few intimates among men of his class, but loved to visit with the farmers and men with whom he had grown up in the town of Dearborn. Life to him seemed bounded by the moralities of a small town, moralities of kindness, of doing your job as well as it can be done, of hating waste in any form, especially hating personal vices like smoking, drinking, or gambling. To him the banker was an exploiter, the railroads were the last word in inefficiency, and should be owned by the government and operated for service, while the land-owner was a non-producer who seized in increased rentals all of the gains which Ford gave to his workers in higher wages. War was the most immoral thing of all. It was caused by international bankers, by munition-makers, and by a parasitical, exploiting class.

Later during the war I had conferences with him on labor supply while Commissioner of Immigration at Ellis Island. I was in his office when Madame Rosika Schwimmer was announced. She was evidently expected. Mr. Ford asked me to remain during the discussion. Madame Schwimmer presented her plans for a peace ship. She had sounded out the neutral countries of Europe, had sympathy, she said, from the belligerent nations; they would welcome some move that would end the *impasse*. Henry Ford was the one man in the world who could dramatize peace; he alone could bring the boys out of the trenches before Christmas. Her arguments appealed to Mr. Ford's sympathy but not to his mind. He hated war, hated those who were responsible for it, but such an enterprise was outside of his experiences. He wanted to escape the conference. From time to time he would disappear. When he returned he seemed irritated that she was still there. He called in his attorney and asked his opinion, not eagerly, but with the listlessness of a man being crowded to something he did not want. His attorney disapproved, and he himself finally decided against it. But Madame Schwimmer hung on. The following day she won out. I think Mr. Ford was lured into the enterprise against his will, his judgment, and his desires by the plea that there was a possibility, a bare possibility, that he might be the means of saving human lives.

I came to know Amos Pinchot, who for many years had been a Progressive Republican, an intimate friend and supporter of Mr. Roosevelt and the liberal insurgence within the Republican Party. Mr. Pinchot was known as a man of culture, idealism, and democratic sympathies, with an interest in industrial questions, and a political creed of his own that led him into conflict with his old party associates and friends.

Later when Morris Hillquit was a candidate for the mayoralty of New York City, Mr. Pinchot took an active part in the campaign. He made a number of speeches, and always explained his independent position. He was not a socialist, but believed in Mr. Hillquit, and worked for him as an individual. This position so frankly stated was not accepted, if indeed it was even understood, by his old friends. Mr. Pinchot was called a socialist, and any other name that came handy. He had been guilty of a serious social offense; had dared to differ from his class, and for this he was made to suffer. He has continued, however, to maintain his convictions, giving of himself and his wealth to the causes in which he believed.

Dudley Field Malone, whom I occasionally met as director of the Institute, became a close political associate later, as Collector of the Port of New York, to which office he was appointed by President Wilson. He was gifted with extraordinary ability as a public speaker, a richly endowed personality, and a generosity that went out to causes only less whole-heartedly than it went out to personal friends. He was a magnetic personality in any group. He chose to identify himself with the woman's party, members of which were being imprisoned in Washington for picketing the White House. He had campaigned for President Wilson, had spoken for suffrage, and had given women's organizations which he addressed assurances of President Wilson's support to the suffrage amendment. I was with him in Washington on his return from a call on the President where he had pleaded the women's cause; he had pleaded for the redemption of his own promises and the promises of the President as well. As a result of this difference with President Wilson he resigned from the Collectorship of the Port of New York. He felt that his personal honor was involved by the President's refusal to support the amendment. This act of Dudley Malone, so generally misunderstood, like that of William Bullitt at the Paris Peace Conference, was one of the most heroic political acts with which I am familiar. It involved a breach with a most promising career, with close friends, and with public opinion as well.

The years from 1911 to 1914 were a happy interim for me. Working with college men and women who were convinced that the old order was breaking up, living in a world that had confidence in literature and in the power of ideas, it seemed to me that a new dispensation was about to be ushered in. A half-dozen monthly magazines had built up their circulation on disclosures of corruption and economic wrong; Lincoln Steffens, Ida M. Tarbell, Ray Stannard Baker, Charles Edward Russell had the attention of America; forums were being opened in the churches, city reformers were springing up all over the country. A dozen insurgents had been elected to Congress; direct primaries, the direct election of United States senators, the initiative and referendum were being adopted, while municipal ownership, labor legislation, woman suffrage, and the single tax seemed but a short way off. It was good form to be a liberal. Conservative lawyers, bankers, and men of affairs stepped out from their offices and lent their names to radical movements. They presided at meetings and contributed to causes. Branches of the Intercollegiate Socialist League were being organized in the colleges, woman suffrage was enlisting the most prominent women of the country, President Roosevelt was providing catchwords for radicals to conjure with, while Woodrow Wilson was taken from the cloisters of Princeton to be made governor of New Jersey, to be later elected to the presidency.

"The new freedom" was to replace the old serfdom of bosses, the younger generation was to achieve the things that had been denied my own—a generation ignorant of the old Egypt of small capitalism, aware of the cruel feudalism of the new. The political renaissance was now surely coming. It would not stop with economic reform; it would bring in a rebirth of literature, art, music, and spirit, not unlike that which came to Italy in the thirteenth century after the *popolo grasso* had made their pile and then turned to finer things. The colleges were to lead it; it was to have the support of the more enlightened business men; it would call forth the impoverished talents of the immigrant and the poor. The spirit of this young America was generous, hospitable, brilliant; it was care-free and full of variety. The young people in whom it leaped to expression hated injustice. They had no questions about the soundness of American democracy. They had supreme confidence in the mind. They believed, not less than I had always believed, that the truth would make us free.

CHAPTER XXV

ELLIS ISLAND

DURING the summer of 1914 I received a letter from President Wilson tendering me the position of United States Commissioner of Immigration at the port of New York. I was happy in the work as director of the People's Institute. The subject of immigration did not interest me greatly, and I knew very little about it. But Ellis Island is a principality. It lies in lower New York harbor, opposite to the Aquarium, which in earlier days was Castle Garden. The Commissioner has a force of six hundred men under him, and in normal times as many as five thousand immigrants passed through the island in a single day. There are two big hospitals and a fleet of boats. The Commissioner is a presidential appointee and responsible to the President alone.

The appointment made an appeal to something in me which has always been fundamental, something which stirred me in the university, led me into the social settlement, urged me into politics, impelled me to work for parks and playgrounds in Cleveland, and landed me in the People's Institute in New York. All of my activities have been part of a lifelong interest in the changing and improving of conditions that result in suffering or injustice. My passion for the city, in fact, all my writing, has been but the expression of this enthusiasm for improved environment. My admiration for Tom Johnson had sprung from the same hope and the same faith.

I hesitate to give a name to something that has been instinctive in me; whether it should be called the spirit of reform, or humanitarianism, or sentimentality, or the dreaming of dreams, or the seeing of visions depends entirely on the way one looks at life.

My interest in political reforms was not personal, it was economic. It was related somehow to a better ordering of things; to freeing the individual so that he could achieve all that was in him. That had been my chief enthusiasm in connection with the People's Institute. I wanted the hidden talents that I found on the East Side released; talents that were hungering for music, for literature, for artistic expression. And I had organized orchestras, choral societies, pageants, had developed dramatics, and had seen with my own eyes the unexplored abilities of scores of young people set in motion, when the opportunity for it was provided.

Ellis Island was an opportunity to ameliorate the lot of several thousand human beings. It was also an opportunity to do the work I liked to do. No doubt I thought I wanted to do this work for the sake of the immigrants. Probably I wanted to do it to satisfy my own instincts. Here on a small scale was an environment to be changed and improved.

I was wholly ignorant of official bureaucracy, of its jealousies and resistances to change—an ignorance, as it turned out, that was an advantage to me, for had I known the psychology of the permanent employee and his power, I should have hesitated before initiating the changes I had in mind to humanize the island. For I had heard Ellis Island referred to at Cooper Union as the Island of Tears. It was a storehouse of sob stories for the press; deportations, dismembered families, unnecessary cruelties made it one of the tragic places of the world.

I had an unfortunate introduction into my position, which was the most important in the service. Shortly after my appointment a dinner was given to the Secretary of Labor, Mr. W. B. Wilson, on the anniversary of the creation of the Labor Department. I was asked to make a speech. I spoke with enthusiasm on the department, which I described as the most important in the government. It was concerned with labor, women, children, the adjustment of labor disputes. I warmed honestly to the subject and expressed my pleasure at being associated with the immigration service.

I was followed by Ethelbert Stewart, a big, Jove-like person, with a terrible impediment in his speech. He was then statistician of the Bureau of Labor Statistics. Stuttering badly, he began:

"I have been moved by Mr. Howe's fresh enthusiasm. Many of us felt as he feels when we entered the service. I am reminded of a story about a man who was committed to an insane asylum." His stutter grew worse. "When he arrived, the attendant began taking everything from him—his keys, his knife, finally his watch. The man resisted. Pointing to the wall, the attendant said: 'But you don't need a watch here—there's a clock.'

"'Is the clock right?' the insane man inquired.

"The attendant assured him that it was.

"'Well, if it's right,' he said, 'then what in hell is it doing here?'"

Then Stewart sat down. Every one gasped. I did not understand the significance of the story, but every one else apparently did. The Commissioner-General of Immigration was angry. He never forgave Stewart.

I was a marked man from that night on. Not alone because of the implication in the speech or the comparison involved, but because of a conflict of purposes. Official changes which I recommended were turned down; my correspondence remained unanswered; I developed the habit of writing my letters and then going to Washington to get an answer. The Commissioner-General, an Americanized Italian, was as untrained in administrative work as I was in higher mathematics, and his consciousness of his inexperience led him to refuse to take any action at all. His table was piled mountains high with undespatched business, with records of men and women held in immigration stations awaiting his decision. He argued by pounding the table, swinging his arms, and evading the issue. In this way he refused to face a problem. When I asked for an assistant woman commissioner to look after the cases of women and children and had finally induced Miss Grace Abbott, of Hull House, Chicago, to accept, I found the position filled one morning by a woman dependent on a job-hunting congressman; she was utterly ignorant of immigration and had a New England morality that made her a nuisance to everybody, and a telltale tongue that carried her to Washington with every conceivable mare's nest that she could uncover.

During the next few years I learned how we were governed by petty clerks, mostly Republicans. The government was their government. A Cabinet official was to be respected, but he was to be made to know his place. He must not think that he could change things and disorganize the department; it had been so for years, it would remain so. Even Presidents came and went, but the permanent official, protected by the Civil Service regulations, was there for life. He hoped for a little more salary, dreamed of a little more power, eventually a place farther up the line as chief clerk. Then he would repay some of the slights he had received.

This was the administrative state—the state that often shapes political action, that conspires with congressmen. In a generation's time, largely through the Civil Service reform movement, America has created an official bureaucracy moved largely by fear, hating initiative, and organized as a solid block to protect itself and its petty unimaginative, salary-hunting instincts. America has paid a heavy price for its permanent classified service. In Washington at least it would be better if we had the spoils system, with all of its evils, in those offices that have it in their power to shape policies, to control executive action, and to make the state a bureaucratic thing. In the State Department, the Treasury, in the War and Navy Departments, this is especially true. Even the Labor Department is tory-minded in its personnel; I found, for the most part, only a petty struggle of groups and individuals to retain and exalt their own power.

On the island there was resistance to change. I had to blaze my way through division chiefs to know what was going on. Finally, I posted a notice in a dozen languages that any immigrant and any official could come to me directly. I posted other notices explaining to the aliens their rights. After repeated failures to get action from Washington, I printed a whole code of rules and displayed them conspicuously about the island. It was as easy to make a hundred changes at one stroke as a single one. Once the order had been issued, the burden was on the bureau to change. The orders stuck; they were never rescinded. And easy access to my office ended many abuses.

I set myself to changing the reputation of the island. I meant that it should be a kindly place to the million-odd people who in normal times passed through its gates each year. Instead of a prison, it should become a place of temporary detention. Aliens were allowed a great deal of freedom. For the first time men and women were permitted to be together in the detention rooms. The war lengthened the period of detention into months, so I opened

a school for children. Outside playgrounds were
equipped, and the immigrants were permitted to go
on the lawns. This aroused an indignant protest.
The lawns had been made at great expense, the officials said. They made a beautiful approach to the
island. I replied that live babies were more precious
than live grass, and took a good deal of satisfaction
in seeing the lawns trampled under foot. On Sunday
concerts were given by immigrant groups, which
readily co-operated with me in caring for their na-
tionals. The Italians arranged to have Caruso sing
on Italian day.

I took down high iron screens that suggested a
prison, refused to permit cells to be used for solitary
confinement. When disputes arose in the detention
rooms which seemed to threaten serious disorder, I
talked things over with the aliens. Always there was
some just cause for complaint, over the food, over
harsh treatment. During these years there were hundreds of persons detained as immoral cases, scores
who had had a criminal record at home. Nearly one
million aliens passed through the island during the
five years I was there. For a time there were two
thousand Germans detained as war prisoners, and for
nearly a year there were a hundred-odd Reds arrested
in different parts of the country and portrayed as the
most dangerous of anarchists, organized to overthrow
the government by force. Yet during these years
there was never a controversy that was not allayed
by a friendly conference, and all told scarcely half a
dozen instances of disorder, disturbance, or outbreak
of any kind.

I found the immigrant well worth the interest he
inspired. He was helpless and confused; he responded
to any kindness and was far better material than I
had anticipated. The British gave the most trouble.
When a British subject was detained, he rushed to

the telephone to communicate with the consul-general in New York or the ambassador at Washington, protesting against the outrage. When ordered deported, he sizzled in his wrath over the indignities he was subjected to. All this was in effect a resentment that any nation should have the arrogance to interfere with a British subject in his movements. All Englishmen seemed to assume that they had a right to go anywhere they liked, and that any interference with this right was an affront to the whole British Empire.

The Irisn and Italians appealed to me most. They trotted down the gang-plank with their packs on their backs, with an air of assurance that they must be welcome anywhere. They had a dignity of their own, different from other European peoples. When ordered deported, they took their misfortunes with a resignation that commanded my respect and admiration.

For over a year things went well on the island. The newspapers gave space to the new ideas that I had introduced, the attempt to care for the thousands of aliens who, as a result of war, found themselves without a country, wards of the United States Government. I spoke before chambers of commerce, clubs, colleges, and universities. I took an active part in the movement to Americanize the alien, especially in trying to interpret his wants, as opposed to the wants which his self-constituted guardians thought he ought to have.

I was happy in my work of humanizing Ellis Island.

CHAPTER XXVI

BUSINESS AS USUAL

THEN something happened. It happened so quickly that I did not understand it. I could not fathom its significance or sense its power. In Cleveland I had been shielded by Tom Johnson's commanding personality. He took the blows; I was one of his seconds, on the edge of the ring. And the fighting had been for the most part fair. Now I was to enter the ring myself. It was a new experience to me to be a principal in the fight.

Some years prior to my appointment the New York *Globe* had made a sensational attack on the condition of food supplied the immigrants on the island. It asserted that the concessionaire supplied poor food, that he made a fortune out of his contract, which carried with it the right to sell supplies to departing aliens as they left the island for Western points. *The Globe* had forced an investigation by the department, which it asserted had never been efficiently conducted. One of my predecessors as commissioner had been involved in the feeding contract and had left office under a cloud. I was warned that the concessionaires on the island had power and influence with Congress. But all I could see was a number of business men with a handful of employees and an investment of a few thousand dollars in their plants. Surely there was nothing formidable in such an outfit. Certainly I should have the support of Congress, of my superiors, of public opinion in cleaning up any objectionable conditions. Everybody, I assumed, wanted the alien protected; everybody wanted the administration to be as kindly as possible. I had the food supervised, and came to the conclusion that it was wrong for private contractors to enjoy concessions on government property, especially in the case of the food contractor, to whose interest it was to push the sale of food and depreciate its quality.

Fortified with my investigations, I went to the department and members of Congress, and urged that the government should feed the immigrant itself. There was no great difficulty with the plan, for the government fed the patients in the hospitals, and the plant was already installed. The Secretary of Labor approved the suggestion, and an amendment providing for it was inserted in a pending appropriation bill. It authorized the department to feed the aliens directly after it had compensated the existing concessionaire for his investment.

The morning following the adoption of this amendment the New York papers carried reports of a savage attack made on me by a New York congressman. He said that I was a Socialist and a radical; he made a number of other charges against my administration. Obviously his information had been obtained from the food contractor.

When reporters showed me the story, I said that possibly the solicitude of the congressman over conditions at the island was due to the fact that he had long been the attorney for the food contractor who had been ousted from a very profitable contract by the change in the law.

Then the storm broke. It did not let up for four years.

I found that seventy thousand aliens were being landed every year in Hoboken instead of being brought to Ellis Island. They lost time. They were fleeced by hotels, by baggagemen; they were lured into houses of prostitution and saloons, and in the end many of them were brought to Ellis Island by circuitous routes on their way to Western-bound trains. They and their baggage were handled over and over again; they were left unprotected on the streets. It often cost them what little money they had. All this would have been obviated had the aliens been landed directly at Ellis Island, where they were under government protection and were placed on outgoing trains by inspectors detailed for that purpose.

I urged that these passengers be landed on the island directly from the steamships, where the abuses could be stopped. Instead of investigating the subject and issuing an order, the Commissioner-General called a hearing at Ellis Island on the proposal. The propriety of the change seemed so obvious that I assumed it would be ordered as a matter of course. On the day of the hearing the island was swamped with a hungry crowd protesting against the proposal. They came not only from Hoboken but from New Jersey and New York. Powerful interests had been enlisted; there were railway and steamship agents, hotel-keepers, expressmen, representatives of the New York Chamber of Commerce. Hundreds of people were angrily aroused at the suggestion that they should be deprived of their prey. Representatives of the Hoboken Chamber of Commerce said it would cost Hoboken at least five hundred thousand dollars a year. Hotel and express men claimed almost equal losses. They looked upon the money which they took from the alien as a vested interest. It was sacred. They were callous to the suggestion that the prevailing system meant a needless loss to immigrants of hundreds of thousands of dollars a year. These considerations were not even noticed in the discussion. Money was at stake. It was to be taken from Americans. Why in the name of Heaven should anybody be concerned over the alien?

The order for the change was never made.

I found that the transcontinental railroads divided the incoming aliens among themselves by a pooling arrangement. Many were taken West over the most circuitous routes. Some were first taken to New York; there they were kept in cheap lodging-houses. Then they were put on a boat to Norfolk, where they were transferred to trains carrying them to Cincinnati, Chicago, or Western points. They lost days of time, often they reached their destination late in the night without friends to meet them. They were open to all sorts of graft on their unprotected arrival.

Here was another instance of "fraud and loss," from which it was the duty of the government to protect the alien. Quite obviously this abuse should be stopped. Aliens should be sent West by the most direct routes; they should not be sent around Robin Hood's barn because the railroads decreed that no single road should get the bulk of the traffic. But, despite my urging, no action could be secured to end the abuse.

I found that aliens in this country were losing large sums of money through irresponsible bankers, with whom they made deposits, bought exchange, or purchased tickets for themselves or their friends. I detailed secret-service men to investigate, and unearthed losses of twelve million dollars in a single year in New York alone. The worst offender fled the country as a result of the investigation. I sought to put these fly-by-night bankers out of business by a State law that would require inspection by the banking authorities, but I was never able to make any headway with the suggestion nor could I get any support at Washington.

The steamship lines were required to pay for the care and detention of aliens whom they had brought to the country, but who were ordered sent back. Deportees frequently had to be cared for in the government hospitals at Ellis Island.' Many were detained for weeks and months by serious illness. The steamship companies were paying a nominal sum fixed many years before for hospital service. I had the cost of the hospitals worked out by accountants on a per-diem basis, and then went to the department and secured an order fixing the charges on the basis of cost. It increased the revenues of the bureau by hundreds of thousands of dollars. But it organized the hostility of the steamship companies.

Unconscious of the interrelation of all these interests with one another, with New York congressmen, with bureaucratic officials, I had built a fire which needed only a spark to start a blaze.

The attempt to deprive the food contractor of his concession started the conflagration. It was taken up by others. I was called a Socialist; Socialism meant all kinds of things to the congressional mind. I was accused of admitting immoral women, who had been ordered deported; of permitting too great freedom on the island, of tolerating gambling. Yet every congressman knew that I had no more power to admit an alien ordered deported than he had, and that the demands of the War and Navy Departments for Ellis Island had led to the admission of many people on temporary permits. Yet these statements, magnified in head-lines, were carried all over the country by the press, to be followed by screaming editorials picturing the immorality of the island. Such basis as there was for these charges was founded on investigations which I had made myself months before, but which had revealed nothing. The gambling charge related to some Chinamen found playing fan-tan; the other charges were quite as inconsequential.

A detained alien for whom I had shown some consideration came to me and made an affidavit that he had been offered five hundred dollars to swear that he had discovered me in a compromising position at the island one night.

"But I have never spent a night at the island," I said.

He knew that. The commissioner had a suite of rooms on the island, and if the story could be started in the press it would be sufficient. It could be used in Congress; it would be difficult to disprove it. That was all that was needed, he said, to distract attention from the things I was doing.

I went to the chairman of the Committee on Immigration in the House and demanded a thorough investigation. The committee took exhaustive testimony. It compelled the congressmen to appear and give their evidence. It made a report which not only dismissed all the charges, but concluded with the statement that under my administration discipline had been improved, aliens were better treated, and many economies had been made.

A few months later a congressional election came around. I sent a letter to the New York congressman who had led the attack on the floor of Congress, asking him to meet me in a series of three debates in his district and repeat the charges he had made in the open, where he would have to either substantiate them or be subject to libel proceedings from which he was protected by the privileges of the House. The challenge was accepted. The meetings were held in the open streets in upper Manhattan the week before the election.

When I arrived at the place designated for the first meeting, the streets were blocked. I was thoroughly angry, at home with the subject, and in a mood to fight. We spoke from an automobile. I made a short speech, and then demanded that the congressman should answer a dozen questions which

I first read and then handed to him as I closed. He never got very far in his speech. Some one demanded that he answer the questions. Did he consider it honorable for a member of Congress to serve as attorney for private interests that had contracts with the government? Another asked if he did not think it cowardly for a man to take advantage of his privileged position on the floor of Congress to make libellous charges which he need not substantiate. Another asked what he would have done with hundreds of aliens packed in Ellis Island and held there because of the war.

When the election returns came in the congressman was overwhelmingly defeated. I believe he did not carry a single precinct. He was one of the prominent leaders of the House, a member of the rules committee, and might conceivably have been chosen Speaker had he been re-elected.

CHAPTER XXVII

HYSTERIA

THE administration of Ellis Island was confused by by-products of the war. The three islands, isolated in New York harbor and capable of accommodating several thousand people, were demanded by the War Department and Navy Department for emergency purposes. They were admirably situated as a place of detention for war suspects. The Department of Justice and hastily organized espionage agencies made them a dumping-ground of aliens under suspicion, while the Bureau of Immigration launched a crusade against one type of immigrant after another, and brought them to Ellis Island for deportation. No one was concerned over our facilities for caring for the warring groups deposited upon us. The buildings were unsuited for permanent residence; the floors were of cement, the corridors were chill, the islands were storm-swept, and soon the ordinary functions of the island became submerged in war activities. Eighteen hundred Germans were dumped on us at three o'clock one morning, following the sequestration of the German ships lying in New York harbor. The sailors had been promised certain privileges, including their beer, which was forbidden by law on the Island. Several hundred nurses were detained for their training prior to embarkation; each day brought a contingent of German, Hungarian, Austrian suspects, while incoming trains from the West added quotas of immoral men and women, prostitutes, procurers, and alleged white-slavers arrested under the hue and cry started early in the war, with the passage of the Mann White Slave Act and the hysterical propaganda that was carried on by moralistic agencies all over the country.

I was the custodian of all these groups. Each group had to be isolated. I became a jailer instead of a commissioner of immigration; a jailer not of convicted offenders but of suspected persons who had been arrested and railroaded to Ellis Island as the most available dumping-ground under the successive waves of hysteria which swept the country.

In the conflict with concessionaires I was sustained by the conviction that I was right. I was fortified with evidence and could face the department, committees of Congress, or the public in my fight to clean up the island. In the case of the thousands of suspects I was merely a custodian; those aliens that had been tried at all, had been tried by drum-head court martials, and such evidence as there might be was not on the island. The justice or injustice of their conviction was no affair of mine; I had no authority to examine the evidence, to concern myself with their stories, to do other than carry out orders, which were to deport aliens when directed to do so, quite irrespective of their guilt. But the testimony on which men and women were held was so flimsy, so emotional, so unlegal in procedure that my judicial sense revolted against the orders which I received. I quarrelled with the Commissioner-General of Immigration, who was working hand in glove with the Department of Justice; I harassed the Secretary of Labor with protests against the injustice that was being done. I refused to believe that we were a hysterical people; that civil liberties should be thrown to the winds. But in this struggle there was no one to lean on; there was no support from Washington, no interest on the part of the press. The whole country was swept by emotional excesses that followed one another with confusing swiftness from 1916 to 1920.

The first of the outbreaks had to do with immoral aliens. The Rockefeller Foundation had made exhaustive studies of prostitution. Congress enacted the White Slave Act. The press played up every arrest that suggested organized vice, and soon the country was convinced that it harbored an army of white-slavers, mostly recruited from south and central Europe. Prosecutors, chambers of commerce, red-blooded editors were carried away by this emotional righteousness. Prostitution, it was assumed, was an alien vice. It was an immigrant traffic. This crusade, like subsequent ones, needed only a spark to set aflame racial hatred that is to-day manifesting itself in the Ku Klux Klan. The white-slave traffic was assumed to be highly organized and financially powerful. It was said to have representatives in foreign countries, and to be linked into an international system, like chain stores, with procurers in villages, towns, and cities. Women were said to be held as virtual slaves by procurers; they were sold as so much merchandise; they were shipped from place to place and used in the most inhuman ways by men who trafficked in their virtue. For over a year America seemed convinced that our social and political life was honeycombed with a vice traffic that was threatening the foundations of the nation.

I do not know whether there was any more organized vice in the country in 1916 than there is to-day. Intelligent agents of the government said that there was no such system. Certainly I could find no evidence of the things portrayed in the press. Of the thousands of arrests made, the number of men and women who might be classed as white-slavers or procurers was very small. Many of them were held on slight evidence of guilt. Certainly there was little official evidence to substantiate the assumption that our morality was being undermined by commercialized vice organized into an international system by the most depraved of alien promoters.

In time this hysteria came to an end. Official raids were discontinued. The press ceased to feature the subject. But as a result of arrests I became the custodian of hundreds of men and women, mostly from southern and central Europe, who could not be deported because of the war and could not be held at Ellis Island because it was not fitted for permanent detention. That I was bound to execute the laws was evident. That I should use my official power to get rid of people without evidence, and because some individual or group said they were undesirable, was abhorrent to my ideas of legal ethics and my sense of responsibility to my oath of office. I listened to the personal stories of the arrested men and women. Many said they had never had a hearing. Others insisted that there had been no interpreter to translate their testimony. Many were arrested under suspicious circumstances, due to the close living of immigrants in tenement-houses, while others were gathered in to satisfy some labor controversy, or in connection with a conspiracy by one alien to get possession of the property or business of another. The records helped little, for the alien had had no counsel, and the procedure was ex parte. Trials had often been without witnesses for the accused, without attorneys, without the aid of friends, and in many cases the alien knew very little as to what it was all about.

In an effort to get at the truth, I asked a group of prominent women from New York to come to the island and listen to the evidence of the arrested women. They would not talk freely to me. Possibly they would talk to other women. The group consisted of my wife, Mrs. Mary Simkhovitch, Miss Lillian D. Wald, and a number of other women con-

nected with social work. I preserved a number of
the reports made by the committee. They ran as
follows:

"Mary ——, a Roumanian, lived in Chicago. Had
gone to call on an uncle; had been arrested in his
tenement; had been tried by an inspector who could
not speak her language. She had not been represented by counsel, and in a few days had found herself at Ellis Island. Said that she had not been permitted to see her friends, that the inquiry had been
carried on in a language that she did not understand,
and that she did not know up to that time why she
was being sent back home."

"Sarah ——. Lived in St. Louis. Husband a
drunken painter who had failed to support her. She
had left home once or twice and gone back. She had
an infant baby and had been evicted from her apartment. She had been driven by despair and had
picked up a man on the street. The evidence confirmed her story. It was her only offense, so far as
the records showed."

"——, an Italian girl, had been married in Algeria
and brought to this country. Her husband had taken
her clothes away from her and had kept her in confinement. She had been forced by him to receive
men. She was arrested and brought to the island.
The husband had not been arrested."

"A Dutchman from Holland had a butcher business in Hoboken. Had left his wife in Holland eight
or ten years before without getting a divorce, or with
some irregularity in the divorce proceedings. Had
lived with a woman in Hoboken for a number of
years and had four children by her. They were living

as man and wife and apparently had the respect of the community. Inquiry disclosed the fact that a partner in the business, reading of the activity of the immigration authorities, had seen an opportunity to steal the business. He had filed a complaint and provided the evidence. The man, woman, and children had been arrested and were to be sent back to Holland."

"A stenographer from Knoxville, Tenn., had been seduced by her employer. He had grown tired of her and had advised the immigration authorities. She had been sent to Ellis Island."

There were more damaging cases than these, but the great majority of the women were casual offenders who would not have been arrested under ordinary circumstances. In many instances their misfortunes were the result of ignorance, almost always of poverty.

The committee studied these cases, not as the inspector had done, seeking to find some technical guilt, but to understand the circumstances, to weigh character and consider the possibilities of finding work either temporarily or until the end of the war. Their work was like that of the police courts, where a probational system has been introduced, or the marital relations courts which have been established in many cities.

With this report in my possession I proposed to the Secretary of Labor that casual offenders whose offense did not involve the commission of a crime should be paroled. Responsible persons or organizations would report on their conduct until they could be deported at the close of the war. The plan was approved, partly because of its humanity and partly because it was becoming impossible to carry on the work of the island in its crowded condition. Hundreds of men and women were paroled. They reported to me in person or through the parole officer, and careful records were kept of their behavior. The great majority of them made good. Some of them married. Before leaving the island I asked for a report of these cases from the legal department, and was advised that not more than a dozen had been rearrested, and that the vast majority were responding to the consideration that had been shown them.

Hysteria over the immoral alien was followed by a two-year panic over the "Hun." Again inspectors, particularly civilian secret-service agents, were given carte blanche to make arrests on suspicion. Again Ellis Island was turned into a prison, and I had to protect men and women from a hue and cry that was but little concerned over guilt or innocence. During these years thousands of Germans, Austrians, and Hungarians were taken without trial from their homes and brought to Ellis Island. Nearly two thousand officers and seamen from sequestered German ships were placed in my care. Many of them had married American wives. They conducted themselves decently and well. They were obedient to discipline. They accepted the situation and they gave practically no trouble. They were typical of the alien enemies the country over that were arrested under the hysteria that was organized and developed into a hate that lingers on to this day.

Again I had either to drift with the tide or assume the burden of seeing that as little injustice as possible was done. I realized that under war conditions convincing evidence could not be demanded. I accepted that fact, but not the assumption that "the Hun should be put against the wall and shot." From our entrance into the war until after the armistice my life was a nightmare. My telephone rang constantly with inquiries from persons seeking news of husbands and fathers who had been arrested. On my return home in the evening I would often find awaiting me women in a state of nervous collapse whose husbands had mysteriously disappeared, and who feared that they had been done away with. I furnished them with such information as was possible. On the island I had to stand between the official insistence that the German should be treated as a criminal and the admitted fact that the great majority of them had been arrested by persons with little concern about their innocence or guilt and with but little if any evidence to support the detention.

Within a short time I was branded as pro-German. I had to war with the local staff to secure decent treatment for the aliens, and with the army of secret-service agents to prevent the island from being filled with persons against whom some one or other had filed a suspicious inquiry.

It is a marvellous tribute to the millions of Germans, Austrians, and Hungarians in this country that, despite the injustices to which they were subjected and the espionage under which they lived, scarcely an Americanized alien of these races was found guilty of any act of disloyalty of which the entire German-American population was suspected or accused.

The final outbreak of hysteria was directed against the "Reds" the winter of 1918–19. It started in the State of Washington in the lumber camps, and was directed against members of the I. W. W. organization which had superseded the more conservative craft unions affiliated with the American Federation of Labor. There was a concerted determination on the part of employers to bring wages back to pre-war conditions and to break the power of organized labor. This movement against alien labor leaders had the support of the Department of Justice. Private detective agencies and strike-breakers acted with assurance that in any outrages they would be supported by the government itself. The press joined in the cry of "Red revolution," and frightened the country with scare head-lines of an army of organized terrorists who were determined to usher in revolution by force. The government borrowed the agent provocateur from old Russia; it turned loose innumerable private spies. For two years we were in a panic of fear over the Red revolutionists, anarchists, and enemies of the Republic who were said to be ready to overthrow the government.

For a third time I had to stand against the current. Men and women were herded into Ellis Island. They were brought under guards and in special trains with instructions to get them away from the country with as little delay as possible. Most of the aliens had been picked up in raids on labor headquarters; they had been given a drum-head trial by an inspector with no chance for defense; they were held incommunicado and often were not permitted to see either friends or attorneys, before being shipped to Ellis Island. In these proceedings the inspector who made the arrest was prosecutor, witness, judge, jailer, and executioner. He was clerk and interpreter as well. This was all the trial the alien could demand under the law. In many instances the inspector hoped that he would be put in charge of his victim for a trip to New York and possibly to Europe at the expense of the government. Backed by the press of his city and by the hue and cry of the pack, he had every inducement to find the alien guilty and arrange for his speedy deportation.

I was advised by the Commissioner-General to mind my own business and carry out orders, no matter what they might be. Yet such obvious injustice was being done that I could not sit quiet. Moreover, I was an appointee of the President, and felt that I owed responsibility to him whose words at least I was exemplifying in my actions. My word carried no weight with my superior officials, who were intoxicated with the prominence they enjoyed and the publicity which they received from the press. The bureaucratic organization at the island was happy in the punishing power which all jailers enjoy, and resented any interference on behalf of its victims. Members of Congress were swept from their moorings by an organized business propaganda, and demanded that I be dismissed because I refused to railroad aliens to boats made ready for their deportation. I took the position from which I would not be driven, that the alien should not be held incommunicado, and should enjoy the right of a writ of habeas corpus in the United States courts, which was the only semblance of legal proceedings open to him under the law.

In maintaining this position I had to quarrel with my superiors and the official force at the island. I faced a continuous barrage from members of Congress, from the press, from business organizations, and prosecuting attorneys. Yet day by day aliens, many of whom had been held in prison for months, came before the court; and the judge, after examining the testimony, unwillingly informed the immigration authorities that there was not a scintilla of evidence to support the arrest. For in deportation cases it is not necessary to provide a preponderance of testimony, or to convince the court of the justice of the charge; all that the government needs to support its case is a "scintilla" of evidence, which may be any kind of evidence at all. If there is a bit of evidence, no matter how negligible it may be, the order of deportation must be affirmed.

Again the pack was unleashed. No one took the trouble to ascertain the facts. The press carried stories to the effect that I had released hundreds of persons ordered deported. I had released aliens, but in each case I had been ordered to do so by the courts or the bureau. I had observed the law when organized hysteria demanded that it be swept aside. I had seen to it that men and women enjoyed their legal rights, but evidently this was the worst offense I could have committed. A congressional committee came to Ellis Island and held protracted hearings. It listened to disaffected officials, it created scare head-lines for the press, it did everything in its power to convince the country that we were on the verge of a nation-wide revolution, of which the most hard-boiled inspectors sent out by the bureau had reported they could not find a trace. When I went to the hearings and demanded the right to be present, to cross-examine witnesses and see the records, when I demanded that I be put on the witness-stand myself, the committee ordered the sergeant-at-arms to eject me from the rooms.

As I look back over these years, my outstanding memories are not of the immigrant. They are rather of my own people. Things that were done forced one almost to despair of the mind, to distrust the political state. Shreds were left of our courage, our reverence. The Department of Justice, the Department of Labor, and Congress not only failed to protest against hysteria, they encouraged these excesses; the state not only abandoned the liberty which it should have protected, it lent itself to the stamping out of individualism and freedom. It used the agent provocateur, it permitted private agencies to usurp government powers, turned over the administration of justice to detective agencies, card-indexed liberals and progressives. It became frankly an agency of employing and business interests at a time when humanity—the masses, the poor—were making the supreme sacrifice of their lives.

I had fondly imagined that we prized individual liberty; I had believed that to Anglo-Saxons human rights were sacred and they would be protected at any cost.

Latin peoples might be temperamental, given to hysteria; but we were hard-headed, we stood for individuality. But I found that we were lawless, emotional, given to mob action. We cared little for freedom of conscience, for the rights of men to their opinions. Government was a convenience of business. Discussion of war profiteers was not to be permitted. The Department of Justice lent itself to the suppression of those who felt that war should involve equal sacrifice. Civil liberties were under the ban. Their subversion was not, however, an isolated thing; it was an incident in the ascendancy of business privileges and profits acquired during the war—an ascendancy that could not bear scrutiny or brook the free discussion which is the only safe basis of orderly popular government.

CHAPTER XXVIII

LIBERALS AND THE WAR

I DO not know why I suffered so much from this particular hysteria and the cruelties incident to it. It was partly traceable to the treatment I had personally received, partly to an instinctive love of liberty and the rights of individuals to their opinions. These rights were essentially Anglo-Saxon rights. I assumed they were prized by everybody. But I think it was the indignities suffered by friends that aroused me most. People came to me from all over the country, I received hundreds of letters, the telephone at my office and in my home was in constant use by people appealing for help or information as to their friends. All of them were seeking a refuge which could only be found in a government official. Few people know of the state of terror that prevailed during these years, few would believe the extent to which private hates and prejudices were permitted to usurp government powers. It was quite apparent that the alleged offenses for which people were being persecuted were not the real offenses. The prosecution was directed against liberals, radicals, persons who had been identified with municipal-ownership fights, with labor movements, with forums, with liberal papers which were under the ban. Many of them were young people, many were college men and women.

Members of the group whom I had known so intimately as director of the People's Institute, and whom I had felt were such promising evidence of the new movement that was rising, were in constant trouble. Many of them were intimate friends. They

278

in turn had friends. I was an official prop to which they clung. They wanted protection, wanted me to take their cases to the President.

I was part of this liberal movement. To me it was a renaissance of America rising from the orgy of commercialism. And I could not reconcile myself to its destruction, to its voice being stilled, its integrity assailed, its patriotism questioned, especially by a war that promised to give these democratic ideals to the world. I saw this youth movement driven under cover; like children when first punished, it did not understand. It was subjected to strain, to espionage; it found itself oppressed by a government that it loved far more fervently than did the secret agents that spied upon it. These young liberals felt that they had done no wrong, so far as America was concerned they would do no wrong. Some of them lived with indictments hanging over them; all felt a sentence suspended over their enthusiasms, their beliefs, their innermost thoughts. They had stood for variety, for individuality, for freedom. They discovered a political state that seemed to hate these things; it wanted a servile society, a society that accepted authority, so long as it was respectable authority, without protest.

The crushing of this movement and the men responsible for it made me hate in a way that was new to me. I hated the Department of Justice, the ignorant secret-service men who had been intrusted with man-hunting powers; I hated the new state that had arisen, hated its brutalities, its ignorance, its unpatriotic patriotism, that made profit from our sacrifices and used its power to suppress criticism of its acts. I hated the suggestion of disloyalty of myself and my friends; suggestions that were directed against liberals, never against profiteers. I wanted to protest against the destruction of *my* government, *my* democracy, *my* America. I hated the new mani-

festation of power far more than I had hated the
spoilsmen, the ward heeler, the politicians, or even
the corruptionists who had destroyed my hope of
democracy in Cleveland. I had cherished a free city,
but I cherished a free people more.

I did not question but that war necessitated the
subordination of the individual to the state, but felt
that we could have waged war quite as successfully
if we had taken a stand like that taken in England,
where men were allowed greater freedom of opinion.
In England those who questioned were respected in
their right to question. I prized liberty at home
more than I feared danger from abroad, and felt that
our own citizens could be safeguarded without our
liberties being destroyed.

And I was officially part of the system. I was part
of this government, very much a part, for I was the
custodian of hundreds of persons whom I knew to
be innocent. That I was shielding them as individuals did not satisfy that part of me that wanted to
protest against the wrongs that were being done.
This was the personal problem that weighed most
heavily on my mind. I was fighting a battle new to
me—a moral battle that went to the bottom of things.
In Cleveland I had been merely a lieutenant; now I
had to act for myself. Previous problems had been
easy; this involved the pragmatic one of sticking by
my job and doing what I could to protect people. I
had rarely lost a night's sleep in my life; now I could
not sleep. And I began to be afraid. The telephone
became to me an evil thing. I felt a sense of oppres-
sion in that I was not doing what the crowd demanded; the fact that I was aiding men and women
in their legal rights in an orderly way gave me little
comfort.

For months I lived in a state of fear. I feared
something impending, something mysterious that

hung over me. I had secret-service men in my employ; I had come in contact with them from other departments, I knew their ability, their ruthlessness; worse than that, I knew their honest patriotism, that was far more to be feared than dishonesty. There were men from private detective agencies who had been taken into the government service. They did as they were told, manufactured evidence, clubbed men, terrorized them by third-degree methods. A congressman from New York came to me and said that the Rules Committee of the House was framing up charges against me. They were false, but he saw no reason for opposing them. "I had never done anything for him," he said. And the charges were serious. I brooded over these fears, over the hostility of the bureau, of the island, of the press. I had never encountered anything like it before.

One evening in Washington, after the Armistice but when the Red panic was at its height, I dined with Doctor R——, a distinguished Johns Hopkins diagnostician and psychiatrist. We had known one another for some time. Over the dinner he said: "Howe, you're sick. I wonder if you know it."

I protested sound health.

"No," he replied, "you're sick. There are a lot of liberals like you. Some became war-mad and deserted their groups; some stuck by their convictions and were punished; others tried to adjust themselves as best they could to the war. There's only one way you can straighten yourself out; blurt out what you have in your mind. Say what you think about the things that bother you. You have been living through a conflict that can only be gotten rid of through the confessional. Make an opportunity to get it all out of your system."

As I thought over Doctor R——'s advice it gave me comfort. A few evenings later, dining with a group of war officials at the Cosmos Club in Washington, I acted on it. Some reference was made to the war.

"Now that it's over," I said, "suppose we all tell the truth. Every one of us has done something he is ashamed of. We have violated our principles, done cruel things. All of us have been lying in some way or other. And many of us have been cowards."

There was protest from the table. My auditors had no part nor lot in my guilt. They had no nefarious estimate of themselves. But I felt better, and the next day I repeated the performance. I kept on telling the same story whenever the occasion offered.

Doctor R——'s diagnosis was correct. Confession had been good for me. My fears began to disappear. I recovered health when I recovered honesty—not entirely, for I could not erase from my mind the things I had done; the fine edge of courage was dulled. Accusations of self against self had sunk deep during those years and created a sense of shame. The fears that had possessed me would not be wholly exorcised. Even now I feel that, should the occasion arise, they would return and possess me, even though their political significance has entirely disappeared.

My attitude toward the state was changed as a result of these experiences. I have never been able to bring it back. I became distrustful of the state. It seemed to want to hurt people; it showed no concern for innocence; it aggrandized itself and protected its power by unscrupulous means. It was not my America, it was something else. And I think I lost interest in it, just as did thousands of other persons, whose love of country was questioned, and who were turned from love into fear of the state and all that it signified. Possibly the falling off in the number of voters, numbered by millions, is in some way related to this disillusionment, this fear of the state which came into existence during these hysterical years.

CHAPTER XXIX

PARIS AND THE WORLD

MY contacts with the President during the war had mainly to do with the prosecution of liberals, who had delayed their approval of his war declarations, assuming as a matter of course the right to question. His acquiescence in the suppression of opposing opinions was incomprehensible to me, as was his apparent approval of private agencies identified with the Department of Justice, and his assent to the indiscriminate inhumanity that fell under my notice at Ellis Island. Nor could I understand the appointment to positions of high trust of the kind of men whom he had vehemently denounced in his "New Freedom"; his turning departmental activities over to business men of the exploiting Wall Street type, who were even, in many instances, his known enemies.

It was difficult to see him on such questions. Tumulty guarded his door vigilantly. The President had no time; he had appointments from morning until night, five minutes for this man, three for that—he would show me the day's schedule. When the subject was an open one and I was given a place on the crowded list, Mr. Wilson received me, as he did other men, attentively, apparently interested in my statement. He was scrupulously attired, trim and erect, even debonair—every inch the gentlemanly President. And master of every subject. He would listen for a moment, then take up the matter, state it in a few phrases better than I had done—and treat the interview as ended. By taking the initiative he protected himself from divergent views, from discussion

of questions that he had settled. Congressmen said
that they had the same experience of his anticipating
their words, knowing more of the subject than they
did, and disposing of opposition by a fluency and in-
cisiveness and directness that left them floundering.
I would go away with a feeling that there was nothing more to be said; the subject was closed, it could
not be debated. But I was confused and unconvinced
by this new aspect of the President, aware that I had
come up against a stone wall; he understood the cases
of arrested liberals, but he seemed determined that
there should be no questioning of his will. I felt that
he was eager for the punishment of men who differed
from him, that there was something vindictive in his
eyes as he spoke. And I could not understand his
apparent hatred of men who persisted in their belief
in his own liberal opinions of 1916. At the same time
he wrote me letters breathing his old belief in freedom. That was the Woodrow Wilson that I knew,
my model of the university statesman; the new intolerant one was a product of the war.

Early in the war I wrote to the President about the
Near East. I was intensely interested in that part of
the world which began with Constantinople and ended with Persia, including Egypt, Syria, Mesopotamia,
and the control of the Mediterranean. I felt that
here was the origin of the war, here was danger to the
British Empire, to France, and to the allied cause.
If Germany could split the Allies as she planned to
do in the Near East, the British Empire would be
destroyed. My Anglo-Saxon instincts were strong
enough to revolt at this. I did not want Germany to
take the place of England and America in their dom-
inance of the world. I did not believe the war propaganda, did not accept the singleness of German
guilt. Still something within me was aroused at the
thought of German ascendancy in the world. The

thought of America seemed to be fixed on the western front; our minds were being filled with hatred and desire for revenge. Vistas of permanent security and peace that the President's eloquence painted were unrealizable, to my mind, unless the problems of the Near East were taken into account. Here was the tinder-box of Europe, the source of repeated modern wars. Over its control Russia, England, and France had warred and negotiated from the time of Napoleon. The Kaiser had bent his energies to the control of Turkey, Asia Minor, and the eastern Mediterranean, with the object of splitting the Franco-Russian Alliance and breaking up the British Empire through outposts menacing the Suez Canal and the Indian Ocean. This was the military objective of the Bagdad Railway and the German *Drang nach Osten*.

I was full of the subject and urged it repeatedly on President Wilson's attention, in long letters to which his replies were far more satisfactory than any talks I ever had with him. Years before, when I was practising law in Cleveland, I had been attorney for a Cleveland firm that installed water-tight doors and compartments operated from the bridge on battleships. I had been to England, France, and Germany to negotiate the sale of patents to munition-makers. Our government had spent millions of dollars in installing the devices on battleships. Yet neither the government, the United States naval commander who had perfected them, nor the directors of the company, of whom I was one, saw any impropriety in selling the installations to other countries with whom we might later be at war. This was the practice of munition-makers. Improvements in machines for killing people were disclosed to friend and foe alike.

On this somewhat less than praiseworthy mission some five years before I had renewed acquaintance in Germany with Wilhelm Muehlon, an intimate friend of my student days at the University of Munich. Then handsome and popular, renowned as a duellist, leader of his university corps, he had since risen rapidly in the Foreign Office, and was at the time of my visit one of the directors of the firm of Krupp. In conference with him and his associates, I heard reference to the Bagdad Railway, to the conquest of the Near East, and the vast resources of Asiatic Turkey, the future German hinterland, where cotton was to be grown to free German industry from America and England, harbors were to be built, and a great market developed for German wares. I heard references to the military significance of the Bagdad Railway. It was to menace the British Empire in Egypt, Persia, and Mesopotamia; to open India, Australia, and the Far East to easy conquest.

In Paris, negotiating with French munition interests, I heard similar discussions. The Bagdad Railway was in the diplomatic mind of Europe. France and England were endeavoring to control it, or frustrate its completion. It was an acute international problem for twenty years prior to the war.

From this time on the problems presented by the Near East were never erased from my mind. I read widely on the subject; followed the Morocco controversy; familiarized myself with British imperialism and the Mediterranean's strategic importance to the empire for food, for raw materials, and for free contact with Australia, India, and China. In 1915 I wrote *Why War?*, a study of economic imperialism, in which I emphasized the importance of the Mediterranean and the menace of German power in the Near East. I had never forgotten my talks in Germany or the explosions of hatred of German officers over British blocking of the Bagdad Railway at Koweit.

In correspondence with the President I urged on him my conviction of the economic causes of the war; that it was not the Kaiser, nor the Czar, but imperialistic adventurers who had driven their countries into conflict. Secret diplomacy, the conflict of bankers, the activity of munition-makers, exploiters, and concessionaires in the Mediterranean, in Morocco, in south and central Africa, had brought on the cataclysm; glacial-like aggregations of capital and credit were responsible for the war. His vision of peace was only possible with imperialism ended and the world freed from the struggle over the control of backward countries, embroiling now one country, now another. Permanent peace meant that Gibraltar, the Suez Canal, and the Dardanelles should be internationalized; the Bagdad Railway completed by an international consortium, so that Asiatic Turkey might again become as in ancient days a great granary and storehouse of wheat and cotton. I pictured the territory of the old Roman Empire freed from imperialism and developed by international arrangement, with Constantinople a free port and great cosmopolis, serving as the distributing centre of three continents.

I pictured a renaissance of this part of the world, a renaissance in industry, in culture, and in art that would make it again the centre of a civilization of its own.

When the armistice was signed I felt that the international millennium was at hand. The President's idealism had carried the world; his Fourteen Points had been accepted; armies were to be disbanded, armaments scrapped, imperialism ended. Self-determination was to be extended to all peoples, hates were to be assuaged, and peace to reign.

I was ready to embrace a league of nations, even a league to enforce peace. Any international arrangement that would prevent war was worth while. I believed that the negotiators at Paris wanted peace and were willing to make any sacrifices for it; that war was going to be forever ended on the earth.

Such facts as did not fit in with my enthusiastic vision, I suppressed. I found an explanation for wrongs that had been done at home in the end to be attained. America had almost lost her own liberties —that was part of our sacrifice. Surely the President had covenanted for his ideals in exchange for what we had lost. His suppression of liberalism still raised unsatisfied questioning, but of a new dispensation for the world I did not permit myself to doubt. The men in Europe would be of one mind with him; war had all but destroyed civilization, war should not happen again. I was captivated by the President's eloquence and thoroughly believed in his programme. And I wanted to have a part in it; a share in the settlement of the Near Eastern problems. I wanted to be around when the hand of the Western world should be lifted from the peoples of the Near East, the glories of whose ancient civilization I dreamed of seeing restored.

George Creel, of the Committee on Public Information, was, besides Tumulty, the one man who had easy access to the President. We had been friends for years. He was devoted to men whom he liked. He had been devoted to Sam Jones and Brand Whitlock and was passionate in his affection for President Wilson. The Committee on Public Information was his creation; it was to serve as a substitute for censorship, and as such he had proposed it to the President, protesting that he wanted no salary; he wanted only to work intimately and closely with his chief. He organized a propaganda agency, and was largely responsible for Wilson's prestige in the popular mind in Europe. For some reason that

I never understood, Creel's appointment aroused the newspapers; they never quite forgave it. Republican senators took a cruel delight in attacking him, possibly as an indirect attack on the President. Creel in turn hated the President's enemies and was brilliantly profane in excoriating them, particularly Senator Lodge. Mr. Wilson appreciated his devotion and enjoyed, I think, the profane denunciations in which he could not indulge himself.

Creel knew about my interest in the Near East and my pre-war knowledge of Germany. I had called his attention one day to a despatch that I had read in the New York *World*, saying that Doctor Wilhelm Muehlon, one of the directors of Krupp's, had resigned as a protest against Germany's declaration of war. I told him about Muehlon, and suggested that the committee try to secure from him a more detailed statement in regard to Germany's entrance into the war. Later I read with eager interest the series of signed articles that came from my friend from Switzerland. I had wondered about him. As a student he had disliked Prussia and the Junkers, had been emotional and lovable, a poet, philosopher, individualistic radical. The brief visit that had fixed the Near East indelibly in my mind had not revealed his change to me. I had been in the munitions game myself at that time. Had his business connections hardened him? Had he become an apologist of German dreams of conquest? Was he able to endure the clanging militarism of the war lords with whom he lived? The articles that George Creel got from him answered my questions. A few weeks before the war broke, Muehlon had gone to Berlin to arrange for a large loan for Krupp from the Deutsche Bank. Doctor Hellferich, director of the Deutsche Bank and one of Germany's most powerful financiers, said that the loan could not be extended. He gave as the reason for so extraordinary a refusal. war. War was inevitable.

Muehlon returned to Essen, aghast at the conflagration which he foresaw. "The war cannot be localized," he said to Krupp. "Russia, France, England, and Italy will come in. It is too terrible to think of."

"You should not have been told anything about it," was Krupp's reply. "Only three men besides the Kaiser know about the war."

George Creel urged on the President an unofficial appointment that would enable me to go to the Peace Conference. One day he said to me: "The President wants you to go to Paris." There was something more about passport, funds, an assignment to be made when I should arrive. It was not very clear, but it meant definitely to me an opportunity to press my ideas about the Mediterranean. That was what I wanted.

The American mission carried with it vanloads of reports. Colonel House had a group of experts gathered from the universities, many of whom had worked for two years on special details. Each was convinced of the supreme importance of his own assignment. The Hôtel Crillon housed this group, military attachés and others. The first struggle of American experts in Paris was not over establishing peace but over room assignments. Men of social significance, with fine family names, had apparently been given the best quarters; others with important duties were crowded into mansard rooms. Men of no importance had suites with private baths. The Hotel Crillon became a little village, in which each person compared his accommodations with another's and was incensed at discrimination. Questions of personal importance took precedence of idealistic visions.

I went with Lincoln Steffens, whose assignment

also came from the President, to the old Hotel Chatham. Together we spent much of our time in a splendid palace on the Champs Elysées, placed by the French Government at the disposal of newspaper men. Here we made acquaintances, dined, and talked over events with men of all nations. They were mostly cynical, many of them had been through the war; they knew more than the American mission about the political psychology of Europe and the methods of the men told off to make peace. Most of the Americans represented papers hostile to President Wilson.

Shortly after my arrival, Colonel House sent for me and said that the President planned to send a mission to Syria to ascertain the wishes of the Syrians themselves in regard to a mandatory. He desired me to familiarize myself with all the treaties and engagements of the allied powers relating to the Near East, and to hold myself in readiness to leave for Syria at a moment's notice. Doctor Barton, of the Armenian Relief Fund, was to be my associate on the mission.

The assignment called for much preliminary work. I reread the pre-war investigations of the Germans on the Near East. The secret treaties were placed at my disposal by Colonel House and the English authorities, who seemingly approved of the mission. There was no help to be had from the French, who did not want the inquiry made. These secret treaties, like others, had been kept from President Wilson; it was claimed he knew nothing about them until his arrival. They furnished astounding revelations. Our allies, like Germany, scrapped treaties—not with traditional enemies, but solemn agreements with friends and with each other. The documents showed that England and France had pleaded with the King of the Hedjas to throw the Arab forces in with the allied cause, and drive the Turks from Arabia. The Arabs were promised their freedom in exchange; England would get out of Mesopotamia, France would get out of Syria; the whole of Arabia was to be divided into three parts, to be ruled by the three sons of the King of the Hedjas—one of whom, Emir Feisal, was in Paris. Dignified, meditative, richly turbaned, he was there to see that the compact was lived up to. But France and England were unwilling to give up this rich territory. Scarcely was the ink dry on their compact with the Arabs when they negotiated with each other the secret Sykes-Picot Treaty, under whose terms England was to retain Mesopotamia, France was to keep Syria, and Russia take Armenia. Then the Jews asked for Palestine, and Balfour, the gentleman-statesman, agreed on behalf of England that they should have it, although Palestine had already been promised to the Arabs and given to the French. And England, I soon found, was reluctant to hand over Syria to France.

The two most picturesque personages in Paris were Prince Emir Feisal and Colonel Thomas Lawrence. Feisal was one of three sons of the King of Hedjas. Turbaned, impassive, he sat in the great hall of the Quai d'Orsay with the conventional, frock-coated representatives of the powers. Occasionally he said something, usually cryptic, that was flashed among the newspaper men at the Crillon. Among his sayings were:

"When President Wilson spoke about self-determination for peoples, a smile went through all Arabia."

"If Syria is given to France. the Arabs will drive them into the sea."

"Backward peoples are apparently peoples with oil, gold, natural resources, but no guns to protect them."

"The British Government has crowned my father the 'King of the Hedjas.' There is no dignity, no title, no honor that could be added to that of 'Sherif of Mecca.' "

Feisal was accompanied by Colonel Thomas Lawrence. He too provided copy for the press, such copy as it was possible to extract from this reticent friend and protector of the Sherif of Mecca. Colonel Lawrence seemed but a handsome boy. He inspired spontaneous affection from every one who came in contact with him. I have seen Mr. Arthur Balfour approach him at the Hotel Majestic as a father might approach a son.

Lawrence was an Oxford man. After graduation he disappeared in the Arabian desert, where he lived with the Bedouin tribes, learned their language, acquired their culture, and understood their wants. He was termed "The Uncrowned King of the Arabs." When things were going badly with the British in Arabia, Lawrence was sought for by General Allenby, and found in the library in Alexandria. He was made a colonel in the British army, he aided in organizing the Arabian forces, and commanded a machine-gun battalion against the Turks in the desert fighting from Egypt up along the Palestine coast.

It helped one to understand British imperialism to talk with Colonel Lawrence, to see him in his room out beyond the Arc de Triomphe, surrounded by an Arabian ménage. There was repose, detachment, apparent indifference to the rushing to and fro of hundreds of little people planning endless conferences, the settlement of the world's troubles. At the door of his apartment was a Senegalese negro. His face was slashed from personal combat. Prince Feisal was attended by a black slave whom he had carried wounded from the desert on the back of his camel.

Was Lawrence guarding Arabia for the British?

Was he one of the thousands of young men in the British foreign office who forget themselves to forward Britain's empire and protect her outposts from German or Russian penetration? Lawrence gave no hint. Neglectful of honors, indifferent to everything suggestive of personal aggrandizement, he seemed as detached from the Occidental world as was Feisal himself. He spoke as frankly about Britain as he did about the French. The Arabs had a culture of their own. They intended to keep it. He knew the Occident, knew its unworthiness, knew that he would have to fight for the things that had been promised his Arab friends by the Allies to bring them into the war. He and Feisal gave one a sense of the Near East, of its age, its sense of security, its apartness. Arabia had been Arabia for thousands of years. Empires had come and gone, conquerors had fought in turn for its possession. It had been the battle ground of millions; it had known almost every ambitious conqueror from Darius to the Kaiser. Yet Arabia remained Arabia; her customs, her culture, her habits were as they had been thousands of years ago.

To Feisal, and in a sense to Lawrence as well, the Paris Peace Conference was but a moment in a history that went back to the very origin of man.

Colonel Lawrence seemed to share my opinion of allied treachery. He even admitted my suggestion that England coveted Syria or wanted America to take it as a mandate. French occupation of Syria meant control of the entrance to Mesopotamia. Syria menaced the Island of Cyprus and British control of the Suez Canal. England did not want France in Syria. She wanted it herself.

My vision of a free world was clouding. Self-determination for peoples began to ring like an empty phrase. Still I believed that President Wilson had guaranties that would permit him to turn a trick at the proper time and restore the situation. I would not believe that we were going back to the old order; would not credit what I saw about me.

One evening a number of young Englishmen visited me at the Hotel Chatham. They were Oxford and Cambridge men, brilliant, friendly, amiable. A few days later I was invited to breakfast with them. Arriving, I found that I was at the house of Lloyd George; that Philip Kerr, my host, was Lloyd George's secretary. He and his associates, Lionel Curtis, Arnold Toynbee, and others, were known as "Lord Milner's men." They were editors of the periodical known as *The Round Table,* and had organized an imperial conference in each of the British colonies. We talked about the Near East. They, too, were interested in the subject. I took it for granted that they were interested in self-determination for peoples; that they understood, as a matter of course, the crimes committed by imperialistic adventurers in Egypt, Persia, Africa. I talked about my discoveries of conflicting treaties, about the activities of British oil interests in Mesopotamia and Persia. I warmed to the theme of financial imperialism and the necessity of being rid of imperialistic exploiters in order to have permanent peace. I felt that they would help in solving the Near Eastern problem.

It astounded me to find that they scarcely knew the meaning of the words "economic imperialism." Imperialism was not economic, it was a white man's burden. A sacred trust, undertaken for the well-being of peoples unfitted for self-government. The war was in no way related to the conflict of financial interests. Unfortunate things were done sometimes by business bounders—true—but they did not influence the Foreign Office. The flag followed the investor, perhaps, but only because the investor was a British citizen who was sacred wherever he ventured. This imperialism, which was not imperialism, must be carried to the end. It must be carried by Anglo-Saxons, and England was no longer able to carry it alone. She had lost much of her best blood in the trenches; Oxford and Cambridge, which recruited the Foreign Office, had been depleted of a generation of talent. The only country which could be trusted to share the white man's burden was America; America must help. She must carry it in Armenia. There was the crux of that sociable morning talk, as of others. America should take the mandate over Armenia. Propaganda to that end should take root in my mind and be carried back to the President.

"But," I parried, "Armenia is a danger-spot. It is a buffer between Europe and Asia. The power that holds Armenia may have to defend the British Empire in Mesopotamia, Persia, and India—defend it against Turkey, central Europe, certainly against revolutionary Russia. If we should take Armenia we would need a huge military and naval force; we might be embroiled with every power in Europe; certainly we would be embroiled with the Turks and Arabs.

"It looks to me," I ended, "as if America is to be asked to carry the bag; to police Europe and remove from England and France the burden of protecting imperialistic ventures. You are asking us to assume the biggest, most dangerous, and costliest job of all."

The young men admitted the danger. They felt, as all Englishmen whom I met seemed to feel, that America owed a debt to England, much as did Canada, Australia, and other colonies. We ought to be proud to pay our debt to the empire. That America was a colonial dependence, not yet a sovereign nation, seemed to be their fixed idea.

I had seen British university men of this type at

Ellis Island, had met them in Washington and at the clubs in New York. But I understood them better in Paris. The civil service of which they are a part is one of the marvellous things about England. Made up of Oxford and Cambridge men who enter the Foreign Office after the hardest kind of competitive examinations, it forms them into servants devoted, like Jesuits, to the empire. Before the war these men, especially the Lord Milner group, had gone to Canada, Australia, and South Africa. They gave up home, companionship, and everything to which they had been accustomed; they often lived isolated lives in distant places of the world. They mobilized opinion for imperialistic ends. Conservatives or Liberals, the empire was their passion. It was to be served, strengthened, carried on. Where the empire was in question they were impervious to facts, blind to obvious evils, untouched by argument. As administrators they were intelligent and kindly—conceded nothing to self-government, nothing to the aspirations of other people for liberty. England and the empire were one; British citizenship a distinction, like Roman citizenship; to question the empire was to question centuries of sacrifice, the renown of England's most distinguished men. This extraordinarily efficient organization knew everything except the suppressed wants of subject peoples; granted everything to subject peoples except political liberty. It was not willing to dignify by discussion the questionings of others as to the sanctity of England's imperial trust.

As I talked with these young men I reflected on the nature of English gentlemen and Oxford scholars—their unwillingness, perfected by long practice into inability, to recognize issues that touched their economic interests. India, Egypt, Africa, Mesopotamia provided careers for the younger sons of the aristocracy; England was crowded, trade undesirable, the service of the state was their opportunity. To end imperialism was to end jobs, opportunities for preferment. It was like suggesting abolishing the church to the clergy, the army to the military caste, the navy to marines. Men receive unwillingly ideas that destroy a livelihood; and vocal England is a unit in the protection of its privileged sons—they would be left to starve if the colonial service were ended, they would have to compromise their dignity in trade or emigrate as workers.

Another interest touched them in a way they refused to see. England exploited her dependencies; billions of pounds were invested in backward countries, in bonds, in oil, in diamond and gold mines, in rubber plantations. The landed aristocracy was the investing class. It kept aloof from things economic at home; business was vulgar, outside of recognized interests. The bombardment of Alexandria or the Boer War was not in any admissible way related to loans, to gold and diamond-mine owners. Yet when the British purse was touched, the investing class felt the hurt. Then the press spoke, the Foreign Office responded, Britain bristled, gunboats were despatched; the cry was that the rights of British citizens were in danger. In reality British pounds sterling were affected. Economic reasons for imperialism were consistently ignored. Even the Labor Party had a confused veneration for the empire, a veneration springing from tradition. Oxford young men wanted our dough-boys to do their policing, to help protect economic interests that they dignified as sacred. That was the objective of the Armenian drive; America's duty was always being held before my eyes.

Representatives of French interests talked no bunk. They were always realistic. They were opposed to our mission to Syria. Syria was French in influence; France claimed it from the time of the Crusades. She had contracts with the British for exclusive control that were exhausting to Syria. France had the prior right to own and exploit everything. Every business concession had first to be offered to her before it could be offered to others. I talked with men from the Sorbonne, with military men and experts. They saw nothing wrong in the contracts, even though the Syrians had not been consulted. France must take and keep all that she could get. She used her possessions for business exploitation—true; as recruiting-grounds for military power—it was obvious. I recalled her exploitation of Algiers and Tunis, the conquest of Morocco by French bankers, and inquired about the Sykes-Picot Treaty. The French shrugged their shoulders. Great Britain had gotten her territory; France would take hers. The only regret was that Great Britain had the most valuable spots. The French treated the blacks with consideration—they were needed for the protection of the republic, and their land and markets were needed for French business. The French point of view was straightforward. It embodied complete historical realism. France could only protect herself by force. President Wilson was a dreamer, his ideals were foolish or worse. France would prepare in every possible way for war that was inevitable; imperialist possessions where black troops were recruited was one important way.

About the Turks, whom the Allies had promised to drive into Asia, the French were equally succinct:

"They owe us money," was their summary of the Turkish question—"huge debts contracted before the war. If we drive out the Turks and take Constantinople, there will be no Turks left to pay our debts. The Turks must keep Constantinople."

England's attitude was that Constantinople must remain British to save it from Russia. Turks were better than Russians in that debated city, better than the French. The Greeks should be invited in to help strengthen British power.

Allied opinion about the Bagdad Railway, which I had visualized as a great international highway to open up a rich storehouse of lands, was that it should be left to rust. It had done enough damage already; completed, it would disturb the balance of power. What would happen to British shipping interests if the freight of Europe travelled by rail? What would happen to the Suez Canal, the majority of whose shares were held by the British?

Only Emir Feisal, the Arabs, and Colonel Lawrence showed any interest in my vision of a Near East relieved from exploitation. And I was not sure sometimes of Colonel Lawrence. Was he also possibly a part of England's mysteriously efficient civil service? The Arabs wanted their land and their culture. If there must be a mandate they would prefer an American one; failing that, British. Their estimate of France in Syria was: "Better a Turkish hell than a French heaven."

At the suggestion of Colonel House I started for Syria, with instructions to pick up my associate, Doctor Barton, at Rome. The Rome express was packed; men stood in the unheated corridors for thirty-six hours. Doctor Barton was not in Rome; possibly he had gone on to Brindisi. I pushed on to Brindisi, there to take a destroyer for Constantinople, from which point we were to be taken to Syria. In Brindisi the hotels were crowded to the last bed. It was bitter cold and raining. Troops of every nationality and every color swarmed the streets, drunk and sober. I had a large sum of money on my person given me by the State Department.

An Italian cab-driver undertook a search for a bed, and finally stopped at a dark alleyway, of which every Italian city has so many, and dove into the unlighted passage. I followed, and finally came to a halt in a wine-room filled with drunken sailors. The driver explained that I wanted a room, and the host took my bags and started up a series of dirty stairs to the top of the tenement. He threw open a door and motioned to a double bed, already occupied by a rough-looking customer, who might have been of any color or nationality. There were a dozen men in the room and more to come. I retreated and caught my Jehu before he had gotten away. It was nightfall before I found a bed. Wet and cold I crawled into it.

My dreams that night of a free Mediterranean, renewing its glories under the protection of an allied consortium, were confused with drunken sailors, with dark-skinned murderers, with filthy wine-rooms and bitter, inhospitable weather. Alternating with chills and fever, the Arabs, French, or English could have Syria and the Syrians for all of me. If the Lord's chosen people wanted Palestine, they could take it for themselves.

Unable to trace Doctor Barton, with the French hostile to the mission and in control of Syria; convinced that America was wanted in the Near East only to pull the chestnuts out of the fire for England and assume responsibilities that would embroil us forever in European affairs, I returned to Paris to lay the situation before Colonel House. A one-man effort under any circumstances would be of little value; if moral effect were desired it should be on a more imposing scale. If such a mission were sent, it should have power to get the information desired from the people themselves. A well-organized commission was later created, with Charles R. Crane as its chairman. It made an exhaustive study and valuable report which conformed in the main to my own opinions.

But America's gesture to the Syrians had no influence on the Peace Conference. As elsewhere, lands and peoples had been disposed of while the war was in progress. The Sykes-Picot Treaty had partitioned the Near East. In the partition the Arabs got nothing.

France took Syria, England Mesopotamia. Palestine went to the Jews. The Arabs had driven back the Turks and had perhaps saved the British Empire. Their sacrifices were ignored; agreements were thrown to the winds and betraying friends took possession of their ancient towns and countryside. The Arabs rebelled; their rebellion was crushed by the same friends with aeroplanes and machine-guns. Emir Feisal, son of the desert, was exiled to Switzerland. A free Mediterranean was the idlest of dreams.

One by one other men despaired. Lincoln Steffens was interested in Russia; President Wilson had spoken generously of Russia's right to have revolutions if she saw fit. Lenin talked Wilson's language as to self-determination and ending imperialism. The Prinkipo Conference was organized as a friendly overture to Russia. It failed. One day Steffens and I were with William Bullitt, a liaison official, whose business it was to keep the American mission informed as to what was going on. Bullitt had an engaging personality. He knew Europe, had been connected with the State Department during the war. Steffens suggested a mission to Russia, a mission that understood the Bolshevik point of view, that could talk its language. Bullitt liked the idea and dictated a memorandum about it to Colonel House. Two days later Bullitt asked Steffens if he would go to Russia with him; if so, could he be ready immediately? The plan had been approved by Colonel House; it was only necessary to get the sanction of Lloyd George. The next day that had been secured. I saw Bullitt and Steffens off. They went to London; from London by British aid they reached Russia. They were sympathetically received by Lenin, and returned to Paris to make their report. The mission had been successful. The Russians had acceded to the allied memorandum; a rapprochement seemed established; Russia was to come back into the family of nations. Bullitt and Steffens were elated. A great advance had been made toward international amity. For some reason or another they could not see the President. Lloyd George received Bullitt and the report, but later denied that he knew of the mission or had given his consent to it. No explanation for his change of front was ever offered. That Lloyd George had approved of the mission was obvious to all. It could not have left France, could not have landed in England, could not have secured conveyance to Russia but for British aid and approval.

Truth meant little at Paris. Paris did not expect men to tell the truth. The President worked in a net of duplicity; he was surprised when apparently satisfactory agreements turned into betrayals of his position. His tasks were cruelly difficult; he attempted them for the most part alone. Aided only by memoranda on a sheet of paper, he went into conference with men who knew personally every detail of the subjects under discussion. The American experts who furnished the President's data were competent; they did thorough work, but they were like an army which was not facing its enemy.

Some time after the return of the Russian mission William Bullitt resigned. He felt, he said, that he could not face himself longer in the world of duplic-

ity in which America was being ensnared. Several
other experts withdrew with him.

One of the clearing-houses of the Peace Conference
was the Press Club on the Champs Elysées. There
journalists and experts of all countries dined and
gossiped. Official secrets, ill kept at the Quai d'Orsay, reached the Press Club. Back-stairs influences
were known. Hidden dictators were named, those
who stood behind Lloyd George and Clemenceau,
with powerful press interests. Sir Basil Zakharoff
and the munition-makers moved across the canvas,
as did French steel, Persian oil, hungry concessionaires. Their power was a gigantic shadow, recognized
but little understood. Officially Paris was not interested in things economic. It was fixing boundaries,
agreeing on reparations. The President was not
interested. Nor were Balfour, Lloyd George, or Clemenceau—ostensibly. But economic forces moved
the conference, like players about a chess-board.
Boundary-lines were shifted to include harbors, cop-
per, oil, mineral resources. Races were split, natural
demarcations ignored. The imperialist interests that
had kept the world on edge for thirty years before
the war were making a killing; they would end the
old controversies; would sanction their loot by treaty
agreements; perhaps rivet them by the League of
Nations. The British Admiralty wanted oil; it had
talked oil for years. British maritime prescience saw
that oil was the fuel of to-morrow. The French steel
trust wanted a grip on coal and iron ore, to gain
command of the Continent and strip Germany of
her war-making power. Munition-makers were busy.
They were getting ready for the next war.

At the Press Club men talked about these things.
Seasoned pressmen displayed, like devil's showmen,
monstrous wares. "The French steel trust wants
the Saar and the Ruhr," they would say. "French

security will be the plea, but the objective is monopoly of iron and steel. Back of the steel combine are the Paris banks and the Paris press.

"England fears a French monopoly of iron and steel. It wants oil. It wants Mesopotamia, Persia, and southern Russia. England depends on fuel for industrial life and naval power.

"The British have won their prizes by arms. The French have not acquiesced in them. When they do, Britain will have to acquiesce in French control of the Ruhr, for which France is now preparing."

"Japan uses Oriental methods. Her representatives file reservations to every decision of the council. They qualify acceptance to French, English, and Italian claims. Japan will finally demand Shantung with its iron-ore deposits as her price for acquiescence."

The Press Club was cynically certain that war, not peace, was being prepared for at the Quai d'Orsay.

One evening at dinner a friend of President Wilson's, a man thoroughly conversant with the conference, said despondently:

"It is impossible to tell yet whether the peace is being drafted by the international bankers or the munition-makers. It is not being drafted by America."

America had no business at Paris. That was the outstanding thing about which we almost all agreed. President Wilson should have stayed at home. We were amateurs, amateurs seeking to right the world by moralistic appeals; we had fought as religious crusaders, and, like Joshua, had expected the old world to fall at a trumpet-blast. Our emotions were honest, the sacrifice genuine, whole-hearted, but Europe only smiled at our naïveté. The righteousness of Wilson was one of the Allies' greatest assets. Confronted with the realism of old Europe, it was almost childish. It was the morality of the church seeking to function against alarmist war lords, ministries tenacious of power, lords of finance—all moved by elemental motives of individual, class, and nationalistic aggrandizement. The evangelism of Wilson had turned America from her traditions; it made no impression on the realism of the old world.

My still-born vision of the Near East was the child of kindly American ignorance. It partook of our righteousness; possibly it was the idlest dream of all. Only a Europe dedicated to renunciation would have considered it. And old Europe was thinking of spoils and the next war.

CHAPTER XXX

WOODROW WILSON AT PARIS

WHEN Woodrow Wilson landed in France he was hailed as a Messiah. His presence would bring in the millennium. His photographs cut from newspapers had a place beside the highly colored representations of the Virgin Mary in peasants' cottages of France, Italy, and Spain. People knelt by the side of the railway when his train passed. Men even expected a new economic order. They dimly hoped for deliverance from war, a deliverance that was to come through the great American emancipator, Woodrow Wilson. For a time Lloyd George, Clemenceau, and Orlando were apprehensive of this veneration; it was whispered that Wilson might appeal to the people, and the people might repudiate their rulers. He might continue to talk to the world as he had talked from Washington; might refuse to confer, to barter, to sit in secret sessions.

At Paris, President Wilson stood on a pinnacle. He had lifted the world to his own idealism, and the world seemed ready for a Messianic dispensation.

By choice he stood alone. He was without commanding advisers. His aides were inconspicuous men. He was without a secretary, was unprepared as a host. It was necessary to reach him with important communications through a White House servant. He had only the scantiest knowledge of Europe, of the men whom he had to meet. He professed to be ignorant of the secret treaties that confounded his pledges. The Peace Conference was to be a personal affair; he hoped that it would be largely personal to him and Mr. Arthur Balfour. It was to be guided by *his* Magna Carta, the lineal issue of other great Anglo-Saxon charters, beginning with the barons at Runnymede and ending with Thomas Jefferson. Men had conquered with the pen as well as with the sword. He would bring liberty to a distracted world by the pen. He would bring it alone.

England fed this isolated grandeur. And England knew Woodrow Wilson better than did we. She knew him as she knows so many things that no other country thinks it worth while to know. She had studied his written words; had penetrated into his hidden psychology. She knew his strength and his weakness. England had sent Mr. Arthur Balfour to Washington to win him to the war. Mr. Balfour was the statesman-philosopher, the model of President Wilson's university aristocrat. He best represented the England that Mr. Wilson knew from Walter Bagehot. The England he had written about, the mother of America. The Balfour family had always been a family of rulers. They had no interest in trade. They knew nothing of the vulgarity of practical politics. Other British emissaries had been picked with the same insight. And England bowed to the Messianic Wilson; she accepted him on his own measure of himself. The King received him with sovereign honors at Buckingham Palace. Peers, commoners, people claimed him as their own. The press sanctioned his idealism as the idealism of English peoples. They seemed to accept his leadership of the world.

While England swelled this Messianic vision, France pricked it. The Paris press was cynical; under government direction it sneered. Daily editorials questioned the President's vision of himself. Clemenceau said: "God gave us Ten Commandments—we have not followed them; but Wilson has given us

Fourteen." His reference to the "tin Jesus" was quoted all over Paris. It stung. A master of dramatic art, he played on France's sufferings, on her moderation. Balfour, the man on whom Wilson relied, was first of all a Briton. He spoke as a philosopher but acted as a politician.

The President had a contempt for Lloyd George, which he incautiously expressed; and he came to have a hatred of Clemenceau which the latter took no pains to assuage. To these men Woodrow Wilson was impractical, naïve. His peace without victory had aided in breaking down German morale. His idealism had deceived the world and helped to win the war. But why did he think his words were different from other war propaganda? It was ridiculous that he should think them so important; his Fourteen Points so sacred. They had never been agreed to, anyhow.

The secret treaties were now brought forward; plans for the distribution of the spoils, for the dismemberment of Germany, the destruction of middle Europe. Mr. Wilson professed to have no knowledge of the secret treaties, which confounded all his pledges, although they had been printed in America. He was indifferent, if not irritated, over imperialism, and was wholly unprepared for criticism and attack from sources from which he had least expected it. Neither France nor England felt gratitude; rather they felt resentment that we had not come in earlier. We had made money from their necessities. That, too, could not be forgotten. Among his confrères he was an inexperienced colonial, to be confused, outwitted, played on; now a savior of the world, now an obstructionist to speedy peace, now an ingrate to the sufferings of England and France. That it was primarily their war, not ours; that we had come in because of appeals for help; that we had abandoned

310 THE CONFESSIONS OF A REFORMER

our traditions and made our own sacrifices, was a point of view to which they were impervious. That we had made these sacrifices because we sincerely believed that they too wanted an end of war, received no credence.

The President's Fourteen Points had no supporters. England would not even consider his freedom of the seas; command of the seas was protection to her empire. She would not renounce conquest. Conquest was a word she did not know. Her empire was a trust, a sacred burden, which could not be discussed. She had seized her winnings by war in Africa, in Mesopotamia, in the islands of the sea. She had gained control of the raw materials of the earth. She would hold them as her spoils. They were not open to disposition by the Peace Conference.

France would draw a cordon about Germany— Poland, Czechoslovakia, the Baltic States, and the Balkans. Austro-Hungary would be dismembered and new countries created. France needed allies, more enemies of Germany. Italy would have the Adriatic; Greece demanded Smyrna, part of Turkey. Japan would have Shantung; she had taken it herself from Germany.

The President was unable to cope with the men about him, who used every device to confuse, to cheat him. He did not trust his advisers. He could not possibly know the significance of what was being proposed, of decisions made, of the things he concurred in. He wanted approval, but was met with a sneer; he reached out for support, but found deceit.

And when he had delivered his sermon he had exhausted his armor. When he abandoned one principle he abandoned all.

As the discussions wore on he became fearful of disorder, of revolutions that were everywhere impending. Russia had gone Red, also Hungary. Germany was filled with revolution. There were communist uprisings in Berlin, Munich, Düsseldorf. Italian workmen were threatening to seize the factories. Everywhere in Central Europe the peasants were seizing the land. Ireland was in a ferment, so were India and Egypt. There was even revolutionary talk in England. The world must be stabilized quickly, or all Europe might go Red. Wilson had made gestures to Russia before leaving America. He repeated them on arriving in France; but Russia was a red ogre to France, the enemy of civilization to the Paris press. His fears were constantly played on. There was but one security, and that was in the old order, the old rulers. A stable France would help Europe. A French cordon between Germany and Russia would stem the revolution. President Wilson was always restive on things economic, on subjects of which he was not himself a master. His economic pictures were those of the early days of the American republic, days of more equal opportunity. That was his vision of the new freedom. Europe did not want the ballot; she wanted food. The revolutionary movement was coming from the submerged classes. Their leaders said that his state must be wholly destroyed.

A thousand cross-currents confused and exhausted him. And he was facing this confusion alone. He could not delegate responsibility, and when his aides acted he seemed to resent their importance. With the exception of Colonel House, he had chosen a mission to take orders, not to share in honors. The years of devotion of Colonel House were said to have been cancelled by the attention which he received.

For the first time in his political life Woodrow Wilson was compelled to do battle with equals, who knew every detail of what was being discussed, but of which he had only the superficial information provided on a sheet of paper. He had expected an afternoon tea; he found a duel. He expected to dictate; he descended to barter.

Conflict disclosed his loneliness, his fearfulness, his hatred of men who challenged his power. Conflict disclosed the Wilson who had bewildered liberals while he was President; who turned on old friends, who hated Cabot Lodge, who excoriated imperialism, and seized Haiti and Santo Domingo and sent battleships to Vera Cruz. It disclosed the Wilson who sanctioned the hate propaganda, the Wilson who imprisoned men who quoted him against himself. When he himself was subjected to a personal test, he abandoned the ideals he had held before America.

Mr. Wilson could not bear criticism. Criticism brought his reveries of himself under inspection, and he cherished these reveries. He shielded them, nursed them, lived with them. His dreams had to be kept intact. They had to be respected by others. Of all men he should have been the most solicitous of our Anglo-Saxon liberties. He knew each step in the long struggle for their realization, and should have prized them as delicate and precious things. Yet after he had decided for war, he allowed to other men scarcely a day in which to change their opinions as had he; he denounced as "wilful men" members of Congress who did not accede to his superior wisdom; he set the Department of Justice in motion to speedily imprison men for saying one day the things he had said the day before. At Paris I asked his closest friend why Mr. Wilson had appointed Mr. Henry White as the Republican member of the Peace Commission when every consideration of expediency suggested the appointment of a man acceptable to the Senate, the treaty-confirming power. He replied: "If President Wilson could have found a man whom the Republicans hated worse than Henry White, he would have appointed him."

Had the President remained a Messiah, content with approval from himself alone, he might possibly have won. He might have failed, but his failure would have been a Messianic failure in keeping with his vision of himself. It might have upset governments, widened revolutions; it would have left an imperishable influence on the world.

But he chose to barter. When he began to barter, he lost all; he lost his own vision of himself, and he had to keep this vision of himself intact. It and his principles were all that he had brought to Paris.

A man less idealistic would have been betrayed as he was betrayed, but he would have been a better bargainer. He would have used America's financial power. He would have brought pressure to bear. He might have threatened. He would have descended more frankly to the world in which he found himself. But the evangelist could do none of these things frankly, and the President was an evangelist.

The peace the President had promised to the world would not come through the treaty. That was clear. Possibly his peace might be saved through the League of Nations, but the League of Nations with him as its first president. That suggestion was held before his eyes. He was again led up to the mountain-top. To secure this new agency of the millennium and his own leadership he made new concessions, but concessions brought him no rewards. They did not soften the cynicism of the Paris press. They did not check imperialistic adventures. They had no influence on Lloyd George or Clemenceau. There was no price that he could have paid that would have satisfied the men who for four years had planned the partition of the world under treaties that double-crossed each other and that violated every assurance that had been given to America. And the League of Nations, which issued like the Treaty of Versailles, was a league of conquest rather than a covenant of freedom. It was an international sanction of servitude to make permanent the conquests of the war. Like the Treaty of Versailles, it provided a moral approval of economic and imperialistic exploitation. It was this that was offered President Wilson in exchange for his ideals; it was this that was urged upon America, for with America sanctioning the league there was no great power left to sympathize with or assist the aspirations of subject peoples.

Mankind needs evangelism as well as achieving statesmanship. Had Wilson remained the evangelist he might have broken Clemenceau and Lloyd George. But he chose political power. As the politician he failed. But his words carrying promise of a new dispensation fell on soil that had been made ready by the pledges of the war and the common sufferings of peoples. And the winged words of the President ripened these aspirations into revolution in Ireland, in Egypt, in Mesopotamia, in Africa, in India. As an evangelist he achieved what he possibly least wanted to achieve. He helped to free Ireland. He heartened the Egyptians, the Arabs, and the Indians. He set aflame fires that are slowly driving the white men from other people's countries. It was as an evangelist that President Wilson realized his reveries of himself. As an evangelist he takes his place among the great men of history.

President Wilson's sense of insecurity, when outside of his study, made him vulnerable. He was unwilling to face defeat. He would not face failure. To escape failure he sacrificed principles. To save appearances he made gestures against Italy over Fiume, against France over Syria. His constant struggle was to preserve the semblance even when the substance was lost.

Criticism exhibited failure; it exhibited it to Mr.

Wilson as it exhibited it to the world. He threatened to leave Paris if the French press was not curbed.

At home many of his constructive measures were sacrificed to stop criticism. He gave way on important sections of the federal reserve system, against the advice of men whom he should have trusted, and in so doing converted it into a private rather than a public agency. Under criticism he sanctioned railway legislation and rate increases that he would not have considered in the early days of his administration. When assailed by the press and by special interests, he sought to re-establish himself by giving way. When his advice to the people in the congressional elections of 1918 was ignored and a Republican Congress returned, he seemed eager to punish the public for its acts. It was then that special interests were permitted to take possession of the government; the Department of Justice became ruthless in its activities, and privileged business became most arrogant in its power. When his pride was affronted he was likely to retaliate blindly, even on his friends. He broke with devoted supporters, Colonel House and Mr. Tumulty, over breaches of this kind that involved no personal disloyalty. He broke with Secretary Lansing as he did with Secretary Lane. Even the assumption of power by an adviser was treated as personal disloyalty.

President Wilson's political life could almost be written about his supersensitiveness. It is one of the most dangerous qualities a public man can have; it leads to the sacrifice of the public, to retaliations, to inability to co-operate. This is especially true when it arises from a sense of insecurity. Then it is that men create fictions of themselves, that they only half believe. It is their half-belief that makes them so sensitive.

When President Wilson returned to America the

people were ready to accept his failures and understand the cause. It was his assertion that he had brought back the peace he had promised that turned the tide. The people did not believe what he said. They heckled him in his meetings. They forced him to see himself. It was then that his strength gave way, his health broke. He lost his vision of himself when he discovered that it was no longer held by others. The pinnacle from which he fell was within himself. That was the tragedy of the Peace Messiah.

President Wilson remains one of the world's great men. He saw life in great principles; he knew what the distracted world needed. His phrases won permanent victories; they inspired peoples; possibly they won the war. He left humanity better for what he said; he enriched it by the unsullied idealism of his messages. He missed being one of the world's great heroes by choosing to be something other than what he was. He would not remain what his instinctive self would have chosen to remain, a maker of ideals by which other peoples should chart their course.

CHAPTER XXXI

UNLEARNING

I HAD been unlearning a great part of my life, sometimes with pleasure, sometimes with pain. The process had begun at Johns Hopkins, where I lost my Meadville moralities. At Cleveland my university categories of "good" people and "bad" people had been challenged; Tom Johnson gave me a picture of economic freedom that displaced the confusion I had gotten from books; with him I had seen the unrealities of the Constitution and of the political machinery with which we were compelled to work. The war had changed an abiding faith in the state into questionings of it. Ellis Island had disclosed hysterias, hatreds, passions of which democracy was capable; Washington had revealed the willingness of men to make profit from the sufferings of the people.

There remained the leader, Woodrow Wilson; he kept the fires of my faith burning. And at Paris I had lost him.

The fairly good, comfortable world, with its respectabilities and illusions, that I had cherished all the way from Meadville, had begun to crumble.

Paris made some things clear.

The scholar was not leading. He did not know what it was all about.

The liberal could not save the world. He wanted to patch.

Facts were of little value. Paris had all the facts in the world. Van-loads of facts. Tons of experts' reports—an army of experts.

Men did not believe in the truth. They lied quite frankly. Sacred pledges were scraps of paper. Men smiled at America's morality. All Paris enjoyed Clemenceau's reference to America's "tin Jesus."

Herd morality in international affairs was not morality at all in my sense of the word.

The Peace conferees were men of my class.

There was only one thing that Paris understood. That was conquest. Clemenceau, Lloyd George, Italy, Japan were intent on it. And conquest meant plunder. The reporters in the press gallery were alert when plunder was discussed. They yawned when Wilson spoke. The Messiah was unpopular at the Quai d'Orsay as in the Press Club.

There were realists in Paris; these facts that I had painfully discovered were the A B C of their political philosophy. Like scientists they saw through unrealities. They gave me keys that unlocked mysteries; clews that explained things that I had only half understood. I began to see the political world in which I had lived as an astronomer sees the universe, as the microscopist sees the atom. It was one. There was cause and effect; the problem was to find the universal cause. There was disease; the problem was to find the universal cure.

And thinking things through I began to see similarities, parallels, universal conditions. The scholar had failed at home as he had failed abroad. Facts were of little value; morality did not guide men. In America, as in Europe, there was conquest, plunder. Plunder was the universal object of men who made war on the city, on the state, on the nation, as it was the object in international wars. Conquest meant war; plunder meant force. The weapons men used were inconsequential.

The Great War was one kind of war; the struggles in Cleveland, San Francisco, Toledo, Ohio, Wisconsin were another kind of war. I had followed these wars as a magazine writer, had used war terms, but only as metaphors. Now I saw they described realities. Men made war on people of their own blood as they made war on other peoples. They made war with corruption as they made war with machine-guns. Democracy had been violated at home as it had been violated in Belgium. War had many disguises, many weapons; ballots or bullets, press propaganda or poison-gas, but it was always war. There was one class in the counting-room, another in the trenches. In America men made war to obtain wealth that they did not create; to enjoy privileges they could only enjoy through war on the political state.

In Europe men had so bent the state to private ends that the World War had come as a consequence. To realists at Paris it was a collision of economic forces. Paris admitted that the war was economic; French generals in the occupied territory spoke to me of its economic cause as though it were a truism. Guilt would have to be restated. It was not personal, it was impersonal and economic.

Wars were made back home. They could only be ended back home. The world was ruled by an exploiting class that ruled in the interest of the things it owned. Tories and liberals, landlords and capitalists, all looked upon the political state as did the spoilsman; it was a thing to give them private gain.

Existing governments could not end war. They were ruled by men who wanted things that made for war. The League of Nations could do little. It represented the states ruled for privileges. The League of Nations could not rise higher than its source. It was like the good government movements of America, the Municipal Association in Cleveland. They wanted to cure corruption without getting rid of the cause of corruption, as men in Paris wanted to get rid of war without giving up its causes. They would not recognize that corruption at home came from franchises, just as war abroad came from conquest. My class either would not or could not see beyond its own interests. It had failed at home; it had failed abroad.

America could not aid the world toward permanent peace. Our alleged ideals did not operate at home, they could not operate abroad. Our State Department was thinking in terms of oil in Mesopotamia, of oil in Mexico, of gold and railroads in Haiti and Santo Domingo. The press did not talk of putting Europe to work, it talked in bankers' terms of loans, interest, getting our money back. We could not send representatives of the American people to Geneva; we could only send the kind of men we put in the Cabinet at home. Righteousness meant getting off the backs of people; it meant extending to backward nations the same liberties we enjoyed at home. Until we, ourselves, were ready for renunciation, we would not ask other peoples to begin the process. To end war we must begin at the cause; we must begin at home.

I had seen many of these facts before but had not understood. I had encountered exploitation, but had seen it in terms of individual men. I had not lived consistently in my mind, my instincts had double-crossed it—as my mind had double-crossed them.

Why had I not seen the universality of war before? Why had I followed President Wilson so unreservedly as I had followed him to Paris?

Facing realities about the world, I began to face myself. I began to take stock of what I was, as opposed to what I thought I was. And I began to understand why I had never thought things through before. One thing was quite clear. I had never been a pioneer. Authority had always been necessary to me. In my boyhood it had been the neighbors; what "they" would say, they being respectable, Republican, church-going people. At Johns Hopkins, my professors. I had always had a leader and a herd. I had abandoned one authority for another—in that, as I look back over my life, there had been original movement of my mind. But I had been a lieutenant, not a leader. I had courage to follow. At Ellis Island I had found it hard to stand alone.

And at bottom I was a moralist; not a realist, not a scientist. My education had halted when in conflict with certain authorities. I had not learned to pursue the truth to its ultimate. I had not gotten rid of the old classifications established in my youth. From Meadville on people had been "good" and "bad" for me. The stubborn assumption remained that educated, well-to-do people, of Anglo-Saxon stock, agreeable socially, were "good." At Johns Hopkins I learned that democracy needed to be saved; I was pleasantly convinced that these people, of whom I was one, would save it. Johns Hopkins gave, in part, voice and dignity to preconceptions I had brought from home. Tom Johnson had roundly disposed of my "good" people. When I asked him to separate himself from politicians and line up with the Chamber of Commerce and the Municipal Association, he had said to me: "The good people, as you term them, can't support me. This fight cuts too deep. It touches too many interests, banks, business, preachers, doctors, lawyers, clubs, newspapers. They have to be on one side. And it isn't my side. They will be against me. The only people who can be for me are the poor people and the politicians, who will have to follow the poor when the people get started."

I listened to him, followed him because I loved him, and saw part of the truth that he saw; but this about my sort of people I never believed. I was devoted to Tom Johnson and accepted him; but I continued to care for the approval of my class, prized its good opinion, suffered from its ostracism.

In New York I stayed with it. I enjoyed membership in clubs, social contacts incident to my work as director of the People's Institute. It was good form to be a liberal; it involved no sacrifices. Indeed, it gave distinction. I never lost my feeling of being one of the elect, of helping to keep America true to the ideals of the fathers. I believed that the things I wanted would come about in time; that they would be brought about by liberals—liberals as represented by the New York *Nation*, the *New Republic*, the insurgent group in Congress. I was confident that peace societies would end war. I believed in discussion; in the writing of books and magazine articles, in making speeches. We liberals had the truth. If we talked it enough and wrote it enough, it would undoubtedly prevail. By eloquence and reason abuses would be ended; the state would be cleaned up. I believed in the mind and in facts. Facts were a Rock of Gibraltar. We had them—facts about government ownership, about free trade, about land.

The one thing I had clung to all these years was a belief in my class convinced by facts. It was mind that would save the world, the mind of my class aroused from indifference, from money-making, from party loyalty and coming out into the clear light of reason. I now began to see that men were not concerned over the truth. It did not interest them when economic interests were at stake. The mind was as closed to facts as a safety-deposit vault. There was a sign outside: "Do not enter here."

Aside from a few young men, I could not remember a person of prominence in the ten years' war in Cleveland who had been converted from his class by intellectual appeals. It had been a war of classes.

Municipal ownership, the single tax, free trade

had no more supporters in the clubs and among respectable people than they had twenty years before. There were certainly fewer believers in free trade, for in my youth the colleges had been filled with men who had taught free trade; the New York *Nation* had a large free-trade following. It was a mark of intellectual distinction to belong to the free-trade group.

I had built my life first around conventional morality, then about the mind. Conventional morals did not prevent men from making war, from corrupting the state, from destroying democracy. There were as many different kinds of morals as there were groups that held them. And the morals men held were in some way shaped by the things they wanted, by their economic interest, by the class in which they worked and lived. There was a group morality for the small town, for the university man, for the banker and the business man, for the lawyer and the doctor, for the politician and grafter, for the men who stood behind the politicians and profited from their grafting. And conventional morality seemed to find no difficulty in justifying these differing codes even to the extent of bringing on a cataclysmic war that had all but destroyed humanity.

And the mind had failed as completely as morals. Men did not think when social problems were involved. They did not use the mind. It refused to work against economic interest. This was so obviously true that I wondered it had not been stated. The mind worked with wonderful precision in the production of wealth, in the making of machines, in the realm of science, in all those fields where men were achieving their own lives and instincts. But when logic, evidence, convincing facts pointed one way and individual or class interest pointed another the mind closed itself to reason and refused to function. The world had not been saved by morality.

Apparently it had little to hope for from the human mind.

But I made one reconciling discovery: my dreams —the things I wanted—were still alive under the ruins of most of what I had thought. I had wanted, since Johns Hopkins, to change things. Freedom seemed to me the law of life, and the single tax the most nearly perfect expression of it that had been given to the world. I would have accepted a lot of evil to get free trade, to end private ownership of the railways, to bring in the single tax. I had had no liking for Socialism; did not want to see struggle, initiative banished from the world. I liked these things and wanted rather to see them released, wanted every one to enter the race on equal terms, with no favoritism, no handicap; no advantages due to birth or ownership. I wanted a world of equal opportunity.

I wanted, too, an orderly world—a world that had the distinction that aristocracy gave; all of the personal distinction of individualism, and all of the wealth that human ingenuity could create, dispensed as its creators desired. I had no fear of great wealth, provided it was the creation of man, of his brain no less than his hands. I had no fear of freedom; rather I liked it, but I wanted the freedom to be open to all, wanted the color, the variety, the waste of a world that produced in abundance and spent as abundantly as it produced.

I still wanted all this. But I had been wrong about the way to get it. My own class did not want such a world. And there was but one other class—the workers—those who produced wealth by hand or brain. Would labor want to end this universal war, would labor want a universal peace, would labor want the kind of world I had long wanted, a world of equal opportunity, a world in which the wealth created would be enjoyed by those that created it? It seemed to me that labor would want these things. Labor could not serve privilege, as privilege could only be enjoyed by the few. By necessity labor would serve freedom, democracy, equal opportunity for all.

My faith in the "goodness" of my class died hard, but its death did not leave me insolvent. My ideals were still undimmed; I had found a class whose interests ran hand in hand with the things I desired. And once the blinders were off, it seemed that my distrust of people not of my own class had little foundation. There were new leaders with vision and confidence. The movement seemed historically inevitable. Political power had been in continuous drift from the few to the many for a hundred years; first from the king to the nobility, then from the nobility to the landed aristocracy; from the landed aristocracy the drift continued to the commercial classes. The next step was the last and it could not be stopped. Labor had to make its own fight, it had to use its own power; the place for the liberal was in labor's ranks.

At fifty I saw myself as I saw the political state. I had lost the illusions I had spent a lifetime in hoarding. I had lost illusions of myself. Much of my intellectual capital had flown. Drafts on my mind came back indorsed: "No funds." But I was still not bankrupt. The new truth that a free world would only come through labor was forced on me. I did not seek it; did not welcome it. But it crowded into mind and demanded tenancy as the old occupants gave notice to leave.

CHAPTER XXXII

WORKING WITH LABOR

LANDING at Ellis Island one morning in the summer of 1919 I saw a struggle on the other side of the slip. Two of my deporting officers were tearing an Italian girl from her father and mother. They placed her in a launch, which steamed out into the harbor, and held her from jumping overboard.

On the way to my office one of the matrons stopped me. "Mr. Commissioner," she said, "they deported the little Armenian girl last night; the one that got away from the Turks and came as a stowaway. She can only be landed in Turkey and she will probably be killed. And I've been put on the night shift because I brought some fresh eggs over to that mother with a sick baby."

At my office I was confronted with an angry group from New York, one of them an attorney. "The three East Indians have been ordered deported," said the attorney. "You promised us that we would be notified of the hearing. They are being sent back to India at the demand of the British Government and they will certainly be shot."

I had given the promise, on assurances from Washington. I had an understanding with the department that aliens should enjoy the right of counsel. I had protested against deporting aliens to devastated areas or countries in revolution. But orders of the Secretary of Labor and agreements which I had with him were ignored by bureau officials.

The next morning I was at the Department of Labor. I went first to the Commissioner-General. I was both angry and profane, for discussion with him was of no value. The action of the bureau was a "damned outrage," I said. It was ordering cruel and inhuman things done; pledges which I had given were being overruled. For once the Commissioner-General sat quiet. I had adopted methods which he could understand. Then to the Secretary of Labor with the whole story of secret deportations, of pledges double-crossed. I suspected that the secretary had been double-crossed, himself. I could not recall the deported girls, but the East Indians should have a trial and be represented by their attorneys. Their order of deportation was stayed. They were not sent back to India.

But I was through. The Red hysteria was at its height. The Commissioner-General and Attorney-General were directing it. I might be asked to carry out any order and be compromised in any promise which I made. There was talk of chartering a vessel and sending a boat-load of deportees back to Russia. Many of them I had personally examined and found held on the most trivial charges. Driven by business organizations back home, congressmen were demanding action, no matter how innocent the victims might be.

I had exhausted my power. Even the secretary was being carried along by the hysteria. High officials in the department had resigned; Louis F. Post, the first assistant Secretary of Labor, was being tried by a committee of the House of Representatives. There were some orders which I would not carry out. And I wanted to be rid of political office that compelled compromise.

The next day I sent for my personal correspondence. I gathered together records of aliens and personal-interest stories that I had been collecting for five years, and which I had planned to use in a book. I sent for a porter, and together we carried them to the engine-room, where I consigned them to the flames.

"I will end that chapter forever," I thought. Then I sat down and wrote my resignation to the President. I left with a feeling of exhilaration. I had entered whole-heartedly into my principality of Ellis Island, hoping to make it a playhouse for immigrants. I left a prison. I recalled what Wendell Phillips said about negro slavery, that it "made a slave of the master no less than the slave."

When I stepped from the ferry-boat in New York I felt that I was through with politics. I had seen the government at close range, with its mask off; it existed for itself and for hidden men behind it, as the realists in Paris had said. It was as dangerous to the innocent as to the guilty. It was frankly doing the bidding of business. At home as in Paris men said: "The ideals of President Wilson had been necessary to win the war, but now that the war is won let us get back to business." That meant using the Department of Justice frankly as an agency to protect profiteers, high officials, and business men who looked upon the government as their own; it meant crushing liberalism by deportations, arrests, a terrorism of fear. This was the democracy that the boys were to come back to from the trenches. There was no place for the liberal in it.

But I could not be rid of the desire for things that I had so long wanted. I saw them as a picture, as I had seen the city when I worked with Tom Johnson; the picture was vivid, photographic. I had always seen things photographically. That was the way I wrote. It was like painting a picture out of the mind. And I had a passionate desire for a society of economic freedom, in which every power and talent of man could function freely. I saw the abun-

dant wealth that could be produced with the land
opened up by taxation; saw this wealth running
freely from one end of the country to the other, with
publicly owned railroads operated for service; saw
the wealth of all the world enriching the culture of
America through free trade. I had a mental passion
for a free society, with the state owning a few industries strategic to its life and functioning more as an
administrative than a political thing. I hated anything that blocked effort, that levied unnecessary
tribute, and interfered with freedom.

My passion for these ideas made inactivity impossible to me. I could not be through with politics.

At Paris I had accepted the new creed of labor; I
had accepted it as a necessity; had accepted it because of its leaders and programme. A new party
was necessary. It was a party of primary producers,
of workers and farmers, of men whose economic interests would exile war from the earth, at home as
well as abroad.

For some weeks I had been reading in the press articles on a new organization formed by the railway
labor-unions. Its purpose was the government ownership of the railroads and their operation by a corporation, the directors of which were to be appointed
by the President, one-third representing the railway
workers, one-third engineering and executive skill,
one-third representing the public. Its author was
Glenn E. Plumb, a Chicago lawyer, who was testify-
ing before Congress and who showed a masterful
knowledge of railroads and the evils of their organization and operation.

I went to Washington and met the leaders of this
movement. I found the railway labor leaders to be
men of ability, understanding, power—great executives. Warren S. Stone of the Engineers, William
Johnston of the Machinists—there were a dozen men

of bigger personality than many of the men I had known professionally or in business. And I found that they were far more scrupulous; they fought fair; they took pride in keeping their contracts; they had the old-fashioned moralities of my boyhood. They were often trapped through their respect for the law, their reliance on old ethical standards.

I became associated with them. They were fearful of radicals, Reds, revolutionists. They wanted change brought about in an orderly way. Radicals in the labor movement were challenging their authority, were sapping their organizations.

I worked with these men for three years. We started a weekly paper called *Labor*, under the editorship of Edward Keating. It was soon self-supporting and reached a circulation of five hundred thousand copies. It takes no advertising; it is devoted almost exclusively to labor and labor policies; is ably edited and exerts a powerful influence.

For a time I had charge of the editorial columns, writing on co-operation, banking, railroads, and guild socialism, which the programme of the Plumb Plan League closely resembled. I travelled, speaking for the Plumb Plan, engaging in joint debates and organizing branches.

My enthusiasms took definite form in a plan for mobilizing the power of nearly two million railway employees. They were intelligent, for the most part well paid, courageous, and independent. Such workers could exert great influence in their communities; if they could mobilize all their power in their own interest they could improve their own standard of living. I was particularly interested in co-operation, labor banking, and direct political action.

The newspaper *Labor* provided a forum for ideas. The Plumb Plan had branches all over the country. There was the organization with which to work, and I threw myself into the movement with eagerness.

For once I was no longer attempting to be in two camps. My convictions and my class were one. As an editorial writer I appealed to men to follow their own interests, to use their collective power for their own well-being. I was no longer appealing to men of my own class to stop exploiting somebody else. I was urging men to free themselves, not persuading some one to give freedom to others. These men had the power if they would use it. They had billions on deposit in the banks. They had great purchasing power and could organize stores, even factories, for themselves. They could join hands with the farmers, and develop direct bargaining. I began to have the same enthusiasm for this vision that I had had for the city. I saw a state within a state, creating its own economic life, massing its own power, using it to build up a co-operative society inside the political state. I had the same kind of dream of order that I had had in the city, only it was the order of a class rather than a locality. It was working with a group whose ideals and interests were alike instead of with men whose ideals and interests were diverse.

My interest in a producers' state recalled Denmark, which I had visited some years earlier in my study of experiments in industrial democracy. I wrote a book about this little state entitled *Denmark: A Co-operative Commonwealth.* It was the story of a country ruled by farmers and workers, men who forty years before had been ignorant, bankrupt, and untrained to political action. They had gone into politics through necessity; the bankruptcy of agriculture had forced political action on them. They had elected peasants and workers to Parliament; had become in time the majority, and filled the ministry with men from their class. They had created a peasant democracy; had all but gotten rid of landlords and capitalists. They stopped spending money on the army and navy and spent it for schools, which had ended illiteracy. There was no ignorance left in this country ruled by peasants. They had almost ended poverty by giving a farm to every man who wanted it and who proved his ability to work it. They had all but exiled middlemen and profiteers. The state owned the railroads and ran them for service at very low charges. These farmers bought and sold co-operatively. They had hundreds of co-operative dairies, slaughter-houses, egg-collecting societies. They had almost gotten rid of capitalists through voluntary co-operation. The landlord had been dispossessed through purchase, and his land distributed among the peasants. Denmark was a living proof of what men in Paris had said: that a diseased society could be brought back to life through the producing classes, and that they, and they alone, would get rid of the things that made for war.

Co-operation gripped me as Socialism had not. It was voluntary, open to individual initiative; it trained leaders and minimized the state. Apparently it achieved all the ends that Socialism promised and left the individual free from bureaucratic control. I saw labor and the farmer rising to political power through the training which co-operation gave. The All-American Co-operative Commission was organized, and I became its secretary. It promoted co-operative stores, published bulletins, and maintained a press service. It was supported by contributions from the railway labor organizations.

The Brotherhood of Locomotive Engineers had long thought of organizing a Brotherhood bank. The organization had millions of funds on deposit in private banks. It had huge insurance funds, and ninety thousand members, most of them well-to-do. They formed the aristocracy of the labor movement. Mr. Warren S. Stone, the Grand Chief of the Brotherhood, employed me on behalf of the organization to investigate banking. I spent six months in this study. I saw the power of credit in private hands, saw its possibilities when dedicated exclusively to productive uses. Credit was power in the modern world; through the mobilization of the credit power of labor co-operative enterprises could be started, homes built, talent encouraged, and men equipped with tools, machines, and capital. And labor had colossal deposits at its disposal, which only needed to be mobilized and dedicated to new ends. I suggested a co-operative bank with dividends limited to ten per cent; a bank that would distribute some of its earnings back to depositors and that would utilize its resources exclusively for productive uses. The governing board of the Brotherhood met and approved the proposal. The bank was organized and opened in Cleveland in 1921 and almost immediately became a recognized success. In two years' time its resources rose to twenty-five million dollars. Subsequently other banks were purchased or organized by the Engineers in New York, Minneapolis, Hammond, Ind., and elsewhere. A coal-mine was developed, two new office-buildings acquired, security companies organized. Ninety thousand men were using their economic power for themselves, as they had previously used their collective power in wage disputes.

The idea of labor banks grew rapidly. The Amalgamated Clothing Workers established three banks on the same model, as did the Railway Clerks and Telegraphers. Other banks were opened by labor groups in New York, Philadelphia, Alabama, California. Soon there were nearly thirty labor banks throughout the country, with resources of close to a hundred million dollars.

My political enthusiasm was now for a party of primary producers. Picturing it, my mind exercised

its old affinity for fortifying facts and ideas. Such a
party was the last step in political evolution. It justified itself historically, scientifically. First, the king
had lost power to the landed aristocracy. They had
ruled during the first half of the eighteenth century.
Then the commercial classes demanded a share in
government and formed their own—the liberal—
party. Tories represented landlords—the old feudal
aristocracy; the liberals, the new commercial interests. Both were class parties, legislating for the
things their members owned. Farmers and workers
formed a natural economic class. They should form
a party, send their own members to Congress. There
was no other way for them to get recognition.

A party made up of primary producers would of
necessity serve the great majority of the people. It
could not serve privilege; privilege could only be enjoyed by the few. Individuals of the new group might
be selfish like other men—dishonest; but collectively
they had to follow the economic needs of their class.
They represented the many, not the few. They
would have to oppose exploiting agencies and the
private monopoly of natural resources.

Bankers thought as bankers, railway-owners as
railway-owners; railway employees thought as railway employees. Labor and the farmer would think
for themselves; they had to think for themselves.
Men did not think disinterestedly in politics; they
followed their economic interests. They were moved
by elemental motives. Like the amoeba going out
for food, man went out for the things he wanted;
sought to satisfy his wants by a minimum of effort.
That was universal in nature. Moral professions
were weaker than instinctive desires.

The instinct of a labor party would be to produce
as much wealth as possible, to distribute it as equitably
as possible; to insure a free field and no favors to

themselves and their children. It was my old dream
of equal opportunity.

Labor leaders, especially Mr. Gompers, resisted
the idea of political action. But the open-shop drive
and railway strike of 1921, together with the defla-
tion of the farmers by the Federal Reserve system,
drove both labor and the farmer into politics. The
Conference for Progressive Political Action, financed
largely by the railway labor-unions, was formed in
1922, to merge these groups.

I became secretary of the organization, which carried on a vigorous fight in the congressional elections
of 1922. We prepared political instructions for primaries and elections; unions were circularized; the
labor executives sent their best men into strategic States—Wisconsin, Minnesota, Iowa, Montana.
They demonstrated real political ability. As a result,
a half-dozen men were elected to the United States
Senate, and nearly fifty to the Lower House. It was
my conviction that labor should begin at the bottom, in city and State elections; that in national affairs it should concentrate its power on congressmen
and build up a labor-farmer bloc in Congress. I
urged the nomination of dirt farmers, actual workers
rather than liberals outside of the ranks. Preliminary
training was essential; it would be gained in city,
State, and congressional elections. Gains of this
kind would not be lost. In time we would have the
group system in Congress; ultimately workers and
farmers, being in the majority, would control it.
Then a third party would come. It could probably
come, I thought, in no other way.

I have never known better political workers than
the rank and file of the labor movement, or executives more intelligent than its leaders. There were
timidities among them, conflict and differences, but
no bitterness.

They were like men learning a new trade, something outside their experience that they would willingly have been relieved of if there were any other way. In the issues they stood for, in the programme they wanted for themselves and others, there was an instinctive desire for right things; for legislation for all of the people rather than emphasis on trade-union demands. There was real wisdom. They threshed things out in the open. Their demands conformed to democracy, to equality, to justice. Criticism of them could not relate to intelligence, justice, or the propriety of their demands; it related rather to too great respect for men, for authority, for things outside their own lives. They feared to move too fast; they were willing to accept favors from others rather than seize rights themselves. That is the weakness of labor. It will remain so for a long time until the old psychology of hope for the individual passes, and labor comes to see that no matter what happens to individuals, it will always be a class by itself. When labor realizes that it has to look after its own interests, as do all other classes, then it will become a menace to the existing party system. Injustice, such as the farmers suffered in 1921 and 1922 by the action of the Federal Reserve banks, the injustice that labor experienced through the decisions of the Railway Labor Board and the "open shop" drive—will drive home this realization. Labor is disinclined to politics. It will be forced into politics and will become politically powerful through the injustice of the existing system. Like other classes, labor prefers to have some one else look after its political activity. It will only cohere through some compulsion outside of itself.

In working with labor I felt a satisfaction that I had never before experienced, and a sense of greater personal integrity. I made friends with men who faced life without confusions. They were the kind of men I had known as a boy, kindly, generous, courageous. They spoke straight and fought fair. With them I wrote without qualifications, without considering whether I would be misunderstood. I think that the locomotive engineers are the finest hundred thousand men in America. A man can only be promoted to a locomotive because of a native power to command. Facing death at every moment, they are fearless and resourceful. They hold in their hands the lives of a train-load of people. And they are always conscious of and responsive to their tremendous responsibility. Epics could be written about the railway engineer; his daily life is necessarily heroic. And rarely is there record of any betrayal of responsibility. The locomotive engineers are the Vikings of modern industrial life. Association with them is one of the outstanding experiences of my life.

The election of 1922 showed that labor could mobilize its power. It showed the possibility of union with the farmers; time alone was needed for the inevitable steps that should bring them into united political action. Reaction had to run its course. Privilege would have to disclose its indifference to democracy before America would accept the inevitable dividing line of politics between those who produced wealth and those who exploited it.

La Follette's campaign of 1924 drew me deeper into the movement. I travelled with him on his speaking-tour. In Boston and Baltimore, Chicago and Detroit, St. Louis and Minneapolis, the largest halls were packed, with thousands of people standing outside. If a political movement could be gauged by enthusiasm, it seemed from the outpouring of people that he was going to receive a tremendous vote. Both the farmers and the workers seemed to be supporting him. Corruption in Washington, the high tariff, high railway rates, the oil scandal, the wide-spread agra-

338 THE CONFESSIONS OF A REFORMER

rian discontent augured victory for his unquestioned integrity. But fear is one of the assets of the prevailing system. People do not always vote as they shout; they do not even vote as they want to vote. Iowa, California, Kansas, Nebraska rolled up their accustomed majorities, for the Republican ticket. But the movement has started. It has a following of nearly five millions; it will require time to overcome inertia. No man can call into being a new party; it will come from economic and biological forces. The people will have to learn to use the ballot as they use their hands and their brains to satisfy their wants. Morality does not change men's politics; my class cannot be brought to do justice; justice will come through the efforts of those to whom it is now denied. Justice has never been given to people; they have had to take it for themselves. From the beginning men have had to fight for equality of opportunity; they will have to fight for it, I believe, to the end.

CHAPTER XXXIII

BEGINNING AGAIN

LIFE in Washington brought me into contact with my Johns Hopkins friend, who had helped me while I was at Ellis Island to get rid of conflicts, poisons, and fears. A diagnostician of minds as well as bodies, he had induced a number of my friends to quit the government service after the war, to change their vocations and follow their instinctive desires. He had a philosophy of healthy living that fitted in with my own incapacity to assimilate uncongenial things. Much that he said was new to me; he talked about mental conflict, bad adjustments, a war that men had within themselves when they were not doing what they wanted to do. He had cured many shell-shocked soldiers. He suggested that I had interests outside of politics; possibly they were more important than the things I was trying to do. He told me that the mind had a way of asserting itself as one fell asleep, as one came to consciousness in the morning. One had reveries of the things one liked, daydreams of what one wanted to do and be.

I knew very well what my reveries were about. They rested me when I was tired. They gave me peace when I was harassed. They were always of an old fishing village on the far end of Nantucket Island, where I had spent many summers; of simple fisherfolk with whom I felt at ease; of a rambling cottage on the edge of the moors into which the sun, rising from the sea, pushed its way in the morning, brighter and gayer and sweeter than sunlight anywhere else in the world.

Satisfied as I was with my new work, there was something I more ardently wanted. It seemed socially indefensible, for it related only to myself. I wanted to live on the Nantucket moors, to be quit of conflict; to live content with simple, friendly contacts, with horses and dogs, with a fire on the hearth. I wanted to build something with my hands; to plant things and see them grow. These reveries were warmer than any other desire. They had something to do with my deeper self. Perhaps they were a throwback to my forbears, to generations of blacksmiths, carpenters, and farmers, men who had lived close to the soil—my people had been peasants in England, Scotland, and Ireland. It may have been the lure of the Scotch moors that called me to Nantucket. Each year I waited impatiently for the summer to come; each fall I left my moorland cottage with greater reluctance.

In the summer of 1920 I had a chance to buy an old farm. On the land were a large farmhouse, a big barn, and a number of other buildings. A plan surged up from somewhere in me that I would build a community; would plant and beautify it, make a free and happy place for myself and my friends. I would have a herd of my own—for along with my desire for personal freedom was a need for people—people who also wanted to escape other herds and be themselves. That was the thing that interested me—finding myself; and I wanted to be surrounded by people who were interested in finding themselves, who wanted to understand life and its meanings.

I laid out a quadrangle on the edge of the moors; cottages were built around it; the barn was turned into a tavern, with an upper story like a sun-parlor overlooking the moors and the sea. There I planned that we would dine, talk, and have music and dances, intimately, informally, as if we were around a fireside. We would have a little world of our own, bounded on four sides by the sea, unconditioned by any other herd than our own; and we would invite people to share it with us who had something to say about the things we were interested in.

James Harvey Robinson came down the first summer; other men came and talked about science, philosophy, literature and art, politics and international relations. A hundred-odd young people came in September on their way to college. The next year the school expanded into ten weeks. Some one named it the "School of Opinion." What I was unconsciously looking for was wisdom; I could not find it alone; I wanted other people to be looking for it with me. I would have liked to call it a "School of Wisdom," remembering Count Keyserling's school at Darmstadt in Germany. But I was inexperienced in knowledge of myself; hesitant about believing in any subconscious urge; my life had always been shaped by the opinions of others, the groups and classes with which I had lived. I had run away from self-questionings; had evaded the solution of personal problems in activities, movements, causes, which had never completely expressed my nature and had sometimes been in conflict with it. I had rationalized about life rather than found it. Building, planting, living in the open, in contact with fishermen, farmers, and workmen, I found a new sort of adjustment. It seemed essential that others should be doing and enjoying the same things; perhaps I wanted them to fortify me in the rightfulness of my enjoyment.

The name "School of Opinion" stuck. It was as good a name as another. I had guesses about the wisdom that I was looking for, not overtly; it might have little to do with facts, statistics, information; less to do with careers and getting on in the world, not much with zeal to make the world better. It had to be gotten mostly out of oneself. Buildings, endowments, and trustees did not aid universities to impart it. Grown-ups like myself found it obscured by various impedimenta of life; young people did not know that academic instruction was bare of it. The School of Opinion should provide an atmosphere of simplicity and intimacy, in which varying opinions, freely expressed, might give hints of wisdom.

The experiment captivated me. Each year my submerged chromozones became more insistent; they asserted themselves in my reveries, in my thoughts of old age. Each year my escape from political activities was of longer duration. Each summer was a new experience of friendship with others and comradeship with myself such as I had never known before.

This long history of changing view-points might seem to argue that I am disillusioned with former convictions and hopes. But the reverse is true.

I still believe in liberalism, I believe in keeping the mind open to everything that is moving. To me liberalism is open-mindedness.

I still believe in education. It is not merely a matter of books or of schools. The best education is derived from life and human contacts. Education can be best gained from great men, not alone from men in educational work.

I am not through with study. I want to study in connection with other books which I hope to write.

I am free from the strain of money-making. I have no desire to be rich or to make more money than is demanded by the simple existence I have chosen.

I believe in ideas; I believe in the single tax as intensely as I ever did, but I think that the single tax as well as other reforms in line with freedom will come through the rise of a new political group that will instinctively demand it.

I began life with a sense of responsibility for my

own soul. I returned to the same sense of responsibility thirty years later. Then my concern was as
to the hereafter; now my concern was pre-eminently
with to-day. Then life was conditioned by fear; now
it is conditioned by desire. I was concerned with the
poverty of others; now I am concerned with the
poverty of my own undeveloped experiences.

Unobligated to movements or to reforms, I find a
kind of verity that I did not know before. I have few
mental conflicts and get a warmth and joy out of life
that are new to me. As a boy I had wanted to be a
newspaper reporter, had abandoned reporting for the
law with reluctance; nothing subsequently gave me
the satisfaction that I got from newspaper work. In a
deeper way I now find the same content in living as I
choose and being myself. I respect my previous activities, and would not want my life to have been without them. I believe in reform, but prefer the reform
that is taking place within myself.

And at fifty-odd, with a conscience that still
troubles me often, I spend my summers on the island
and my winters in Europe. A lifetime spent in making good in material ways, in political struggle, and
moralistic reform, leaves me aware of gaps in personality; of a fashion of perceiving life fragmentarily. I
am committed to such beauty as I can find, to harmony within and without, to friends and the things
I love. I have more to learn than the time that is left
suffices for. Yet I realize that only a beginning is
possible to any man.

INDEX